W9-BOK-616

WITHDRAWN

The History of
American Church Music

Da Capo Press Music Reprint Series
GENERAL EDITOR
FREDERICK FREEDMAN
VASSAR COLLEGE

The History of American Church Music

by

LEONARD ELLINWOOD

Revised Edition

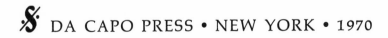 DA CAPO PRESS • NEW YORK • 1970

35646

A Da Capo Press Reprint Edition

This Da Capo Press edition of Leonard Ellinwood's *The History of American Church Music* is an unabridged and slightly corrected republication of the first edition published in New York in 1953. The author has provided a number of footnotes for the present edition.

Library of Congress Catalog Card Number 69-12683
SBN 306-71233-4

Copyright © 1953 by Morehouse-Gorham Company

Copyright © 1970 by Da Capo Press

Published by Da Capo Press
A Division of Plenum Publishing Corporation
227 West 17th Street, New York, N.Y. 10011
All rights reserved

Manufactured in the United States of America

THE HISTORY OF AMERICAN CHURCH MUSIC

Other Works by the Author:

Musica Hermanni Contracti

Works of Francesco Landini

Bio-Bibliographical Index of Musicians in the United States of America
Since Colonial Times (editor)

The Hymnal 1940 Companion (editor)

and numerous articles on Church music and medieval music in

Collier's Encyclopedia

The Musical Quarterly

Speculum

The Cathedral Age

Journal of the American Musicological Society

Music Library Association Notes

Musica Disciplina

The Hymn

The American Organist

The History of
American Church Music

by

LEONARD ELLINWOOD

1953

MOREHOUSE-GORHAM COMPANY

New York

Copyright, 1953, by
Morehouse-Gorham Company
All rights reserved

Printed in the United States of America

To

HOWARD HANSON

Crusader for American Music

Preface

PREPARATION of this *History* began with work on a series of lectures which I gave in August, 1950, at the School of Church Music, Evergreen Conference, Colorado. When Dean Williams first proposed the subject to me the preceding summer, my immediate reaction was one of doubt as to whether there was sufficient material available on the topic, as well as of serious question as to whether or not it would be possible to present it in a positive manner. Earlier impressions, gained through the many aspersions which have traditionally been cast upon American church music, had left me with a fear that most of the subject would have to be covered in a negative manner, a constant condemnation of the bad practices of the past with little that was good to relieve the gloomy monotony.

Once I began to dig into the sources of our musical history, I was pleasantly surprised to find the opposite to be the case. There was much that was worthy, and there were many occasions on which we could well be proud of our musical forebears. It is to be hoped that some of this corrected impression may be conveyed to the reader. While there are many incidents which appear humorous to us today, and many practices which border on the maudlin, fundamentally this work is able to record the sincere efforts of many generations of Americans whose sole aim was to worship God to the best of their musical ability. As will be noted in several specific connections, their seeming lack of taste merely reflected the current European taste, or rather the universal ignorance of the times.

Another illusion which was quickly clarified was that it would be relatively simple to secure material about music in each of the major denominations, as well as in various parts of the country. In point of fact, it soon became questionable as to whether this would turn out to be any broader than a history of music in the Episcopal Church alone. I have striven to avoid this as much as possible but it has been difficult, for there has been relatively little written, or few records preserved, on music in the other churches. Similarly, much more has been recorded of music in the older, Eastern sections of the country than in those sections but a few generations removed from the pioneer days.

In the effort to make this work as comprehensive as possible, I have been greatly assisted by a number of individuals. Many of the persons whose biographical sketches are included in Appendix C have been very helpful, both in conversation and correspondence. I have been aided by innumerable letters from others who have oftentimes been able to clarify or verify otherwise obscure points. What perspective my work does have has been increased immeasurably by the following persons, each of whom has read and commented upon various parts of the work: the late Wallace Goodrich, director emeritus of the New England Conservatory; J. Vincent Higginson, managing-editor of *The Catholic Choirmaster;* Berniece Fee Mozingo, organist-choirmaster of Trinity Evangelical Lutheran Church, Indianapolis; Leo Sowerby, organist-choirmaster of St. James' Church, Chicago; Robert Stofer, organist-choirmaster of Covenant Presbyterian Church, Cleveland; William Treat Upton, professor emeritus of Oberlin College and authority on early American music.

Two facts have been noticed many times in the course of my research. The first is a recurring emphasis on congregational singing, even in the Roman Catholic Church. At first, in the New England colonies and in the special groups in Pennsylvania, the only music was the congregational singing of Psalms and hymns brought over from the old country. But as organs and choirs were introduced, we find, again and again, sermons and lectures stressing the importance of participation by the entire congregation. The emphasis placed on it today by musicians of all faiths has a very familiar ring.

The second fact, and one which should be accentuated, is that throughout our history no church has succeeded in having outstanding music unless it was ready and willing to pay for it. Good music costs money! Money not only for instruments and music scores, but sufficient money to secure competent church musicians who can devote their full efforts toward this end. Throughout the following pages, while there is much evidence of the volunteer choir, there is no sign of any preeminence where the choir, volunteer or professional, was not adequately supported.

This book is not primarily intended as a history of hymnody in America. The subject is well covered in Henry Wilder Foote's *Three Centuries of American Hymnody* (Cambridge: Harvard University Press, 1940) and in the Introduction to *The Hymnal 1940 Companion* (second edition, New York: The Church Pension Fund, 1951). I have here concerned myself only with those aspects of hymnody which have affected the main-stream of our church music. I have likewise omitted reference to the work of the various oratorio societies which have done so much to encourage choral music in its larger forms. They are adequately covered in John Tasker Howard's *Our American Music* (third edition, New York: Crowell, 1946).

With these limitations in mind, it is my earnest hope that the reader will not only find inspiration in this recitation of the manner in which our predecessors "sang praises unto their God," but also encouragement to "sing unto the Lord a new song" in days to come.

L.E.

Washington Cathedral
Whitsuntide 1953

CONTENTS

CONTENTS

ILLUSTRATIONS

ILLUSTRATIONS

Part One

THE COLONIAL ERA : 1494–1820

Let us now praise famous men,
And our fathers that begat us . . .
Such as found out musical tunes
And recited verses in writing.

—ECCLESIASTICUS 44:1, 5

CHAPTER I

In New Spain

THE ARRIVAL of the *conquistadores* to colonize the lands discovered by Christopher Columbus and his fellow voyagers coincided with the "Golden Age" of Spanish culture. The homeland was replete with churches, monasteries, and private chapels where music was held to be of the utmost importance. The Royal Chapel in Madrid, the chapel of the Duke of Calabria in Valencia, and the cathedrals of Seville and Toledo, maintaining establishments the equal of those anywhere else in Europe, were fertile soil for the development of such composers as Cristóbal Morales and Tomás Luis de Victoria.

Coming to settle in the New World as overlords of a native population, the Spaniards brought with them as much of their Old World heritage as could be readily transplanted. The earliest record of their music in the New World is that of the Mass sung by Father Boil, aided by an improvised choir, at La Isabela (northwest of Puerto Plata) on San Domingo, January 6, 1494. The first Dominican cathedral was authorized in 1512; its chapter included a singer and an organist.[1]

Cortés landed in Mexico in the spring of 1519. Five years later, Father Pedro de Gante—"Peter from Ghent"—a Franciscan from Louvain University, established a school at Texcoco for the training of native musicians. He began by teaching the Indians to copy music neatly and clearly. Then, after a year of practice, the study of plainsong began. With his fellow Franciscans, Father Pedro also taught the natives to play and to construct European musical instruments. Soon, Indian singers and instrumentalists were in the service of the Church throughout the territories occupied by Spain. In 1527 Father Pedro moved to Mexico City, where he continued to train native musicians until his death in 1572.[2] There are records of twenty-five music schools in the missions of New Spain during the seventeenth century.

Mexico City and Lima gradually became the principal centers. European choirmasters and teachers served in all the larger cathedrals as they were established, and to them were sent annual consignments of church music and texts from across the Atlantic. An item in the list for the year 1586 mentions music by the distinguished composer Antonio de Cabezón which had been published in Spain only eight years before.

Coopersmith[1] describes the vicissitudes of a typical establishment, the Cathedral of La Vega in the Dominican Republic, with its long succession of Spanish musicians. The early music in the Cathedral of Santiago, Cuba, and that of the principal church of Havana are briefly described by Carpentier.[3] In an account of cathedral music in Mexico City during the sixteenth century, Lota M. Spell[4] describes an unpublished catalog of the choral library in 1589 which listed works by Guerrero, Morales, Victoria, Orlando di Lasso, and Palestrina, as well as many works by the various choirmasters. While most of the cathedral service was performed by European musicians, there are also notable accounts of singing both plainsong and polyphony on the part of the Indian musicians. A few of them even became choirmasters.

Music printing followed close on the heels of other cultural developments. A printing press was set up in Mexico City in 1539. From this press in the year 1556 came the first American printed book to contain music, the *Ordinarium*[5] (Ordinary of the Mass) published by Juan Pablos (see Plate Inside Front Cover). In 1583 there was published the *Psalmodia Christiana,* a collection of hymns and Psalms which had been translated into Aztec by Bernardino de Sahagún. In all, ten such items as these were published in the colonies by 1600. Four years later, Diego López Davalos published a musical setting of the Passion narratives for Holy Week, *Liber in quo quattuor passiones Christi Domini continentur,*[6] by the Spanish composer Juan Navarro. After this, there was a period of over a century before additional music was published, possibly due to the difficulty and cost of procuring materials. The missions continued to copy manuscripts for their own uses, however, and cathedral centers imported from Spain from time to time.

The first activity of this sort within the present limits of the United States of America was at the Mission of San Felipe in New Mexico, where Father Cristóbal de Quinones installed a small organ and began to teach the San Felipe Indians to sing the music of the liturgy sometime between 1598 and 1604.[7] During the following century and a half, through the many Franciscan missions there was laid a love of the Church and its music, especially that of a folk character, that even the extensive deprivations of the nineteenth century failed to erase from Indian hearts.

Typical of the religious folksongs were the *alabados* (Songs of Praise). These were simple folk-hymns in the form of the Spanish *romance,* which could be used on all occasions. The texts were summaries of the essential tenets of the Christian religion, an important means of propagation of the faith among illiterate natives. Many *alabados* were either composed in, or translated into the different Indian languages. The following is a common form which Father Antonio Margil de Jesús (1657-1726) taught from Costa Rica to Louisiana:[8]

Sé alabado y ensalzado El divino sacramento,
En que Dios oculto asiste De las alamas el sustento.

Y limpia la Concepción De la Reina de los cielos,
Que, quedando virgen pura, Es madre del Verbo eterno.

Y el glorioso San José Electo por Dios inmenso
Para padre estimativo De su hijo el divino Verbo.

Y esto por todos los signos Y de los siglos amén.
Amén—Jesús y María, Jesús, María y José.

¡O dulcísimo Jesús! Yo te doy mi corazón,
Para que estampes en él Tu santisima pasión.

¡Madre llena de dolor! haced que, cuando expiremos,
Nuestras almas entreguemos Por tus manos al Señor.

Quien a Dios quiere seguir Y a su gloria quiere entrar,
Una cosa ha de asentar Y de corazón decir:

"Morir antes que pecar! Antes que pecar, morir!"[9]

Juan B. Rael[10] has recorded and published a number of *alabados* from communities along the Rio Grande between Alamosa, Colorado, and Santa Fé, New Mexico, which are still used by members of Los Hermanos Penitentes de la Tercera Orden de San Francisco (the Penitent Brothers of the Third Order of St. Francis). They are sung in Spanish during Holy Week processions, as these flagellants wind through the streets, black-hooded and stripped to the waist, while whipping themselves and bearing wooden crosses.

Another phase of the mission music which has survived in the Southwest is found in the religious pageants, descendants of the Spanish *autos* of the sixteenth century. One of these is the *Comedia de Adan y Eva*; its performance at Mexico City in 1532 was probably the first dramatic presentation in the New World. More popular, and still performed annually in some isolated villages, is *Los Pastores* (The Shepherds).[11] The music is a curious medley of Latin plainsong, Spanish air, and native Indian melody. The following is a description of a modern performance:

> The whole village packs itself in the one-room adobe schoolhouse. Here after an interminable delay, the calico curtain parts for *Los Pastores*. Everyone in the audience is as tense with excitement as if he had not heard the lines since he was a babe in arms.
>
> Shepherds are seated around a little fire. Sometimes a few of the village sheep are brought in and provide a touch of realism as they baa mournfully during the whole performance. Suddenly the Star of Bethlehem, usually a coal oil lantern moved jerkily along a wire, appears, and progresses across the "sky," at least until it becomes stuck in its majestic course and some village men have to rush to its rescue armed with pliers. Meantime the shepherds decide to follow the Star; pick up their shepherds' crooks twined with home-made, tissue-paper roses and sling their wanderers' pouches over their shoulders.

[6]

Then the trouble begins. Everything gets in the way of their progress —one of their own lazy members and the devil, himself, wearing red or black tights with a long tail to which is fastened packs of firecrackers. Even a holy hermit armed with a corn-cob cross cannot cope with the representative of evil. The arguments go on hour after hour in resounding Spanish. Often the village poet gets in a few sly digs at the storekeeper who has charged too much and the villager who has ploughed his field on Sunday.

The shepherds get nowhere until the Archangels Gabriel and Miguel appear. Then the evil one is vanquished and disappears, still shouting terrible Spanish imprecations, into a red calico hell. At that the smallest villagers take their heads from under their mothers' shawls and dare look again at the stage.

Actors, villagers, and the Archangels burst into triumphant hymns. Singing, they move on to Bethlehem, which is represented by a manger scene in the village church. Here in a green-wattled bower hung with the best rugs of village weaving is *El Santo Niño* on his pallet of straw, surrounded by his blue-robed mother and St. Joseph.

At midnight the little altar blossoms with lighted candles. The villagers drop to their knees on the hard-packed adobe floor. From the hand-carved choir-loft roll the ancient responses and the old, old Spanish hymns.[12]

In 1769, Father Junípero Serra founded at San Diego the first of the twenty-one California Franciscan missions. He was an ardent musician, and it was not long before the Indians of the West Coast were likewise being taught the plainsong and other melodies of the Church. Here, too, the *alabados,* with the *Salve, Adoro Te,* and *Santa Cruz* became integral parts of native worship and daily life. Native choirs and orchestras were soon developed which at times obtained a high level of proficiency in both plainsong and choral works. Father Owen Da Silva[13] gives a detailed description of the music in various missions, with biographical sketches of several of the *padre* musicians and a list of the extant music, together with transcriptions of several examples of both folk melodies and composed masses. Among these is the simple but worthy four-part *Misa de Cataluñ,* by Father Narciso Durán (1776-1846).

A more conservative view is taken by Father Zephyrin Engelhardt, who holds that the four-part masses were sung only by the seminarians:

[7]

It is altogether unlikely that Father Tapis [at Mission San Juan Bautista] or any other missionary anywhere bewildered the Indian choir-singers with such a multitude of notes. The mental exertion would have been more than they could endure, and then the singers would one by one have absented themselves.[14]

Father Durán was the outstanding music teacher of the period. His choir book, compiled in manuscript form at Mission San José in 1813, is the most complete collection of mission music available. Its *Prologue* is a valuable testament to the type of musical conditions under which he worked:

When we arrived at this mission, the Ecclesiastical Chant was so faulty that the one song the boys knew, the *Asperges,* had neither feet nor head, and seemed a howl rather than a song. And let us not speak of the Masses, for in telling you, scarcely without exaggeration, that they did not know how to answer *Amen,* you can judge the rest for yourself.

He then proceeds to tell how he trained the Indian boys, reducing notation to as simple a form as possible and using but a few easy tones:

This then, O pious reader, is the method that we have followed for the last three years in performing all the services of the Church, with as becoming a solemnity as can be expected for many years in these very remote parts. . . . In this way I am convinced that music and singing will not degenerate, even if I am absent, contrary to the opinion of some who think that all will die out when I am gone.[15]

He was right: the music did not die out for a full generation after the eclipse of the missions themselves. With the revolution which made Mexico an independent republic in 1822, financial support of the missions fell away. In 1834 the territorial legislature in California passed an abortive act secularizing the missions and making possible the gradual sequestration of their lands. A required inventory at Mission San Juan Bautista in May, 1835, showed the contents of the choir loft to be valued at one thousand and sixty dollars Mexican, or two and one-half times that of the library which contained one hundred and eighty-two volumes! American occupation, and confirmation of mission property-rights in 1855, came too late to preserve more than a few remnants of the labors of over two generations of Franciscan missionaries. The Reverend Francis Mora, the second secular priest of Mission San Juan Bautista, has told how *ca.*1856 the faithful Indian choristers came to him, asking to be locked up overnight on Saturday in order that they might avoid the white-man's "fire-water," and so be in condition to sing the mass on Sunday.

Robert Louis Stevenson has left this vivid picture of the final generation of mission musicians trained by Father Durán and his fellow monks, written in the fall of 1879:

> Only one day in the year [November 4], the day before our Guy Fawkes, the *padre* drives over the hill from Monterey; the little sacristy, which is the only covered portion of the church, is filled with seats and decorated for the service; the Indians troop together, their bright dresses contrasting with their dark and melancholy faces; and there, among a crowd of somewhat unsympathetic holiday-makers, you may hear God served with perhaps more touching circumstances than in any other temple under heaven. An Indian, stone-blind and about eighty years of age, conducts the singing; other Indians compose the choir; yet they have the Gregorian music at their finger-ends, and pronounce the Latin so correctly that I could follow the meaning as they sang. The pronunciation was odd and nasal, the singing hurried and staccato. "In saecula saeculo-ho-horum," they went, with a vigorous aspirate to every additional syllable. I have never seen faces more vividly lit up with joy than the faces of these Indian singers. It was to them not only the worship of God, nor an act by which they recalled and commemorated better days, but was besides an exercise of culture, where all they knew of art and letters was united and expressed. And it made a man's heart sorry for the good fathers of yore who had taught them to dig and to reap, to read and to sing, who had given them European mass-books which they will still preserve and study in their cottages, and who had now passed away from all authority and influence in that land—to be succeeded by greedy land-thieves and sacrilegious pistol-shots.[16]

CHAPTER II

Metrical Psalmody

A MONG all the people of the Protestant Reformation in Europe
during the sixteenth century, save for the Bohemian Brethren and the followers of Martin Luther, the Psalms were
deemed the sole suitable vehicle for singing the praise of Almighty
God. Since representative groups of almost all of the various movements sought refuge from persecution in the New World, the many
facets of their psalmody found expression here, some as transient as
were their colonies, others more enduring.

The French, or Genevan, Psalter evolved between the years 1539,
when the Strassburg *Aulcunes psaulmes* was published, and 1562,
when Theodore de Bèze completed the metrical versions in French
which had been initiated by Clément Marot, with tunes adapted by
Louis Bourgeois.[1] The first of the metrical psalters to be developed,
the French Psalter was also the first to reach the shores of America,
being brought over by the short-lived Huguenot expeditions of 1562-
1565 to Florida. Baird comments that, thanks to the pleasant relations
between the French and the Indians,

> . . . long after the breaking up of Laudonnière's colony, the European,
> cruising along the coast or landing upon the shore, would be saluted
> with some snatch of a French Psalm uncouthly rendered by Indian
> voices, in strains caught from the Calvinists.[2]

In other settlements along the coast during the subsequent century,
from Charleston, South Carolina, to Oxford, Massachusetts, the French
Psalms were sung by Huguenots as long as they maintained their own

separate services. There is no indication, however, that the French Psalter was ever reprinted in the American colonies. This is so presumably because few Huguenot groups long retained their identity; they rather tended to merge with Anglican congregations after a few years.

In 1566, only four years after the French Psalter had been completed, it was translated into Dutch verse by Peter Datheen, likewise adapted to the Bourgeois tunes. This version soon became the official song-book of the Reformed Church throughout the Netherlands. Thus when the first church was organized in New Amsterdam, in 1628, by the Dutch and French settlers jointly, they were able to sing together in their respective languages.[3] This Reformed Protestant Dutch Church, the present Collegiate Reformed Dutch Church of New York, continued to use the Datheen Psalter until 1767, when, after the introduction of English preaching, Francis Hopkinson[4] was commissioned to adapt English words to the traditional tunes. In 1847, Dutch "Seceders" under the Reverend A. C. Van Raalte brought the same Bourgeois tunes to their Michigan settlements, where they are still sung, to the exclusion of all other music, in the Christian Reformed Churches.

The Reverend Francis Fletcher, who was the chaplain with Sir Francis Drake on his famous voyage around the world, refers several times to the Psalm-singing on board ship. Since Drake sailed from England in 1577, they undoubtedly used the Old Version of Sternhold and Hopkins, with the tunes published in the original edition of John Day, 1562. During the five weeks of midsummer, 1579, when the expedition was laid up for repairs in what is now called Drake's Bay, just north of San Francisco, Fletcher writes that the Indians visited the camp frequently,

> In the time of which prayers, singing of Psalmes, and reading of certaine Chapters in the Bible, they sate very attentively: and observing the end at every pause, with one voice still cried, Oh, as greatly rejoycing in our exercises. Yea they tooke such pleasure in our singing of Psalmes, that whensoever they resorted to us, their first request was commonly this, *Gnaáh,* by which they intreated that we would sing.[5]

When the Pilgrims landed at Plymouth in 1620, they brought with them an English psalter which had been compiled by Henry Ainsworth and published at Amsterdam in 1612. During their stay in the Netherlands, these "Separatists" had become familiar with the Bourgeois tunes in the Dutch Psalter. Consequently, the Ainsworth Psalter made wide use of these tunes, nineteen out of a total of thirty-nine being thus derived. Its use persisted, without "lining," at Plymouth until 1692,[6] supplying a higher musical standard than was found elsewhere in New England.

The Old Version was brought to Jamestown by the first settlers of 1607, who used the music settings of Thomas Est, 1592. When the Massachusetts Bay Colony was established, 1628-30, the Ravenscroft tune-book of 1621 was used.

Dissatisfaction with the Old Version was rife on both sides of the Atlantic. It was, however, considerably easier to make changes in a young, theocratic colony than in the conservative homeland. Consequently, it was not long before a committee of New England clergymen was appointed to prepare a revision of the metrical Psalms. This appeared in 1640 as *The Bay Psalm Book*, published by Stephen Daye in Cambridge—the first book of any sort to be published in the English colonies in North America.

Page 13 quotes Psalm I from the versions used in the New England Colonies: the Old Version, Ainsworth's Psalter, and *The Bay Psalm Book*. The variants are interesting, but the modern reader is likely to prefer the Old Version in spite of its ill-repute.

John Eliot, the "Apostle to the Indians," shared in the preparation of *The Bay Psalm Book*. In 1661, he prepared a versification of the Psalms in the Algonquin language which was bound with his famous Indian Bible. Here again, as in Florida and California, the Indians took to Psalm singing. Over twenty years later, in 1687, the Reverend Increase Mather wrote that "the whole congregation of Indians praise God with singing, and some of them are excellent singers."

While it found a certain amount of conservative opposition, *The Bay Psalm Book* soon became widely accepted. It went through twenty-seven editions in New England before 1762, and approximately twenty more in England during those same years. But there was so little demand for new music that no music editions were published until 1698, and then only a few familiar tunes were included: *Litchfield, Canter-*

1
The man is blest that hath not bent
to wicked read his eare:
Nor led his life as sinners do,
nor sat in scorner's chaire.

2
But in the Law of God the Lord
doth set his whole delight:
And in that law doth exercise
himself both day and night.

3
He shall be like the tree that growes
fast by the river side:
Which bringeth forth the most pleasant
fruits in her due time and tide.

4
Whose leaf shall never fade nor fall,
but flourish still and stand:
Even so all things shall prosper well
that this man takes in hand.

5[!]
So shall not the ungodly men,
they shall be nothing so:
But as the dust which from the earth
the winds drives to and fro.

6
Therefore shall not the wicked men
in judgement stand upright:
Nor yet the sinners with the just,
shall come in place or sight.

For why? the way of godly men
unto the Lord is known:
And eke the way of wicked men
shall quite be overthrown.

—Old Version

1
O Blessed man, that doth not in
the wickeds counsell walk:
nor stand in sinners way; nor sit
in seat of scornful-folk.

2
But setteth in Jehovah's law
his pleasureful delight
and in his law doth meditate,
by day and eke by night.

3
And he shall be, like-as a tree,
by water brooks planted;
which in his time, shall give his fruit
his leaf eke shall not fade;
and whatsoever he shall doe,
it prosp'rously shall thrive.

4
Not so the wicked: but as chaff,
which winde away—doth drive.

5
Therefore, the wicked shall not in
the judgement stand—upright:
and in th' assembly of the just,
not any sinfull—wight.

6
For, of the just, Jehovah he
acknowledgeth the way:
and way of the ungracious
shall utterly—decay.

—Ainsworth

1
O Blessed man, that in th' advice
of wicked doeth not walk:
nor stand in sinner's way, nor sit
in charge of scornfull-folk.

2
But in the law of Jehovah,
is his longing delight:
and in his law doth meditate
by day and eke by night.

3
And he shall be like to a tree
planted by water—rivers:
that in his season yields his fruit,
and his leafe never withers.
And all he doth shall prosper well.

4
The wicked are not so:
but they are like unto the chaffe,
which wind drives to and fro.

5
Therefore shall not ungodly men
rise to stande in the doome
nor shall the sinner's with the just,
in their assemblie come.

6
For of the righteous men, the Lord
acknowledgeth the way:
but the way of ungodly men,
shall utterly decay.

—Bay Psalm Book

bury, York, Windsor, Cambridge, St. David's, Martyrs, St. Mary's (Hackney), Old 100th, 115th, 119th, and 148th.

This was the period which Millar Patrick refers to as "The Great Eclipse."[7] No new English or Scottish Psalm-tunes came into common use from 1635, the year that *London New (Newton)* appeared in the Scottish Psalter, until after 1698 when the New Version of Tate and Brady provided the fresh incentive to help break the iron fetters of tradition.

It is difficult for us today to realize how extremely narrow our Puritan forebears were in their attitude toward church music.[8] Not only must all music be limited to the singing of the Psalms of David in metrical form—chanting the prose Psalms was abhorrent to them—but serious questions were raised as to whether even these should be sung to man-made tunes. The metrical Psalms were considered by some so sacrosanct that they could not be rehearsed; the tunes must rather be learned with practice-verses.[9] Even the tunes were sometimes regarded as holy, so that men

> put off their hats, and put on a great show of devotion and gravity, whenever Psalm-tunes were sung, though there were not one word of a Psalm.[10]

Rehearsals were better held in the village taverns than in the meeting-house, in spite of the attendant temptations.

In order to clarify the issues involved for the New England conscience, the Reverend John Cotton published a tract in 1647 entitled:

SINGING OF PSALMES A GOSPEL ORDINANCE. OR A TREATISE, WHEREIN ARE HANDLED THESE FOURE PARTICULARS:

1. Touching the Duty it selfe.
   . . . Singing of *Psalmes* with a lively voice, is an holy Duty of God's Worship now in the dayes of the New Testament.

2. Touching the Matter to be Sung.
   . . . We hold and believe:
   1. That not only the *Psalmes* of *David,* but any other spirituall Songs recorded in Scripture, may lawfully be sung in Christian Churches. . . .

[14]

2. We grant also, that any private Christian, who hath a gift to frame a spirituall Song, may both frame it, and sing it privately. . . . Nor do we forbid the private use of an Instrument of Musick therewithall.

Neither doe we deny but that in the publique thanksgivings of the Church, if the Lord should furnish any of the members of the Church with a spirituall gift to compose a Psalme upon any speciall occasion, he may lawfully be allowed to sing it before the Church, and the rest hearing it, and approving it, may goe along with him in Spirit, and say Amen to it.

3. Touching the Singers.

1. Whether one be to sing for all, the rest joining only in Spirit, and saying, Amen; or the whole congregation?

2. Whether women, as well as men; or men alone?

3. Whether carnall men and Pagans may be permitted to sing with us, or Christians alone, and Church Members?

4. Touching the Manner of Singing.

. . . It will be a necessary helpe, that the wordes of the *Psalme* be openly read before hand, line after line, or two lines together, that so they who want either books or skill to reade, may know what is to be sung, and joyne with the rest in the dutie of singing.

As to thus "lining out" the Psalms, Cotton pointed out:

We for our parts easily grant, that where all have books and can reade, or else can say the *Psalme* by heart, it were needlesse there to read each line of the *Psalme* before hand in order to singing.

Deacons who could "line" the Psalm by intoning on pitch, to say nothing of giving a pitch suitable to the range of the tune, were in great demand, but too seldom obtainable. The introduction of choirs stopped the practice of "lining out" in New England by the end of the eighteenth century, but it still persisted elsewhere for many years.[11] The change did not come without pathetic scenes; at Worcester, for example, the town voted on August 5, 1779,

That the singers sit in the front seats in the front gallery, and that those gentlemen who have hitherto sat in the front seats in said gallery have a right to sit in the front and second seat below, and that said

[15]

singers have said seat appropriated to said use. Voted, that said singers be requested to take said seats and carry on the singing in public worship. Voted, that the mode of singing in the congregation here, be without reading the psalms line by line to be sung.

The Sabbath succeeding the adoption of these votes, after the hymn had been read by the minister, the aged and venerable Deacon Chamberlain, unwilling to desert the custom of his fathers, rose and read the first line according to the usual practice. The singers, prepared to carry the alteration into effect, proceeded without pausing at the conclusion. The white-haired officer of the church, with the full power of his voice read on, until the louder notes of the collected body overpowered the attempt to resist the progress of improvement, and the deacon, deeply mortified at the triumph of musical reformation, seized his hat, and retired from the meeting-house in tears. His conduct was censured by the church, and he was for a time deprived of its communion, for absenting himself from the public services of the Sabbath.[12]

The First Presbyterian Congregation at Mendham in Morris County, New Jersey, was more conservative; in 1791 the Session "Voted to sing half the time without reading."

The role of parish clerk, precentor, or deacon, as he was variously designated, persisted in many churches even after the practice of "lining out" the Psalms was abandoned. In Episcopal churches, the parish clerk had the additional duties of giving out notices and of leading the congregation in the responses. A description of the clerk's duties at St. Michael's Church, Charleston, South Carolina, is quoted on page 44. This was designed to encourage congregational participation, although it more often had the opposite effect. The clerk was frequently paid a regular salary, but usually wore no distinctive dress save for a large wig. He was given a small desk located either in front of the larger, minister's desk or beneath the pulpit. Plate I shows a typical "three decker" still in its original position in the center aisle of Trinity Church, Newport, Rhode Island. The wineglass pulpit is above, with the minister's desk below it, and the clerk's desk still lower, nearer the floor level.

Today we stand to sing the hymns, and, in nearly all places, to chant or read the Psalms. The eighteenth century, however, sang its metrical Psalms while seated. For Episcopalians, the change came in

1814, when at the General Convention of that year the House of Bishops proposed, the House of Deputies concurring, a direction for standing during the singing of the metrical Psalms.[13]

CHAPTER III

Singing Schools and Early Choirs

WHILE it is rather easy to describe the extreme paucity of tunes, and the consequent impoverished state of church music around the year 1700, it is more difficult to evaluate the causes for conditions which prevailed at that time.

First and foremost must be considered the stifling effect of the cultus of psalmody, as described in the previous chapter. There was little incentive to learn new music when a small number of old, familiar tunes would fit all the metres used, and when the music of worship was limited to the few Psalms sung by the congregation. How restricted the music thus remained, even in a relatively liberal work, may be observed in the Proposed Prayer Book issued by a committee of Episcopalians in 1785. Bound at the back of the book was a group of 84 selections from the metrical psalter, together with 51 other hymns: for 135 texts, there were but 18 tunes provided.

Foote[1] points to the isolation and hardship of pioneer life as the basic cause for this wide-spread musical illiteracy, but actually conditions differed little from those prevailing in England and Scotland, in either rural or urban communities. Underlying the entire problem was a basic lack of music education. Psalmody had relied on the oral tradition, had avoided the use of professional musicians, and had found its musical level at the lowest common denominator of quality. Its *ne plus ultra* was the music of the masses, *i.e.,* the congregations, be they musical or nearly tone-deaf. Consequently, congregations of 1720 were able to sing far fewer tunes than those of 1620. The solution lay in a

Henry A. Curtis

PLATE I. The Three-decker Pulpit, Trinity Church,
Newport, Rhode Island

St. Michael's Church, Charleston, S. C.

PLATE II. The Choir-loft and Organ, St. Michael's Church, Charleston, South Carolina

program of music education through the formation of singing schools giving instruction in music notation as well as in rote singing.

It must be distinctly realized that although each county in England supposedly had its professional cathedral choir, there were never any such choirs brought over to this country. Individual musicians migrated, but wherever choirs were established they began with untrained, amateur voices and proceeded to build their own tradition with no professional choirs to provide models for comparison. Seventeenth-century psalmodists had not felt the need for choirs, but as musical conditions grew steadily worse, the younger, more progressive ministers took steps to develop "regular singing"—singing by rule, or notes—with the aid of select groups of singers segregated in galleries or side pews.

Throughout the eighteenth century the rear choir-gallery was an architectural feature common to churches of all denominations. It provided space not only for the singers but also for the organs and other instruments used to accompany the singing. Across the front of the gallery there was frequently a long music rack, designed to hold the singers' tune-books. Such a rack may be seen in Plate II, which shows the rear gallery of St. Michael's Church, Charleston, South Carolina.

The Reverend Thomas Symmes, in his pamphlet *The Reasonableness of Regular Singing: or Singing by Note* (1720), writes of singing schools in the early days of the Massachusetts Bay Colony, as well as of music study at Harvard:

> Music . . . was studied, known and approved of in our College, for many years after its first founding [in 1636]. This is evident from the Musical Theses, which were formerly printed; and from some writings containing some tunes, with directions for singing by note, as they are now sung; and these are yet in being though of more than sixty years' standing.

One wonders if these tunes could have represented a first effort at creative music in the colonies. The writings referred to were destroyed when the Harvard Library was burned in 1764, so nothing further is known of them.

Symmes, who signed himself "Philomusicus," followed this pamphlet with two others: *Concerning Prejudice in Matters of Religion* (1722), and in the following year, *Utile Dulci. Or, A Joco-Serious Dialogue, concerning Regular Singing: Calculated for a Particular Town, (where it was publicly had, on Friday, Oct. 12, 1722) but may serve some other places in the same Climate.* . . . His purpose was "to encourage Singing Meetings in the Town in the long winter Evenings," presumably in Bradford, Massachusetts, where he was minister from 1708 until his death in 1725. While his *Dialogue* was written in an attempt to eliminate conservatism with ridicule, it does summarize the principal objections to "regular singing":

1. It is a new way, an unknown tongue.
2. It is not so melodious as the usual way.
3. There are so many tunes we shall never have done learning them.
4. The practice creates disturbances and causes people to behave indecently and disorderly.
5. It is Quakerish and Popish and introductive of instrumental music.
6. The names given to the notes are bawdy, yea blasphemous.
7. It is a needless way, since our fathers got to heaven without it.
8. It is a contrivance to get money.
9. People spend too much time learning it, they tarry out nights disorderly.
10. They are a company of young upstarts that fall in with this way, and some of them are lewd and loose persons.

Typical is his reply to the fifth "complaint":

> . . . If the Papists sing a better Tune, or with a better Air, than we do, I'd as soon imitate them, and a thousand times sooner, than the Honestest man among you that had no skill in singing. . . . Your usual way of Singing would much sooner dispose me to fall in with them, Because the Quakers don't Sing at all, and I should be out of the Noise of it; and the Papists sing much better. . . . You may depend upon it, that such as are not willing to be at the Cost of a Bell, to call the People together on the Lord's Day, and of a Man to ring it . . . will never be so extravagant as to lay out their Cash . . . to buy Organs, and pay an artist for playing on 'em.

Another of the dozen pamphlets published during this decade of controversy was *An Essay Preached by Several Ministers of the Gospel*

[Peter Thacher, John and Samuel Danforth] *For the Satisfaction of their Pious and Consciencious Brethren, as to Sundry Questions and Cases of Conscience, Concerning the Singing of Psalms, in the Publick Worship of God* (1723). Like the other essays, this was liberal—it favored new tunes if they were dignified, permitted women to sing, encouraged the participation of young people, and allowed part-singing. It was, however, opposed to the use of organs.[2]

Not all clergy, however, were liberal; the Reverend Samuel Niles at South Braintree, Massachusetts, found himself part of a small minority in his church who were opposed to the new way. The resultant controversy was aired in the columns of *The New England Courant* beginning in March, 1722.[3] The climax came two years later, and the *Courant* of February 10, 1724, reported:

> We have advice from Brantrey, that 20 persons at the South Part of the Town, who are Opposers of Regular Singing in that Place, have publickly declar'd for the Church of England.

It would appear that Niles' supporters had deserted in the very direction that Symmes' objectors thought the "regular singing" was taking.

Material for the new way was provided by the Reverend John Tufts, of Newbury, Massachusetts, in a brief manual published *ca.* 1712. The original title is not known, but the third edition, published at Boston in 1721 and containing 12 pages with 28 tunes, was called *A Very Plain and Easy Introduction to the Singing of Psalm Tunes*. One wonders if he could have known Thomas Morley's famous *Plaine and Easie Introduction* of 1597. Tuft's little work, usually found bound with copies of *The Bay Psalm Book,* went through eleven editions, for it filled a real need. Its brief instructions were derived from Ravenscroft and Playford; the tunes were harmonized in three parts, using letters rather than notes, on a staff with rhythm indicated by dots. Tufts' *Introduction* not only marked the beginning of the reform in singing, it was also the first book on music instruction to be published in the Colonies.[4]

This work was followed by a more detailed text using diamond notes with bar-lines, written by the Reverend Thomas Walter of Roxbury, Massachusetts, with "A Recommendatory Preface" signed by Increase Mather and fourteen other leading ministers of the older generation. Entitled *The Grounds and Rules of Musick Explained*, it was published at Boston in 1721 on the press of James Franklin. The printer's younger brother, Benjamin, was an apprentice in the shop at the time.

Gould[5] has described how singing schools were organized. When the singing had become insufferable in a given church, either the minister or interested members of the congregation would form a committee to secure subscribers to underwrite the school. They then proceeded to select a teacher and hire a place for the meetings of the school. According to Gould, this was frequently located in the village tavern for want of a better place. Singers were expected to come with their own candles, and with a board to hold both candle and music book. Instruction consisted of the simple elements of notation, followed by basic voice-placement exercises, sung by rote. As soon as possible the class would undertake the learning of new tunes. Since financial support was nearly always limited, few schools ran for more than twenty-four evenings. The group was then expected to be ready to take its place in the choir loft on the Sabbath, either with the older members, or as the nucleus of a new choir where none had existed before. In the Appendix to his *Church Music in America*, Gould lists 115 such schools which he taught in New England and in New York State between 1799 and 1844.

Gould's picture may be warped to a certain degree by his own experiences. We find records of many city churches maintaining a regular singing school and furnishing a room in which to hold it. Thus the session of the Old South Church, Newburyport, Massachusetts, voted £40 in 1795, and in 1807 appropriated still more money "for a singing school for the benefit of the church."[6] At Westfield, New York, singing schools were held from time to time in a Sunday School room, while at Lancaster, Ohio, they met in the basement of the church. Records of the First Church of Christ (Congregational) at New London, Connecticut, in 1797 show "To one Quarter's Tuition of Singing School beginning 17th of July and ending 17th of October as per agreement with the Singing Committee £3-5-0." The sum was paid to George Harris, who taught over a period of three years. During these same years, it was also voted "that the Loos Contribution Collected the

Courant year be appropriated to the use of Encouragement and supporting of Singing." In 1807, the church officers paid ten dollars "for 20 nights use of Mason Hall @ 50 cts."[7]

Several of the more prominent tune-book compilers and teachers of singing schools are discussed in Chapter VI. Andrew Adgate (d. 1793) was active at Philadelphia with a school which, in 1787, became the Uranian Academy. His special programs of church music are detailed in Sonneck's *Early Concert Life in America.* Andrew Law (1748-1821) taught in Connecticut and as far south as Baltimore. He advocated placing the melody in the soprano, or treble, part, and was a pioneer in the development of "shape-notes."[8] His *Art of Playing the Organ* (1809) was reprinted in 1819. Daniel Read (1757-1836) was active in New Haven and the Connecticut Valley, and was the most popular composer of fuging tunes.[9]

An interesting description of what must have been typical of eighteenth-century choirs is given by the Reverend Samuel Gilman, the author of "Fair Harvard," in his *Memoirs of a New England Village Choir; with Occasional Reflections, by a Member* (1829). Although fictitious names are used, the scene is supposedly laid in Atkinson, New Hampshire, during the author's youth, immediately after 1800. The *Memoirs* describe the petty jealousies and rivalries over the leadership of the choir, the duties of which consisted merely in giving out the pitch and singing lustily but accurately to encourage the less talented members. The "bass viol," probably a violoncello, and a clarinet furnished the only instrumental accompaniment.[10] The choir loft was in the rear gallery behind the congregation, but was reached by stairs on either side of the gallery which were completely visible from the congregation, so that any straggling or other eccentricity promptly became the subject of intense gossip. At a point in Gilman's narrative where the choir was making a fresh start after a period of decline, singing meetings were held in private houses on two or three evenings of each week "for practice and improvement."

The early eighteenth century saw the beginnings of an interest in instrumental music in the Colonies.[11] While this had no immediate effect on the churches, the use of a pitch-pipe and bass viol in the singing schools gradually led to their introduction in the church choirs.

[23]

Kenneth H. MacDermott[12] has shown how the gallery orchestras in England grew out of the destruction of organs during the Commonwealth. As will be noted in Chapter VII, there were no colonial organs at that time. Nor is there evidence of the use of other instruments until the following century, and then seldom more than three appear to have been used together.

None of the early American tune-books indicate the key-note to be sounded on a pitch pipe, but the *Federal Harmony,* 1794 edition, contains "Directions for pitching a tune by a concert pitch pipe." These indicate that the pitch was given to each part separately. MacDermott[13] states that frequently the singers used the phrase "Praise ye the Lord" as each took his pitch.

Foote[14] cites several instances where reference is made to the "town's viol" in New England village records. Although at first they met with the same conservative opposition that "regular singing" had—meeting-houses which used them being referred to as "catgut churches"—the bass viols eventually became known as "the Lord's fiddles" to differentiate them from the dancing-master's violins, "the devil's fiddles." Gould writes of the use of the violoncello (the "bass viol") much as the organ was later used:

> We have heard all the routine of playing the tune before commencing the singing, and interludes between the verses, by a single violoncello. But this, being done by a skillful hand, was, on the whole, rather interesting.[15]

With a widened repertory of Psalm-tunes there came also a gradual widening of the texts acceptable to the congregations. Isaac Watts' *Hymns* and *Psalms of David Imitated* were familiar to the more cultured clergy of the Colonies; several of the New England clergy, such as Cotton Mather and Benjamin Colman, corresponded regularly with Watts. Benjamin Franklin published Watts' *Psalms* in Philadelphia during 1729, but complained two years later that they remained unsold on his shelves. During the seventeen-forties, however, several editions of Watts' works were published in various colonial cities, attesting to their later acceptance.

John and Charles Wesley arrived in Georgia as youthful missionaries for the Church of England in 1735. They brought copies of Watts' and the New Version, as well as Count Zinzendorf's *Gesang-Buch der Gemeine in Herrnhut*, acquired from their Moravian shipmates on the voyage.[16] During their three-year stay in the colony, John Wesley prepared his first *Collection of Psalms and Hymns*. It was printed by Lewis Timothy at Charleston, South Carolina, in 1737, and was the first of a long series of Wesleyan hymnals. Indicative of its initial reception is the fact that Wesley was promptly haled before the Savannah grand jury and charged with introducing "into the church and service at the Altar compositions of Psalms and hymns not inspected or authorized by any proper judicature."

George Whitefield's evangelism during the years 1739-1741 brought about wide acceptance of the newer texts. The "Great Awakening" had begun in 1734 at Northampton, Massachusetts, under the preaching of Jonathan Edwards, who wrote of the singing:

> Our congregation excelled all that I ever knew in the external part of the duty before, generally carrying regularly and well, three parts of music, and the women a part by themselves. But now they were evidently wont to sing with unusual elevation of heart and voice, which made the duty pleasant indeed.[17]

Choirs and singing schools could not long be content with the small number of tunes bound with *The Bay Psalm Book*. The first of the new, larger works, published at Philadelphia in 1762 by James Lyon,[18] was entitled *Urania: Or a choice collection of Psalm Tunes, Anthems, or Hymns, from the most approved authors, with some entirely new. . . .* Lyons included at least six tunes of his own. There were some two hundred pages of music, handsomely engraved but badly edited. About half the tunes were in the new fuging style. This collection was followed in 1763 with Francis Hopkinson's *Collection of Psalm Tunes*, prepared for Christ and St. Peter's Churches, Philadelphia.[19] The following year, Josiah Flagg brought out, in Boston, *A Collection of the best Psalm Tunes . . . to which are added some Hymns and Anthems; the greater part of them never before printed in America*. The plates were engraved by Paul Revere.

These collections were but the beginning. By the turn of the century, over 130 such collections had been published in various cities up and down the coast.[20] Already anthems were beginning to be mentioned in the title pages—testimony to the progress which American choirs were even then making.

CHAPTER IV

Fuging Tunes

IN 1764 there appeared the first of a series of works issued by Daniel Bayley [Bailey] (1729-1792), a potter, publisher, and organist of St. Paul's Church, Newburyport, Massachusetts:

A NEW AND COMPLEAT INTRODUCTION TO THE GROUNDS AND RULES OF MUSICK IN 2 BOOKS:

Book I. Containing the Grounds and Rules of Musick: Or an Introduction to the Art of Singing by Note, taken from Thomas Walter, M.A.

Book II. Containing a New and Correct Introduction to the Grounds of Musick, Rudimental and Practical; from William Tans'ur's *Royal Melody;* The Whole being a Collection of the Choicest Tunes from the most approved Masters.

The work was prefaced both by the "Recommendatory Preface" signed by the fifteen clergymen found in earlier editions of Walter's work, and also some "Thoughts on Music: By Dr. Watts." Among the "choicest tunes" are three of a new type called fuging tunes: *St. Luke's,* in four parts, and *St. Martin's* and *Morning Hymn* in three parts.

Tans'ur's work was published in several editions during the next few years, its popularity aiding the spread of the fuging tunes. It had been first published in England in 1734, under the title *The Complete Melody, or Harmony of Zion.* In 1755 it became *The Royal Melody Compleat.* The third edition was reprinted in Boston by W. M'Alpine in 1767. We quote the title page in full because of the picture it gives of church music toward the end of the colonial period:

ROYAL MELODY COMPLETE, OR THE NEW HARMONY OF
ZION, CONTAINING

I. A new and correct introduction to the Grounds of Musick, Rudimental, Practical, and Technical.

II. A New and Complete body of Church Musick, adapted to the most
select portions of the Book of Psalms, of either Versions; with many
fuging chorus's, and Gloria Patri's to the whole.

III. A new and select number of Hymns, Anthems, and Canons, suited
to several occasions; and many of them never before printed; set by
the greatest Masters in the World.

The whole are composed in Two, Three, Four, and Five Musical Parts,
according to the nicest Rules, consisting of Solo's, Fuges, and
Chorus's, correctly set in score for Voices or Organ; and fitted for all
Teachers, Learners, and Musical Societies, etc., with a preface on
Church Musick, shewing the Beauty and Excellency thereof.

The fuging tunes, mentioned twice in the title, were well represented
in the collection and included the three published earlier in Bayley's
first work.

There has been considerable confusion in the writings on these
fuging tunes. Actually they are a relic of the polyphonic motets of the
Elizabethan era, with their imitative entrances for each voice part in
turn. Although the Colonies were settled toward the end of that era,
there is no indication that there was ever a musical establishment in
them capable of performing polyphonic motets; still, some of the
Virginia and Maryland colonists must have known them from the
English cathedral services.

Claude Goudimel (*d.* 1572) published a number of motet settings
of the tunes in the French Psalter. The first Scottish Psalter to contain
harmonized tunes was that of 1625. This contained fifteen "common
tunes" in four-part, simple harmonizations, with one other tune, *Bon
Accord,* "in Reports." Ten years later, the outstanding Psalter of 1635
contained harmonizations of both common and proper tunes, as well
as eight tunes "in Reports." These were imitative settings, deriving
their name from the French *rapporter,* "to carry back." Their fugal
treatment turned them into short motets, and they are thought to have
been composed by Edward Millar for use in the Scottish Chapel Royal.
The fuging tunes have also, at times, been called "repeat tunes."

The second edition (1707) of Henry Playford's *Divine Companion
. . . a Choice Collection of New and Easy Psalms, Hymns, and Anthems* contains "a Night Hymn in three parts" which is imitative—
midway between his anthems and the homophonic hymn and Psalm
settings. There must have been others in addition to those of Tans'ur,
for in the preface to the *Parochial Music Corrected* (1762), William
Riley writes of the airs sung by the Methodists:

> Their tunes mostly consist of what they call Fuges, or (more properly)
> Imitations, and are indeed fit to be sung only by those who made them.

Lyons' *Urania* and the two publications of Tans'ur's *Royal Melody*
were the first American printings of fuging tunes. The latter provided
exactly the sort of stimulus needed for ambitious village choirs, so
they are to be found in almost all New England tune-books for
several generations thereafter.

Billings[1] has frequently but erroneously been called the inventor of
the fuging tune; actually his are not even among the most popular
ones of the period, and in recent years some of his anthems have been
mistakenly termed fuging tunes.

Irving Lowens[2] has made an exhaustive survey of around 850 fuging
tunes published between 1761 and 1810. These are all tunes which,
set in either three- or four-part harmony, have an opening homophonic
phrase followed by a polyphonic section using either strict or free
imitation in at least three parts. This section is then followed by a
concluding, homophonic phrase. Frequently, all save the opening
phrase is repeated. Many other tunes suggest the form without exactly fitting the above pattern of polyphonic imitation. Such a tune,
still in popular use although frequently disguised with superfluous
harmonies, is John Francis Wade's *Adeste fideles;* properly, the trebles
alone should sing, "O come, let us adore him," the first time, with the
tenors joining them in fugal imitation when the phrase is repeated,
and with all four parts then coming in together for the final phrases.
Another in common use even today is Oliver Holden's *Coronation,*
first published at Boston in 1793.[3] Here there is no fugal imitation, but
otherwise it is in the same basic idiom; most modern hymnals conceal
its character by doubling the soprano and alto with the original tenor
and bass parts at the first appearance of the phrase, "Bring forth the

[29]

royal diadem." Holden intended that phrase to be sung only by the tenors and basses, leaving the full choir to respond, "And crown him Lord of all."

Lewis Edson's tunes *Greenfield*[4] and *Greenwich,* with Jeremiah Ingall's *New Jerusalem,* were among the most popular fuging tunes; the latter appeared, with three others, in a New England gospel-song collection published as late as 1916![5] When Lowell Mason edited the *Boston Handel and Haydn Society Collection of Church Music* in 1821, he included a few fuging tunes. Similarly in Mason's later collections, *e.g.,* the *Carmina Sacra,* there are a few true fuging tunes, and also a number of the antiphonal type, similar to Holden's *Coronation.*

The fuging tunes were equally popular in the South. Alexander Ely's *Baltimore Collection of Church Music* (1792) contained a high proportion of them. Here, in a predominantly rural atmosphere, they continued to be sung throughout the nineteenth century from such popular shape-note collections as William Walker's *Southern Harmony* (several editions between 1835 and 1854) and Benjamin White's *Sacred Harp* (1844, and other editions to the present time).[6]

Allen P. Britten has analyzed the contents of the tune-books of the period in an effort to characterize their musical idiom.[7] Contrasted with the English tunes of the same period, he found that American composers were, as Billings prided himself, every man "his own carver." Their tunes were more closely allied with folk elements, with more irregular phrases, stronger rhythmic pulse, and more use of the natural minor scale than is found in contemporary English tunes. Unprepared cadences and contrapuntally derived dissonances appear beside hollow fifths, imparting to the music a unique and almost archaic quality.

Otherwise throughout the eighteenth century, American tunes remained in the same basic idiom as those found in the English and Scottish psalters a century earlier. The florid tunes of eighteenth century English Methodism, the best-known example of the type being *Easter Hymn* ("Jesus Christ is ris'n today, Alleluia!"), had little vogue in this country save for a brief decade following 1810. They were soon to be crowded out by the more continental style and influence of Lowell Mason.[8]

[30]

CHAPTER V

Outside the Puritan Sphere

THE QUAKER province of Pennsylvania gave refuge to a number of groups from Central Europe who left their native lands for conscience's sake or were driven out by persecution. They formed distinct communities or congregations in the New World, keeping themselves apart both from their dissenting countrymen and their English-speaking neighbors. For a long time it was believed that the quality of their musical culture had no effect on the colony as a whole; more recent studies, however, have shown many connections by which their influence was spread through all the Colonies.

The first of these was a little band of fifteen Mennonite families which arrived at Germantown in 1683. The following year, a party of Labadists from Friesland settled on the Bohemian Manor in New Castle County. Ten years later, Johannes Kelpius brought a chapter of Pietists to found the community known as the Hermits, or Mystics, of the Wissahickon, on a site now included in Fairmount Park, in the Roxborough section of Philadelphia. During 1719, twenty families of Dunkards, or German Baptists, settled in Germantown—to be joined in 1725 by some of the *Neu-geborenen.* The Ephrata Community, led by Conrad Beissel and Peter Miller, dates from 1720. In 1734, groups of Schwenkfelders from Berthelsdorf and Görlitz settled near Philadelphia. The last and most important body of German Pietists to migrate to colonial Pennsylvania was the *Unitas Fratrum,* the United Brethren—also known as Moravians or Bohemian Brethren—whose members settled at Bethlehem, beginning in 1741.

[31]

Kelpius' group cultivated the monastic life, preaching, teaching, and working in a large garden of medicinal herbs. Their morning and evening devotional services attracted many visitors of varied nationalities and creeds. A manuscript hymnbook with German and English texts and occasional tunes, compiled by Kelpius and several of his brethren, is extant.[1] In 1703, they furnished the choir and instrumentalists for the ordination service of Justus Falckner in Gloria Dei Church.[2]

Gloria Dei, or Old Swedes Church, still standing on the waterfront in Philadelphia in a section formerly called Wicacoa, was consecrated on July 2, 1700. It was the foremost of five congregations which were supplied until 1791 by the Swedish Mission with distinguished clergy from the homeland who maintained the Swedish Lutheran liturgy of their national church, with its high standards of congregational hymnody.

The Mennonites and the Dunkards, like the Quakers, generally opposed instrumental or vocal music as commonly practiced in the church. They did, however, permit the use of a few conservative hymns. In more recent years, Mennonite hymnody has flourished.

The settlement at Ephrata was begun by Conrad Beissel, whose dissent from the Mennonites and Dunkards was on sabbatarian grounds. Beissel, who took the name Father Friedsam, came to Pennsylvania in 1720, in order to join the Hermits of the Wissahickon. Finding that the community had become extinct, he established a similar cloister at Ephrata, in Lancaster County. By 1740, there were 36 brethren and 35 sisters in residence; at the height of its prosperity, *ca.* 1770, the congregation numbered 300 persons. A printing press was set up in 1742 on which some 42 publications were issued, including their own hymnals, tracts, and Bibles. A large quantity of Continental money was printed on this press during 1777 and 1778. Their schools attracted pupils from many of the leading Pennsylvania families, and their leaders were respected scholars, familiars of such men as Franklin, Hopkinson, and Washington. Beissel's successor, Peter Miller, rendered distinguished service to the Revolutionary cause by translating the Declaration of Independence into seven European languages, which were forwarded to their respective countries. Francis Hopkinson penned the following lines *To Peter Miller at Ephrata:*

[32]

'Tis true devotion—and the Lord of love
Such prayers and praises kindly will approve,
Whether from golden altars they arise,
And wrapt in sound and incense reach the skies,
Or from your Ephrata so meek and low,
In soft and silent aspirations flow.[3]

The praises, in antiphonal part-songs, became widely known for
their excellent intonation and pure tone quality. Beissel was outstanding as a director, composer, and teacher of music, and under his leadership the study and practice of music became a distinctive feature of
the Community. The women were organized into three choirs of four
parts each, taking the lower parts as well as the higher ones. Similarly,
the men sang in parts, so that when combined, the mixed ensemble
was in as many as seven parts. Since there is no record of the use of
instruments, we may assume that all of the singing was unaccompanied. The music, much of it consisting of original compositions by
Beissel, was homophonic, but judging by contemporary accounts of
performances, was sung in a free rhythm governed by the accent of
the words. An account of the singing written sometime before 1835
by William M. Fahnstock, M.D.,[4] stated that the tones imitated soft
instrumental music, and were entirely sung in the falsetto voice, which
may account for the striking impression the music had on all visitors.

Beissel's thories on music were published in the preface to the
Ephrata hymnal, the *Turtel-Taube* (1747), and in the *Chronicon
Ephratense* (1786).[5] Judging by the harmonizations of his tunes, he
knew little traditional theory, for there are many parallel fifths and
octaves, with other weak doublings. But his ideas were minutely detailed, so that they could be meticulously followed by the brothers and
sisters. Diet was an important factor, for it was "especially necessary
to know what kinds of food . . . make the spirit teachable, and the
voice flexible and clear." Meat and foods derived from animals were
condemned, as was

butter, which makes indolent and satiates to such an extent that one
no longer feels the need of singing or praying; *eggs,* which arouse
numerous capricious cravings; *honey,* which brings bright eyes and a
cheerful spirit, but not a clear voice.

Of bread and cooked dishes, none are better for producing cheerfulness of disposition and buoyancy of spirit than *wheat* and after this *buckwheat*. . . .

As regards the other common vegetables, none are more useful than the ordinary *potato,* the *beet,* and other *tubers. Beans* are too heavy, satiate too much. . . .

Elsewhere Beissel specified different diets for high and low voices.

A pressing need for musical scores prior to the installation of their own printing press, and continuing even afterwards on a more limited scale, led to the preparation of manuscript choral books which were decorated with elaborate illuminations based on the mystical tulip, pomegranate, lilies, and doves—all popular emblems of Ephrata symbolism. Several of these manuscripts are now preserved in historical collections, one of the finest, a presentation copy from the sisters to their leader in 1745, being in the Music Division of the Library of Congress.[6]

With the decline of the monastic features of the Community at the end of the eighteenth century, its music fell into disuse save in a limited way in the nunnery at Snowhill, Franklin County, until the last of the sisters passed away, only a few years ago. Today, the grounds and buildings of the old community are preserved as a historic shrine.

The Schwenkfelders were another group which produced a number of fine manuscript music-books. They used many of the hymn books of the Moravians, which they gradually augmented with interleaved manuscripts of their own. A number of complete manuscript collections were also compiled prior to the publication of their own hymnal in 1762.[7]

The Moravian immigrants were the spiritual descendants of a distinguished line of Bohemian Protestants from the days of John Hus. By the time of Luther, they had over four hundred churches in Bohemia and Moravia, with others in Silesia and Poland. But the Peace of Westphalia left the Brethren in dire straits, for they had no princes to represent them. Johann Comenius, the famous philosopher and educator, once invited to become Harvard's president, tried in vain to secure adequate aid. His writings were, however, the means of converting Count Nicholas von Zinzendorf, who provided refuge for the fugitive remnants on his estate at Berthelsdorf, in Saxony. Here the

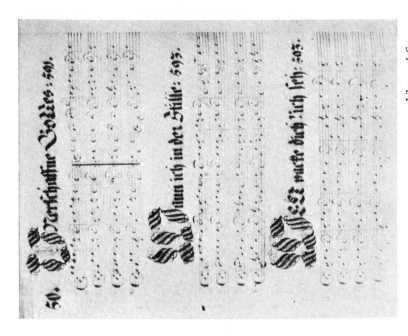

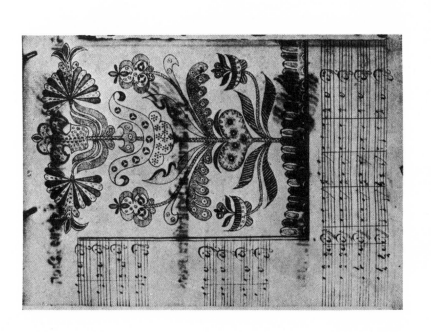

Library of Congress

Plate III. Pages of an Illuminated Manuscript from the Ephrata Community

Francis Hopkinson
(1737-1791)

*Historical Society
of Pennsylvania*

Benjamin Carr
(1768-1831)

Library of Congress

PLATE IV.

Herrnhut was built and the discipline and vigor of the church re-
newed. The first to begin a Protestant hymnody, they had songs for
every act of life. Fresh refugees were received, missionaries sent out,
and even the night-watchman made his rounds to the singing of
chorales.

In 1735, twenty-six of the Moravians migrated to Georgia[8] to begin
work with the Indians near Savannah. Five years later, they moved
to Pennsylvania, where they settled at Nazareth on land owned by
George Whitefield. The following year they purchased a tract of land
on the Lehigh River and began the settlement at Bethlehem, to be
visited that winter by Count Zinzendorf with additional recruits. Filled
with zeal for missions and educational activities, the community
thrived. A report of Bishop Spangenberg to the colonial governor in
1756 stated that the community consisted of 188 married persons and
322 children, with 225 additional single men, 67 single women, and
96 other children who were orphans or boarding pupils. Forty-eight
were absent at the time, engaged in missionary work among the Indians;[9] 54 were preaching or teaching school in other parts of the
American colonies, 62 were tutors or attendants in their own schools.
Ere long, other communities were established at Lititz, Christian's
Spring, Gnadenthal, Friedensthal, Salem in North Carolina, and Hope
in New Jersey.

Wherever the Moravians were, they used music in their daily life.
They sang at meals, in the fields, in the work shops, and while travel-
ing. When a special group engaged on a particular enterprise—such as
a week's camping in the forest to fell timber—they were given a love-
feast, a common meal, with singing, and then a procession with instrumental music to start them on their way. Hymns helped speed the
completion of arduous tasks. They were heroic days, and Bishop Spangenberg's motto was lived in full:

> In commune oramus,
> In commune laboramus,
> In commune patimur,
> In commune gaudeamus.

Polyglot singing was practiced for a few years at Bethlehem, possibly due to the varied nationalities present in the community as well

as a deliberate expression of the universality of the church, which was the Moravian ideal. Thus, at a love-feast on September 14, 1745, the old German carol *In dulci jubilo* was sung in thirteen languages simultaneously by academicians, missionaries, Indian converts, and settlers—people of every strain and race: Bohemian, Dutch, English, French, German, Greek, Irish, Latin, Mohawk, Mohican, Swedish, Welsh, and Wendish.

Naturally, such constant use of music led to intensive practice and the cultivation of musical talents. The Collegium Musicum was formed in 1744, with weekly rehearsals of instrumental and choral music. By 1780, its orchestra consisted of four violins, a viola, and two each of violoncellos, flutes, oboes, horns, and trumpets; its repertory included works by Abel, J. C. Bach, Graun, Haydn, Mozart, Stamitz, and others. Instruments and music were constantly being purchased abroad as well as being copied at home. John Antes not only made violins, but also composed a number of quartets for strings and anthems for church use. Other prolific and not unworthy composers were John Frederick Peter[10] and John G. Herbst. While Philadelphia may have led the country in its concert life toward the end of the eighteenth century, it did not begin to approach Bethlehem in the quantity and quality of its music-making. This is true not only in the field of orchestra and chamber music, but in church music as well. Nowhere in the country could one hear anthems with instrumental accompaniment on the scale used in the Moravian communities.

A distinctive feature of Moravian music which is preserved to the present time is the trombone choir. It cannot be determined when their use was first introduced into the Moravian rite in Europe, but it is known that trombones were brought to this country with the first immigrants to Georgia. They have continued in constant use ever since. The quartet, or choir, consists of treble, alto, tenor, and bass trombones, permitting the chorales to be played in full four-part harmony. Tradition has it that such chorales played in the early morning hours of Christmas Day, 1757, unwittingly deterred an attack by hostile Indians. A schedule of tunes was worked out in the mid-eighteenth century and later printed in the German Moravian Liturgy Book of 1791, which provided special chorales for each occasion in the life and worship of the community. Thus the *Passion Chorale* tune by Hans Leo Hassler was used to announce the death of a member of the community. Such announcement tunes were played from the church tower or belfry. Another use was in the welcoming of distinguished visitors, such as General Washington and his retinue. It was an honored, albeit rigorous service, and the trombonists put in long years of daily devotion to their duties. Grider[11] has recorded the names of the players over a period of a century and a half.

An anecdote which he relates is illustrative of the liberal outlook toward music among the Moravians, in marked contrast with the New England viewpoint described in Chapter II. When a zealous young minister questioned the propriety of using the same instruments in church on Sunday that had been used for secular music the evening before, one of his elders asked: "Will you use the same mouth to preach with today which you now use in eating sausage?"*

Jesuit missions in French America never became as intensive as were the Franciscan missions in New Spain, due in large measure to the desultory and feeble attempts made to colonize the northern regions by the French, as well as to the migratory nature of the northern tribes. Consequently, little has been recorded of musical activities there.[12] In Father Claude Dablon's *Relation de ce qui s'est passé . . .* of the years 1671 and 1672 (Part II, Chapter V, Article III), "De la mission faite aux peuples de la Baye des Puans," the labors of Father Louis André at Green Bay, Wisconsin, are described:

> The reason why he was so eagerly sought was found in certain spiritual songs that he was wont to have the children sing to French airs, which pleased those savages extremely; so that our teachings were published in the streets and cabins, and were received with applause, impressing themselves insensibly on people's minds through these songs.
>
> This success encouraged the Father, and made him resolve to assail the men through the children, and to combat idolatry with souls of extreme innocence. In short, he composed some songs against the superstitions that we have mentioned, and against the vices most opposed to Christianity; and after teaching the children to sing them to the accompaniment of a sweet-toned flute, he went everywhere with these little savage musicians, to declare war on jugglers, dreamers, and those who had several wives. And, as the savages are passionately fond of their

[37]

*The Moravian Music Foundation, since its establishment at Winston-Salem, North Carolina, in 1956, has sponsored an archive, related studies and festivals of Moravian music. See *The Moravian Music Foundation Bulletin* and *Moravian Music Foundation Publications* for details.

children, and will endure anything at their hands, they accepted the reproaches, bitter though they were, that were made them through the songs, since they came from their children's mouths.[13]

In Maine, Father Sebastian Rale trained a vested choir of forty young Abnakis for his chapel at Norridgewock *ca.* 1700.[14]

The Iroquois mission founded in 1668 at La Prairie, near Montreal, Canada, is unique in that it received a papal indult permitting its services to be sung in the Indians' own language instead of in Latin. In 1676 this mission moved to Sault St. Louis, the home of the Blessed Catherine Tegahwitha (*d.* 1689). A century later, the mission moved to St. Regis, where the privilege of the vernacular is still enjoyed.[15]

There is almost no further record of such musical activity until after the Colonial period. Although Maryland was originally founded as a refuge for Roman Catholics from England, nothing is known of early church music there.

The first notice of a festival *Te Deum* being sung in the colonies is cited by the Right Reverend Hugh T. Henry.[16] St. Mary's Church, Philadelphia, founded in 1763, was used by the French and other Roman Catholics connected with the Continental Congress. Here, as reported by the *Pennsylvania Packet* for July 10, 1779, was held at noon on Sunday, the Fourth of July, a commemoration of the Declaration of Independence, attended by the President and members of Congress, where they heard a "*Te Deum* solemnly sung by a number of very good voices, accompanied by the organ and other kinds of music."

In 1787, John Aitken published in Philadelphia *A Compilation of the Litanies, Vespers, Hymns and Anthems As they are Sung in the Catholic Church.* The work also contained treble and bass parts for *The Holy Mass of the Blessed Trinity* and *The Mass for the Dead,* the parts of which were interspersed with the hymns. Other editions with three parts, and with the contents rearranged so that the masses were printed as units, were published in 1791 and 1814. The following are the contents of the edition of 1791, an octavo volume of 181 pages:

The Litany of Loretto [Latin]
Litany [English]
4 additional chant tunes for the Litany.
Komm, reiner Geist.

[38]

Veni Creator [Latin and English]
Pange Lingua [Latin and English]
The Holy Mass of the Blessed Trinity [Latin]
℣ & ℟: *Dominica ad Vesperas* [Latin and English]
Psalms 109, 110, 111, 112, 113, 116 [Latin and English]
Lucis Creator [Latin and English]
Magnificat [Latin and English]
[Anthems in Latin:]
   Alma Redemptoris Mater
   Ave Regina coelorum
   Regina coeli laetate
   Salve Regina
Psalm 50 [Latin and English]
Ave Maria [Latin]
Missa Pro Defunctis [Latin—plainsong]
The day of wrath [English]
Psalm 129 [Latin and English]
Sing ye praises [English—the tune *Easter Hymn*]
Psalm CIV [in English metre]
[Anthems in English:]
   Grateful notes and numbers bring
   Jesu dulcis memoria
   The wonders which God's laws contain
   This is the day which the Lord hath made.
   Alleluia. Young men and maidens [*O filii et filiae*]
   Sing to the Lord a new song
   Lift up your gates
   How various Lord, thy works are found
   King of kings, Lord of lords
   O praise ye the Lord
   O be joyful in the Lord
   Make a joyful noise unto God
   We adore and worship thee
   Through all the changing scenes of life
   Sing unto God
   Let us magnify thee
   Praise the Lord with cheerful noise
   Let the bright seraphim (Handel)
   Praise the Lord Jerusalem
   This solemn feast our joyful songs inspire
   Praise the Lord, O my soul
   I will glorify thee, O God

[39]

Salve Regina: Hail to the Queen [in English metre]
[Latin arias:]
  Confitebor tibi, Domine
  Deus ego amo te
  O anima beata
  Benedicamus Patrem
  O Esca viatorum
  Jesu dulcis memoria
  O Jesu, Deus magne
  O Salutaris Hostia
[Anthem:] *Asperges me*
In die Solemni Missa [with a little polyphony, less instrumental than
  the first Mass]
[Aria:] *O aller höchste Speise*

No composers are indicated for any of the music. Solos and choruses
are clearly noted, but it is not easy to distinguish between instrumental
or vocal parts.

In 1800, the Reverend John Cheverus[17] published in Boston a 72-page
collection entitled *Anthems, Hymns, &c Usually Sung at the Catholick
Church in Boston.* An enlarged edition appeared in Baltimore in 1807
under a slightly different title. Father Cheverus then brought out a
*Roman Catholic Manual, or Collection of Prayers, Anthems, Hymns,
&c.,* Boston, 1803, with subsequent editions in 1807 and 1823.

In 1805, Benjamin Carr, a leading musician and publisher of Philadelphia, brought out his *Masses, Vespers, Litanies . . . composed,
selected and arranged for the use of the Catholic Churches in the
United States of America,* a work dedicated to Bishop John Carroll
of Baltimore, the first Roman Catholic bishop in the United States.
Carr's work included an original mass and a *Te Deum.* A second edition appeared in 1811. Both Aitken's and Carr's collections contained
hymns in English which were identical with those sung in contemporary Protestant services.

The Church of England was well established in Virginia early in
the seventeenth century. With the advent, in England, of the interreg-
num Commonwealth, all worship according to the Book of Common
Prayer was suppressed for over a decade. With the restoration, in 1660,
of not only Charles II but also the Prayer Book and the clergy, the

Church in many of the Colonies entered upon a period of vigorous growth. A century or so later the advance was again halted, this time by the upheavals brought about by the American Revolution. Many clergy and laity, by reason of oath or inclination—or both—remained loyal to the Crown, and were forced to leave the Colonies or suffer deprivation. At the same time, much of the leadership of the Revolutionary cause came out of the colonial Anglican Church. Washington and over two-thirds of the signers of the Declaration of Independence,[18] among them Francis Hopkinson, were Churchmen, and the government of the Episcopal Church in the United States was soon organized along lines similar to those of the new Federal Government itself.

During these years, music in the Episcopal Church differed little from that in the Puritan congregations of New England. The clerk gave out the metrical Psalms from his desk, supported, in some of the larger churches, by a gallery choir. In the smaller chapels-of-ease there was frequently no singing at all, but merely the reading of the Prayer Book offices by the minister and clerk. Where there was a choir, it was often accompanied at an early date by an organ, as will be noted in Chapter VII. Elsewhere, a few orchestral instruments were used. One such instance, in George Washington's presence, is cited on pages 57-8.

A primary characteristic of Episcopal Church music, Anglican Chant, is first noted in Andrew Law's *Rudiments of Music* (1783), "to which are annexed a number of plain tunes and chants," with rules for chanting. Two years later, Francis Hopkinson included three chants with the music in the back of the Proposed Prayer Book of 1785. A passage in a letter from Francis Hopkinson to Bishop White, quoted in part on page 49, infers that the practice was not new. The bishop himself, in a letter dated June 20, 1809, stated,

> Having been, so far as I know, the first clergyman in the United States who introduced chanting into any of our churches. . . .[19]

This claim must be due to a certain amount of provincialism, however, for English-trained musicians in Boston, Newport, New York, and Charleston can hardly have failed to have introduced it. This is indirectly evidenced by the statement of Henry Mason Brooks[20] that chanting was first introduced in this country at Christmas, 1787, in

[41]

St. Michael's Church, Marblehead, Massachusetts—four years after Law's publication. It took hold rapidly thereafter, for chants are to be found in most tune-books published at the end of the century.

The services of Morning and Evening Prayer were used almost exclusively during the eighteenth century, and all of the extant Anglican service music relates to them. The Holy Communion was seldom administered save for three or four times a year—usually on Easter and Whitsunday, and on the Sundays following Christmas and Michaelmas. Not until John Cole's *Episcopalian Harmony* (Baltimore, 1800) do the tune-books include settings of the Responses to the Decalogue, the *Kyrie, Gloria tibi,* and *Sanctus.* Not until after the Oxford Movement do we find the full musical settings of the Communion Service *(Kyrie, Credo, Sanctus, Agnus Dei,* and *Gloria in excelsis)* which are common today.

In at least two Episcopal churches, however, boy choirs were established during the course of the eighteenth century for the purpose of singing the metrical Psalms and the chants of Morning Prayer.

In 1709, Trinity Church, New York, founded a charity school for boys. It met at first in a rented room for secular teaching, and in the porch of the church itself for religious instruction, including psalmody. The first master was William Huddlestone (*ca.* 1663-1726), a local lawyer and a vestryman who was then serving as parish clerk, and therefore responsible for the Psalm singing.[21] He may very well have used some of his forty-eight boys as a group of singing-boys to help with the psalmody in services. They are next mentioned in the vestry minutes of 1739, when it was ordered that someone be employed to teach "such Youth to sing as shall be recommended." Two years later, a Mr. Eldridge was paid five pounds "for his care and pains in having the children taught to sing Psalms.[22] Further references of this sort indicate that a group of singing-boys was used regularly at Trinity during most of the eighteenth century. The practise lapsed for a number of years, however, for when Edward Hodges arrived in 1839 to serve as organist-choirmaster, his choir consisted of but six persons, apparently all adults. In 1843, he was able to secure sixteen music scholarships at Trinity School and thereby restore singing-boys to the Trinity Choir.

Reference will be made in Chapter VI to Francis Hopkinson's work in teaching the children of Christ Church, Philadelphia, in 1764. Nothing further is known as to the extent of their use in services, but of possible significance in this connection is the fact that the manuscript of his *Anthem from the 114th Psalm,* dated 1759, is arranged for two treble parts and a figured bass.

At St. Michael's, Charleston, South Carolina, the establishment of a municipal orphanage in 1791 prompted the rector, the Reverend Dr. Henry Purcell, and his organist, Samuel Rodgers, to turn to this ready source of choir-boy material. Both men had been trained in the English cathedral tradition, and it was only natural that they should attempt to develop their music along those lines. A pew was designated for the use of the boys in the rear gallery, by the organ, and surplices of Irish linen were prepared. Laundry bills for these were paid through the year 1798.[23] In 1793, the boys were permitted to sing at a benefit performance in the local theater. During the next two decades, St. Michael's, with its peal of Whitechapel bells, its Snetzler organ, and its boy choir, maintained the finest musical establishment in the country.

The vestry minutes of St. Michael's afford some interesting pictures of early customs. The following instructions to the organist, still Samuel Rodgers, are dated February 27, 1803:

THE ORGANIST Shall perform the Duties of his Office, which Shall from Time to Time be directed by the Ministers, in the Mornings & Evenings of every Sabbath Day in the year; also on Such Festivals or Holy days, as now are, or shall hereafter be appointed by Authority:— He shall perform on the Organ, at all Times preceding the Services of the Day, the Time usually adapted to the 36th. Hymn, or any other Solemn piece of Music; to begin at the exact Time the Clergyman enters the Desk, & to continue the Music for one Verse only, or for a reasonable Time.—He shall chant the *Venite exultemus* & the *te Deum,* on alternate Sundays; & Shall play a solemn & well adapted Voluntary, preceding the first Lesson; & Shall receive from the Clerk such Psalms or Hymns as the Ministers shall appoint for the Day, in Order to adapt them to suitable Tunes.—He shall not only accompany the Clerk with the Organ, in such Psalms and Hymns as may be appropriated by the Ministers; but shall join the Clerk in the Gloria Patri, which shall invariably be sung after every Sermon; He shall also perform at all

[43]

Funerals, to which he may be invited, accompanying the Clerk with the Organ in the Gloria Patri, which shall always be sung at the Conclusions of Funerals, Psalms, or Hymns: He shall, in Conjunction with the Clerk, instruct such Youth as chuse to attend (who shall be particularly placed under his charge) in the Rules & Practice of Psalmody; & he shall command and require of them, a serious and decent Deportment, during the Time of divine Service: And at the Conclusion of Morning & Evening Service, the voluntary, which he shall play shall be some Piece of *sacred Musick,* of rather *slow Time,* such as will tend to cherish the solemn Impressions made by the pious Exercises of Prayer & Exortation. And lastly, it is fully understood and required that he shall be under the Direction of the Clergymen of the said Church for the Time being, in all such things appertaining to its religious Services—

The directions to the clerk, Samuel Ruddock, read:

THE CLERK shall attend in the Vestry on the Mornings & Evenings of every Sabbath Day in the Year; also on such Festivals and Holy-Days, as well as at all Times when either of the Ministers shall be called to the Discharge of the Duties of their Function in the said Church, in order to receive such Directions as may be thought expedient to be given to him for the Service of the Day. He is hereby directed to chant the *Venite exultemus,* or *Te Deum,* accompanied with the organ: He shall likewise receive from the Preacher of the Morning or Evening of every Sabbath Day, the appropriate Psalms to be sung on the Day; and shall immediately deliver a copy of the said Psalms to the Organist for the purpose of adapting them to suitable Tunes before the Service begins: He shall attend all Funerals and invite to them all such Persons & Families in the City, as shall be directed by the Friends of the deceased. —He shall give Notice to the Officiating Minister, as soon as possible, at what Hour the Funeral is to be; and He is to use every possible Effort that the Corps be moved at that time.—He shall, in Conjunction with the Organist, instruct such Youth of the Church as choose to attend, in the Rules & Practice of Psalmody and Chanting; He shall collect all the Perquisites of the Officers of the Church and deliver to them the established Fees; and He shall not fail in his early Attendance at the Church on the days of Prayer.—And lastly, it is fully understood and required, that he shall be under the Direction of the Clergymen of the said Church, for the Time being, in all things appertaining to the Duties of his Office—

On December 6, 1807,

The Vestry considering the necessity and propriety there is for the Clerk of this church to act in conjunction with the organist in the

instruction & Practice of the Boys in Psalmody & chaunting—Resolved
to allow the Clerk in addition to his former Salary of £50. Per annum
the further Sum of *Fifty Dollars* Per ann. for the purpose of encouraging and exciting his exertions to the judicious fulfilment of this part of
his Duty. This additional Salary to Commence as Soon as the requisite
Number of Boys is obtained to establish the Choir & the Vestry have
notice of the Same.

At the same meeting a committee was appointed to draw up supple-
mentary rules for the regulation of the organist, choir, and clerk. The
following rules were presented one week later:

> 1st. That it be the Duty of the Organist & Clerk to attend at the Church
> every Friday afternoon at   oClock, & every Sunday Morning at
> 9 oClock throughout the Year, for the purpose of Instructing the
> Boys, composing the Choir, in Psalmody & Chaunting; at which time,
> the Boys are required, *Punctually* to attend them.
> 2nd. That the Choir will not be considered as *complete* by the Vestry
> without the *constant and regular* attendance of *Twelve* Boys, at least;
> it is, however, the Wish of the Vestry that as many more than that
> number may attend, as can be Conveniently accommodated in the
> Orchestra [i.e., the choir gallery].
> 3rd. That it be the Duty of the Organist & Clerk to attend diligently
> to the Behavior of the Boys, & to preserve such order & decorum in
> the Orchestra as Shall become the Solemnity of Divine Worship. That
> it be required of the Organist to dismiss from the Choir, any whom
> he shall find, after *repeated adminition,* to be disorderly, rude or
> refractory, or any whom the Rector or Minister of the Church shall
> find to Persist, & shall thereupon point out to the Organist as having
> been observed by him, or them, to *persist* in such behavior—
> 4th. That in order to the removal of any interruption of the Services
> of the Orchestra, No person or Persons whatever be allowed to Set
> therein beside the Organist, Clerk & Choir: And, that the Organist
> & Clerk be requested to notify to any Person, or Persons who may
> ask Permission to set there during the Time of Divine Service, or any
> part of Divine Service, that they are directed by the Vestry *not to*
> *admit* him or them to a Seat there.

In December, 1817, the propriety of the organ voluntary was questioned. The rector, Dr. Frederick Dalcho, addressed the following in-
quiry to a committee of the vestry:

> Will you have the goodness to let me Know in the course of the day,
> the decision of the Committee on the Subject of omitting the Voluntary;

[45]

as it will be advisable to give notice of it to the Congregation tomorrow. It will likewise be necessary to inform the organist of the contemplated change. The following, I believe to be the alteration proposed, & which meets with my hearty Concurrence. To omit the Voluntary on the organ after reading the Psalms for the day of the month, in the Morning & Evening Service, & to Substitute in its place, the Chant of *Gloria in Excelsis.* This Change will certainly be pleasing to the pious part of the Congregation, perhaps to all.

The vestry thereupon resolved to order

the Substitution of the *"Gloria in Excelsis:"* in lieu of the Voluntary, the former being Permitted to be used by the Rubric, & the latter not being at all noticed in it.

It should be pointed out that the organ voluntary at this point in the service was characteristic of Episcopal usage only. The custom may have originated in the English cathedral services as a musical interlude to fill the time required for the precentor to pass from his stall to the lectern following the singing of the Psalms and before the reading of the First Lesson. But in the colonial churches the minister remained in his reading desk. The natural urge of organists and congregations to enjoy the expensive instrument in which they had invested was later satisfied elsewhere by the "offertory"—an organ solo played during the collection of the alms of the congregation, a practice still followed in many Protestant churches.

CHAPTER VI

Eighteenth Century Composers

IN SPITE of the popularity of psalmody throughout colonial America, the first known work by an American composer is a secular art-song. Actually, of course, it is impossible to determine who may have been the first American to make up a melody of his own, or who may have been the first deacon, singing-school teacher, or choirmaster to have introduced tunes of his own composition. Most of the following composers were so closely contemporaneous that no single one can truly be said to stand out as the first American composer.

Francis Hopkinson (1737-1791) has been acclaimed our first composer on the grounds that his song "My days have been so wondrous free," was composed in 1759, several years before any American Psalmtunes were published. He himself claimed that distinction in the dedication to Washington of his *Seven Songs* of 1788.[1] Since he was well acquainted with the German-born musicians discussed in the previous chapter, we may assume that his claim was made advisedly. Born in Philadelphia on September 21, 1737, Hopkinson was the first student to enroll in the College of Philadelphia (now the University of Pennsylvania), where he graduated, A.B. 1757, M.A., 1760, and received the LL.D. in 1790. He was admitted to the bar and served as secretary of the Indian Treaty Commission in 1761. Journeying to England in 1766, he returned the following year to engage in political activity. Poet, essayist, satirist, there are preserved many letters which he exchanged with Washington, Jefferson, and Franklin. He signed the Declaration of Independence for New Jersey, later becoming the first

[47]

Secretary of the Navy in Washington's Cabinet. He was admiralty judge for Pennsylvania from 1779 to 1789, and then judge of the U.S. District Court until his death, in 1791. He has been called, next to Franklin, the most versatile American of the eighteenth century.

As an undergraduate, he staged Arne's *Masque of Alfred*. Several manuscripts of original songs and harpsichord works attest his constant interest in music, although he remained essentially an amateur all of his life. He invented an improved method for quilling the harpsichord which attracted considerable attention in European musical circles, being mentioned in Fétis' *Biographie universelle des musiciens*. He also adapted a keyboard to Franklin's famous musical glasses.[2]

Hopkinson deservedly stands near the first of American church musicians as well. The year after Lyon's *Urania*[3] was published, Hopkinson brought out his *Collection of Psalm Tunes* (1763), for the united Christ and St. Peter's Churches, Philadelphia, where he long served as vestryman and warden. Some of the tunes were of his own composition. His continuing interest in the music of his church is shown in the vestry minutes of April 3, 1764:

> . . . the members of the vestry, who frequently attended while the children of the united congregations were improved in the art of psalmody, reported that they had observed Mr. William Young in connection with the secretary, Mr. Hopkinson, to take great and constant pains in teaching and instructing the children; it was therefore unanimously agreed that the thankful acknowledgments of the board be given Mr. Hopkinson and Mr. Young for their kind services which they are requested still to continue.

And again in the minutes of December 10, 1770:

> Mr. Churchwarden Hopkinson having been so obliging as to perform on the organ at Christ Church during the absence of Mr. Bremner,[4] the late organist, the vestry unanimously requested of him a continuance of this kind office, until an organist should be appointed, or as long as it should be convenient and agreeable to himself.

Sometime after 1779 he wrote a long letter to the Reverend Dr. William White (later the first Bishop of Pennsylvania) "On the conduct of church organs," in which he summarized his views on the esthetic side of the organist's work. The letter concludes thus:

[48]

In general, the organ should ever preserve its dignity; and upon no account issue light and pointed movements which may draw the attention of the congregation and induce them to carry home not the serious sentiments which the service should impress, but some very pretty air with which the organist hath been so good as to entertain them. It is as offensive to hear lilts and jigs from a church organ, as it would be to see a venerable matron frisking through the public streets with all the fantastic airs of a *Columbine*.⁵

A few years after the publication of his *Collection of Psalm Tunes*, Hopkinson was commissioned by the Dutch Church in New York to prepare a psalter for them in English which would be adapted to the traditional Genevan tunes.⁶ This was accomplished by judiciously adapting the New Version of Tate and Brady, the resultant work being published in 1767 as *The Psalms of David . . . For the Use of the Reformed Protestant Dutch Church of the City of New York*.⁷ Nearly two decades later Hopkinson edited the music for the hymns at the back of the Proposed Prayer Book of 1785, published unofficially in April 1786. This little work, the beginning of the modern Episcopal hymnal, contained eighteen tunes and three chants.

Among the composer's manuscripts which are still preserved is a collection of songs, part-songs, operatic excerpts, and other pieces, all with harpsichord accompaniment or figured bass, dated 1759 and now owned by the Library of Congress. Of more than one hundred compositions in the manuscript, sixteen are by Handel while others are by Purcell, Boyce, Arne, Hasse, and Pergolesi. At least six are his own compositions, two of them being anthems. The *Anthem from the 114th Psalm,* "What aileth thee, O thou sea," compares favorably with much of the English work of the period, with an occasional touch of the Handelian style. It is written for three voices, with figured bass.

He died in Philadelphia on May 9, 1791, and was buried in Christ Church yard.

William Billings (1746-1800) was the composer who attracted the most attention during the latter part of the century in the field of church music. He was born in Boston and was a tanner by trade. He had little formal education, but was fired with an irrepressible zeal for developing popular singing. He was blind in one eye, with a withered arm and one leg shorter than the other, but with a stentorian voice which drowned out all those near him. His eccentricities caused small boys to torment him upon occasion, but his enthusiasm was contagious, and his tunes had a freshness which made them well liked. He opened a music store in Boston and from 1764 sponsored concerts there. At the same time he traveled extensively in that area, organizing singing schools and musical societies.

Billings' first tune-book, *The New-England Psalm-Singer,* came out in 1770. Its frontispiece, engraved by Paul Revere, shows seven men seated around a table, the whole encircled by "a Canon of 6 in One with a Ground." His defiance of the rules of composition, which he had never bothered to learn, was expressed in the preface:

> Perhaps it may be expected by some, that I should say something concerning Rules of Composition; to these I answer that *Nature is the best Dictator,* for all the hard dry studied rules that ever were prescribed will not enable any person to form an air, any more than the bare knowledge of the four and twenty letters and strict grammatical Rules will qualify a Scholar for composing a piece of Poetry. . . . For my part, as I don't think myself confined to any Rules for Composition laid down by any that went before me, neither should I think (were I to pretend to lay down rules) that any who come after me were in any ways obliged to adhere to them, any further than they should think proper: so in fact I think it best that Every Composer should be his own Carver.

This collection, and the five which followed it, contained only his own compositions. Some were conservative tunes, a few were modest anthems,[8] while many were excellent models of the new fuging tunes. These furnished, under his leadership, a colonial counterpart to the rise of Methodist singing in England. His tunes and anthems appeared on many programs in American cities during the next few decades, and were reprinted in subsequent tune-books for over a generation. His tune *Chester* with its defiant text, became a veritable national anthem during the Revolutionary War. Yet, like many a greater composer, he died a pauper in 1800.

Abraham Maxim (1773-1829), a pupil of Billings, was born in Carver, Massachusetts. His brother wrote that "his heart and mind

Christ Church, Philadelphia

PLATE V. The Choir-loft and Organ, Christ Church, Philadelphia

Frederick J. Miller

PLATE VI. The Snetzler Organ in the Congregational Church
of South Dennis, Massachusetts

were so absorbed in music that he was of little use on the farm." He settled at Turner, Maine, where he taught "reading schools and singing schools." His *Northern Harmony* (Exeter, New Hampshire, 1803) went through several editions and his fuging-tune *Hallowell* was one of the last of its genre to drop out of use.

Oliver Holden (1765-1844) was a native of Shirley, Massachusetts. After service in the Marine Corps, he settled in Charlestown, Massachusetts, and helped to rebuild the town after its burning at the hands of the British. He acquired large real-estate holdings, kept a music store and taught music, was elected to Congress, and became a prominent Mason. For a time he served as minister at the Puritan church which he had built virtually unaided. His organ is preserved in the rooms of the Bostonian Society in the Old State House, Boston. His tune *Coronation* mentioned in Chapter IV as a quasi-fuging tune, is the oldest American tune in general use today.

Philadelphia and Boston were not alone in their cultivation of church music and its composers. William Tuckey (1708-1781) was active at Trinity Church, New York.[9] He had received English cathedral training, having been a vicar-choral of Bristol Cathedral. In 1753 he was appointed clerk at Trinity Church and given the use of the charity school room and also the vestry room two nights a week for his singing lessons. The following year, "Scholars to the number of 56 . . . sung an Hymn suitable to the Occasion." It is recorded that in 1761 he composed and directed "an Anthem on the death of his late Sacred Majesty [George II]." His tunes were included in many collections for several generations. On January 9, 1770, he directed the performance of seventeen numbers from Handel's *Messiah,* the first performance of this work in America. It is not clear how he spent his last years; it is known only that he died in Philadelphia on September 14, 1781, and was buried in Christ Church yard.

In Charleston, South Carolina, Peter Valton (*d.* 1784) was organist of St. Philip's Church from 1764 to 1781, and then at St. Michael's for two years. Prior to 1762 he was deputy organist at the King's Chapel, Westminster Abbey. He advertised subscriptions for the publication of *Six Sonatas for Harpsichord or Organ* in 1768, but nothing further is known about these works. Sonneck[10] also lists his *Ode for the Festival of St. John, Evangelist.* Another Charleston composer was Benjamin Yarnold (*d.*1787) who arrived from London in 1753 to become the organist at St. Philip's Church. He made several subsequent moves, becoming organist of St. Michael's in 1784. Sonneck[11] found notices of an *Anthem and Ode* by Yarnold performed *ca.* 1762.

American composition in both secular and sacred music was admittedly weak in the colonial period. The same, although to a lesser degree, was true of musical composition in the mother country. Even there the art did not flourish during the eighteenth century as it had during the two previous centuries. In America the best efforts in the field of sacred composition came from the various Moravian settlements. Unfortunately, little of their music is generally known today.

CHAPTER VII

The First Organs and Bells

THERE were no church organs in the American Colonies to be destroyed in accordance with the (English) *Orders in Council* of May 6, 1644:

> Two Ordinances of the Lords and Commons in Parliament for the speedy Demolishing of all Organs, Images and all manner of Superstitious Monuments in Cathedralls, Parish Churches and Chapells, throughout the Kingdom of England and Dominion of Wales: the better to accomplish the blessed Reformation so happily begun, and to remove all offences and things illegal in the Worship of God.

Several organs have been described as the very first to be used in the colonies. Actually, the earliest reference we find to organ music pertains to a little known instrument in the Swedish Gloria Dei Church at Wicacoa (Philadelphia). Here, on November 24, 1703, Justus Falckner was ordained to the Lutheran ministry. The service was conducted by the Swedish clergy, with music furnished by Johannes Kelpius and his Mystics of the Wissahickon. Julius F. Sachse, in his *Justus Falckner . . . a Bi-Centennial Memorial,* describes the music:

> The service was opened with a voluntary on the little organ in the gallery by Jonas the organist, supplemented with instrumental music by the Mystics on the viol, haut-boy, trumpets, and kettle-drums. After this they intoned the Anthem: *Veni Creator Spiritus.*

"Jonas the organist" was mentioned a year earlier in a diary, but nothing else is known of him. Nor can anything else be determined about the little organ he used. It had not been in the church at the time of its consecration two years earlier. It is possible that it was a portable instrument brought over from the Wissahickon for the occasion, as there is an account stating that Dr. Christopher Witt and others of the Community built an organ there at an early date.

Actually, Witt did not arrive from England until the following year. He is, however, the earliest organ builder known to have worked in the colonies, and may have been the builder of the organ which Christ Church, Philadelphia, purchased in 1728 for £200 from Ludovic Sprogel, one of the survivors of the Wissahickon Community.[1] When Witt died in 1765, his personal property included an organ valued at £40.

A Swedish organ builder and portrait painter, Mons Gustaff Hesselius arrived in the communities on the Delaware in 1711. It is quite probable that he helped to install the organ mentioned above in Christ Church, also that he constructed the "small, new and fine organ" for Gloria Dei Church in 1740. In 1744, he began an organ for the Moravian Church in Bethlehem which was installed in 1746 by John Clemm (Johann Gottlob Klemm). Partial receipts for this instrument are in the amount of £25, but the original down-payment is not known.[2]

In 1749 a skilled joiner from Saxony, David Tanneberger,*joined Clemm in Bethlehem. They built several organs together in Bethlehem and Nazareth. After Clemm's death in 1762, Tanneberger moved to Lititz where he is known to have continued building organs until his death in 1804. His last organ, at York, Pennsylvania, was being set up when he suffered a stroke and fell from the scaffolding, and it was played for the first time at his funeral. John W. Jordan[3] has compiled a list of twenty-four instruments which Tanneberger built at prices ranging from £40 to £375. One, built for Trinity Lutheran Church in Lancaster, had "twenty registers." Another, built in 1793 for the Moravian Church in Nazareth for £274, contained 421 pipes and was not replaced until 1912.

Another organ builder active in Pennsylvania was Philip Feyring, who built an organ for the new St. Paul's Church, Philadelphia, in 1762. A few years later, he installed one in St. Peter's Church, Philadelphia, which was either another of his own construction or else the organ formerly in Christ Church. In 1766 he was engaged in building

*Organs for America, the life and work of David Tannenberg by William H. Armstrong, was published by the University of Pennsylvania Press in 1967.

or enlarging the Christ Church organ described a few years later as containing twenty-seven stops with 1607 pipes on three manuals and pedals. It is not certain whether or not this included parts of the original organ, or whether all was completed in the construction of 1766.[4]

The first organ in Virginia was brought from England to St. Peter's Church, Port Royal, shortly after 1700; the exact date cannot be established. It was later moved to Christ Church, Alexandria, presumably during the time that George Washington served there as a vestryman and warden. Still later it was used in Trinity Church, Shepherdstown, West Virginia, and St. Thomas' Church, Hancock, Maryland. In 1907, it was transferred to the Smithsonian Institute, where the case is still preserved.[*] This reveals an instrument with a single, five-octave manual, 12 stops, and 25 pipes across the front. At Bruton Parish Church, Williamsburg, the first organ was installed in 1755, in a small gallery above the sanctuary. It is still in use today, incorporated in a much larger instrument of contemporary design.

In New England, the first mention of an organ is found in the diary of the Reverend Joseph Green, who wrote under the date May 29, 1711, "I was at Mr. Thomas Brattle's; heard ye organs." On Brattle's death in 1713, the organ was willed to the Brattle Street Church, which refused to accept it. According to the terms of the will, it was then given to King's Chapel, whose officers proceeded to "procure a sober person that can play skillfully thereon with a loud noise." The first such person was a Mr. Price. He was succeeded the following year by a London organist named Edward Enstone, who served for several years at an annual salary of £30 with the additional privilege of keeping a music and dancing-school.[5] In 1756, the organ was sold and removed to St. Paul's Church, Newburyport, where it remained in use until purchased in 1836 by St. John's Church, Portsmouth, New Hampshire, for the sum of four hundred dollars. In recent years the action has become warped, but the instrument has been preserved intact. In the Spring of 1950, the pipes were loaned to an organ factory where they were placed on a voicing machine and a recording prepared by E. Power Biggs. Original ranks of pipes are known to be an 8-foot stopped diapason and a 2-foot fifteenth. The 4-foot principal,

[55]

*The Organ Historical Society, founded in 1956, has since published much material on the history of American organs in its quarterly journal, *The Tracker*. Cleveland Fisher reports in Vol. XII/1 (Fall 1967) on research concerning the organ attributed to Port Royal, Virginia. Fisher shows that it was built by Jacob Hilbus of Washington, D. C., for Christ Church, Alexandria, Virginia, 1811-1815. It has recently been restored at the Smithsonian Institution.

sesquialtera (3 ranks), and 8-foot dulciana may have been added at some time after the organ left the Brattle home.[6]

Christ Church, Boston—the "Old North Church"—purchased an organ for £320 from William Claggett, who came up from Newport to install it in 1736. It was repaired in 1750 by Thomas Johnston, who rebuilt it in 1752, being required to retain as much as possible of the original organ. In 1759 he completed an entirely new organ for the church, "with an echo equal to that of Trinity Church [Boston]," an organ imported in 1736. Johnston's case is still preserved in the church, but with the addition of two end rows of pipes.[7]

Several early histories of music in New England[8] mention an organ built by Edward Broomfield, Jr., of Boston, in 1745. The instrument contained two manuals and "many hundred pipes, his intention being 1200, but he died [in 1746] before he completed it." It was located in the South Church, but removed to a store for safekeeping during the siege of Boston, where it was subsequently destroyed by fire.

St. Peter's Church, Salem, purchased its first organ in 1743 from John Clark. In 1770 it was exchanged, with a bonus of £50, for an organ built by Thomas Johnston in 1754, modelled after the Trinity organ. In 1819, this Johnston organ was moved to St. Michael's Church, Marblehead.[9]

Charles Theodore Pachelbell was a German organist resident in Boston *ca.* 1730. His employment there is not known, but it is possible that he was Enstone's successor on the Brattle organ in King's Chapel. Virginia Larkin Redway[10] has been able to prove that he was a son of the famous Nuremberg organist and composer, Johann Pachelbell. He was employed in February, 1733, by Trinity Church, Newport, to install and play its English organ, an instrument which remained in use for 111 years. Its specifications were as follows:[11]

Great organ:	Principal	50 pipes
	Stopped diapason	50
	Open diapason	50
	Twelfth	50
	Fifteenth	50
	Tierce bass	25
	Tierce treble	25

	Flute	50
	Trumpet	38
		388
Swell organ:	Stopped diapason	27
	Open diapason	27
	Flute	27
	Trumpet	27
		108

Total: 496 pipes

These pipes have been dispersed, but the oak and walnut case is still used. The console, displaying the legend "Ricardus Bridge Londini, Fecit MDCCXXXIII" is preserved by the Newport Historical Society. In 1736 Pachelbell advertised two concerts in New York City, and on St. Cecilia's Day (November 22), 1737, gave a benefit concert in Charleston, South Carolina.

By 1800 there were approximately twenty organs throughout New England, mostly in Episcopal churches due to the prejudices which still lingered in most Puritan congregations. A notable exception was in the First Congregational Church at Providence, which in 1770, after considerable hesitation and debate, acquired the first "dissenting" organ in New England.

Christ Church, Cambridge, Massachusetts, in 1764 acquired an organ through the interest of the Lord Mayor of London. This was a chamber instrument built by John Snetzler, a German organ maker who settled in London shortly after 1740. Of ninety-four organs which he is known to have built or altered,[12] five were in the American Colonies. At the Battle of Bunker Hill, most of the lead pipes in the Cambridge organ were melted-up for bullets. A contemporary letter describes a service attended by General George Washington and his officers on New Year's Day, 1776:

Unfortunately the organ could not be used. Some of the leaden pipes had been taken out to furnish ammunition for our men at the fight in Charlestown last June, and it was quite out of order, but a bass viola

[57]

and clarionet played by some musical soldiers led the singing which was very good. The strong voices of the many men who thronged the Church made fine music for my ears. . . .[13]

The organ was partially restored after the Revolution and used until 1845. A few pipes are still preserved in a case at Christ Church.

Another of Snetzler's chamber organs is still in use in the Congregational Church at South Dennis, Massachusetts. Its early history is no longer known, but it is thought to have been acquired somewhere in Connecticut when the present building was erected in 1835. The organ has been thoroughly overhauled and an electric blower added, but it remains structurally the same as it was when—according to a slip of paper with the maker's signature inside the rosewood case—"John Snetzler fecit Londini 1762." There are eleven stops on a single manual, with a pedal board containing thirteen notes: G, A-g♯. *Cf.* Plate VI. The registration is:

Stopped Diapason (Treble and Bass) 8′
Twelfth
Fifteenth
Principal (Treble, 4′, and Bass, 8′)
Dulciana, 8′
Clarabella (Treble) 8′
Cornet (Treble) 2′
Open diapason, 8′
Flute, 4′

A third chamber organ, built by Snetzler in 1761, was brought to this country before the Revolution but not unpacked until the end of hostilities. It was purchased in 1784 by Dr. Samuel Bard, founder of Bellevue Hospital and New York's first medical school, for his twelve-year-old daughter, Susannah. In 1816 the latter's daughter, Mary E. Johnstone, loaned the organ to St. James' Church, Hyde Park, New York, where she played it in the rear gallery for twenty-two years. The instrument is now preserved in the museum of the New York State Historical Association in Cooperstown. It has a single manual running 4½ octaves from B to e‴, but sounding G, A, C, D to e‴, with the key for B sounding the G, and the key for C♯ sounding the A. The registration is:

Sesquialtera (Treble and Bass)
Stopped diapason, 8′
Principal, 4′
Fifteenth, 2′
Open Diapason (Treble) 8′

There is also a Snetzler chamber organ of 1742 in the Belle Skinner Collection of Old Musical Instruments, Holyoke, Massachusetts. This was never used in an American church, however, having been purchased overseas by Mrs. Skinner where it had formerly been in the collection of Sir Thornley Stokes of Dublin and the Karl Freund Collection.*

The Dutch Church in New York City installed an organ in 1724, but its subsequent history is not known.

John Clemm, mentioned above in connection with the Moravian organs, was commissioned in 1739 by the vestry of Trinity Church, New York, to build an organ for their west gallery. No exact specifications of the instrument exist, but it is known to have contained twenty-six stops on three manuals. Its installation was completed by August, 1741, and three years later, pedals were added. In 1752, extensive repairs and a few additions were made by the builder. John Clemm, Jr., served as organist for the first three years, but apparently played too many "frivolous" interludes, for in December, 1743, the vestry asked that a "good, sober organist" be procured at £40 per year. This was John Rice of London, who arrived in November, 1744 and served soberly for seventeen years, and thereafter intermittently until 1795.

The Clemm organ was replaced in 1764 by one built in England by John Snetzler, costing ca. £700. This was destroyed in the fire which leveled Trinity Church, together with much of the lower part of the city, in September of 1776. The unsettled condition of the times delayed the replacement of the church until 1788. At that time a new organ was ordered from Hall of London. This was probably the smallest to be used at Trinity, for it contained only nineteen stops on three manuals, and there were no pedals. Nevertheless, it remained in use until 1839.[14]

St. Michael's Church, Charleston, South Carolina, prior to 1762 used

*A 1760 chamber organ by Snetzler, built for Kimberly Hall, Norfolk, England, has recently been acquired by the Williamsburg (Virginia) Lodge.

a chamber organ belonging to a Mr. Stroubell. It was replaced with another chamber organ, borrowed from Mr. Sampson Neyle, which remained until a permanent instrument was obtained from England. This second instrument, which had four whole- and two half-stops, was installed by John Spiceacre (Speissegger), and later repaired for £160. The bicentenary history of Saint Michael's Parish[15] reproduces the detailed but interesting correspondence between the Charleston vestry and their London agents during the years 1766-68 regarding the purchase of a good organ. At the same time their organist, Benjamin Yarnold, wrote Dr. William Boyce, then organist of St. Michael's Cornhill (London), asking his expert assistance in the purchase.[16]

The new organ, built by John Snetzler for £528, arrived in August, 1768, and was installed, at the builder's recommendation, by Spiceacre, who was paid £120 for the installation and for tuning it fortnightly throughout the year. The exact specifications are not known, save that it was a well-balanced, baroque instrument of ca. 1000 pipes, and especially notable for the softness of its tone. It is known to have included a 16-foot open diapason and a stopped diapason on the great, a stopped diapason on the swell, a fifteenth on the great, and also a bassoon and a fourniture. The following list of probable stops is derived from specifications of comparable instruments from Snetzler's shop during this period:

Great:	Open diapason	Choir:	Stopped diapason
	Stopped diapason		Principal
	Principal		Flute
	Twelfth		Bassoon
	Fifteenth	Swell:	Open diapason
	Tierce		Stopped diapason
	Sesquialtera IV		Principal
	Cornet (fourniture)		Cornet
	Trumpet		Hautboy
			Trumpet

The handsome mahogany case, still preserved in St. Michael's modern organ, was typical of Snetzler's larger organs. The display pipes in the front of the case were all speaking pipes, the case being carefully channeled to transmit the wind to them. It may be seen in Plate II.

Spiceacre overhauled the organ in 1792, and again in 1800. In 1833, Henry Erben of New York was hired to add a single octave of pedals, and in 1859 several other stops were added. During the Civil War the organ was boxed up and stored in Radcliffeboro, as it had been endangered by falling shells. After the earthquake of 1886 it was again stored while repairs were being made to the church. Thereafter it continued in regular service, with intermittent repairs and slight alterations, until 1910, when a new instrument was installed by the Austin Organ Company, utilizing a few of the old pipes and the original case. At its last service, the old organ was played by Arthur Speissegger, a direct descendant of the man who first installed it.

St. Philip's Church, Charleston, first acquired an organ *ca.* 1728, which, tradition says, was used at the coronation of George II. Charles Theodore Pachelbell presumably served as organist there from 1738 until his death in 1750.[17] The organ was dismantled in 1833 and replaced by another which was destroyed by fire within a year's time.

Little specific is known of the use of barrel- or hand-organs in American churches. These instruments, which would mechanically play a limited number of Psalm-tunes, had come into use in eighteenth-century England. Brooks quotes the following advertisement in the *Columbian Sentinel* for December 8, 1797:

To the Lovers of Harmony

Dr. Flagg, if a sufficient number of purchasers offer, intends to contract in Europe for the construction of a number of Organs, calculated to play all tunes usually sung in places of worship, with interludes to each Psalm, without the assistance of an organist. Their prices will be various, supposed from 60 to £300.[18]

On the opposite shore of the continent, a barrel-organ of three cylinders was reported in the organ loft of Mission San Juan Bautista in 1829, but there is no indication as to its use in church services.[19]

Reference was made in Chapter III to the attitude which some New Englanders had toward bells. While they are rather outside the scope of this book, it may nevertheless be well to summarize what has been written about our colonial church-bells. The first seems to have been acquired for the meeting house in Cambridge during 1632.[20] Others appeared in various village churches during the remainder of the century, usually within a few years after the permanent church building had been erected.

The first peal of bells in the Colonies, a chime of eight, was ordered by the vestry of Christ Church, Boston, from the Rudhall Foundry in Gloucester, England, in 1742. It was installed in 1745, and Paul Revere, later to receive the famous lantern signal from the same belfry, was one of the young men who rang the changes on this peal. The bells are still intact, having been remounted in 1847 and again in 1894.[21] After the Revolution, the versatile Revere added bell-casting to his other activities. Using the Christ Church bells as models, he set up a bell foundry with his son, Joseph, which from 1792 to 1826 turned out 398 bells.[22]

In 1764 a peal of eight bells from the Whitechapel Foundry of Lester and Pack, London, was installed in St. Michael's, Charleston.[23] These were somewhat heavier than the Boston peal. When the British evacuated Charleston in 1782, the bells were carried away to England in the last ships to leave the city. They were brought back the following year. In 1832 two of the bells were recast. During the Civil War, seven bells were removed to Columbia, where it was thought they would be safer; but the building in which they were stored was fired by Sherman's troops and the bells damaged. The peal was again shipped to England in 1866 and recast, returning to St. Michael's in 1867 where they still ring out over the city.

Philadelphia's most famous and most defective bell is the Liberty Bell. It was purchased from the Whitechapel Foundry for the Pennsylvania State House in 1752. It cracked on its first trial and had to be recast, only to crack again when tried. After a third casting, the bell played its historic role and continued to sound annually on Independence Day until 1835 when it acquired its permanent crack.

Christ Church, Philadelphia, acquired a 700-lb. bell in 1702. It hung for a long time in the fork of a tree beside the church. A smaller, 215-lb. "minister's bell" was given to the church by Captain Herve of the *Centurion* in 1711. At mid-century when the church was remodeled, a steeple was erected and a peal of eight bells from the Whitechapel Foundry installed (1754), costing £560.[24] These are the chimes referred to in the closing scene of Longfellow's *Evangeline*.

Many romantic tales are told about the mission bells of California. Some of them date from 1722, but most of them have been dispersed and lost. The oldest known today is the 1738 bell at Mission San Diego. Although several missions eventually had as many as four or six bells, there is no indication that they were tuned for peals or chiming.[25]

Part Two

1820–1920

O praise God in his sanctuary.
Praise him in the firmament of his power.
Praise him in his noble acts.
Praise him according to his excellent greatness.
Praise him in the sound of the trumpet.
Praise him upon the lute and harp.
Praise him in the timbrels and dances.
Praise him upon the strings and pipe.
Praise him upon the well-tuned cymbals.
Praise him upon the loud cymbals.
Let everything that hath breath praise the Lord.

—PSALM 150.

CHAPTER VIII

The Pages from Which We Sang

I T IS difficult at times for the younger generations to realize what life was like without electricity, when our churches were illuminated not with evenly diffused rays from modern electric fixtures but with sputtering gas jets, kerosene lamps with smoky chimneys, or banks of flickering candles. Similarly, the hymnals and octavo anthem pages from which we sing today differ greatly in format from the music pages which choirs used a century and more ago.

The big parchment graduals and antiphonals, which during the Middle Ages stood on a single lectern before the entire choir, are well known from the specimen pages in our libraries and museums. A number of these, laboriously copied by hand in the missions and cathedrals of New Spain, are still in existence.

With the advent of music-printing in the sixteenth century, motet collections and metrical psalters containing harmonized tunes were printed in England and on the continent. Some were issued in the form of part-books, with separate fascicules for each vocal part, along lines similar to the separate parts used by orchestras and bands today. Others were printed in such a way that a full quartet could read from the same page, with treble and bass on one side, alto and tenor facing the others, and the book held between the singers. A few copies of this music, particularly of the latter type, may have been brought over to the English colonies. European part-books were more common in the cathedrals of Spanish America.

When tune books began to be published in the colonies, as discussed in Chapter III, they were issued in score, much as all choral music is today; but with the tenor part on top, and the treble coming third, above the bass. There was no separate organ part; instead, occasional figured bass indications were given. The standard format for over half a century consisted of board covers with a thin leather back and pages 15 cm. high and 25 cm. wide. (*Cf.* Plates XI and XII.[1])

Most common today among the relics of eighteenth century choirs are the psalters and copies of Watts' and Wesley's editions which have individual parts to the tunes, for the owner's voice only, carefully copied into the end-papers. This practice may have been adequate while only a few tunes were used, but by the beginning of the nineteenth century the repertory was broadening enough so that each chorister needed both tune-book and hymnal. Tune-books continued to be published with only the first stanza of each hymn given until well past the mid-century. Thus the chorister must either have held a book in each hand, or have had a rack in front of him for the tune-book.[2] In a final phase, shortly before they gave place *ca.* 1860 to the modern style of hymnal, a few editions were published with tunes above and full texts below, and with the pages cut so that either tunes or texts could be turned over separately (*e.g.,* Tune 20 being equally available with Text 6 or 59)—a format still used in some Lutheran books. The treble part continued to be printed next to the bass, for the convenience of accompanists, in almost all of the tune-books until the latter passed out of vogue.

Beginning with Lyon's *Urania* in 1762, the modern style of notation was used in all collections except those using shape-notes. *Cf.* p. 101 ff.

Francis Hopkinson's *Collection of Psalm Tunes* for Christ and St. Peter's churches in Philadelphia, 1763, was mentioned in Chapter VI. With the turn of the century, a number of tune-books were published to provide for the specific needs of special churches or denominations, and we find titles such as

John Cole's *Episcopalian Harmony* (Baltimore: 1800)
The First [Congregational] *Church Collection of Sacred Music* (Boston: 1806)
Trinity Church Hymns (Boston: 1808)
Collection of Sacred Music for West Church (Boston: 1810)
Isaac Cole's *Third Presbyterian Church Collection* (Philadelphia: 1815)

Wesleyan [Methodist] *Selection of the John Street Church* (New York: 1820)

These are but a few, selected to show the diversity of churches having their own collections. Jacob Eckhard's *Choral Book* (Boston, 1816) is a published version of a manuscript organ book, dated 1809, which is still preserved in St. Michael's Church, Charleston, South Carolina. (Its contents are discussed in Chapter XI.)

Each tune-book contained not only Psalm- and hymn-tunes, but also a few single and double chants for Episcopal churches, even though the collection was not intended primarily for their use. Each book also contained a few short anthems. For most parish choirs this would constitute the entire repertory, not to be augmented except when a new tune-book was introduced in place of the older one.

To be sure, a few anthems, usually solos or duos concluding with the full quartet, were published as sheet music in quarto format. In this size, anthems and small cantatas continued to be published until the last years of the century. Here again, as with the tune-books, a few churches published collections of anthems and other service music for their own peculiar use. Such was the 75-page quarto collection of anthems and canticles adapted to Unitarian use, *Music of King's Chapel* (Boston, 1835), edited and largely composed by its organist, Thomas Comer. Another such collection was W. C. Peters' *Catholic Harmonist* (Baltimore, 1851; later editions, Boston, 1871 and 1895) which had 146 pages in tune-book format, containing motets, masses, hymns, and chants. Its preface stated that

> The want of a cheap volume of simple music, suitable to the various Festivals of the Church in the United States has long been felt both by the clergy and the laity.

Other churches doubtless had their manuscript books such as the Eckhard manuscript cited above, or the quarto manuscript of service music from Trinity Church, New York, under Edward Hodges. Separate bass and treble parts of this, copied by a Samuel Maynard, November, 1844, are now preserved in the Library of Congress.

The revolutionary change which brought about our modern supply of octavo anthems and other service music, at a price which made it

[69]

possible for each singer to have his own copy, was initiated by Vincent and Alfred Novello with the establishment in England of *The Musical Times* (1844).[3] With this, the Novellos began their series of *Octavo Anthems,* using one each month as an insert to the magazine, which was devoted to news and articles on music, and especially choral music. Coupled with this was the publication, at prices within popular reach, of the standard oratorios, masses, etc., in convenient octavo score, with special organ or piano accompaniments arranged by Vincent Novello. This series, initiated with an edition of Handel's *Messiah* in 1846-7 which sold for six shillings and sixpence per copy, marked the first consistent use of a fully realized thorough-bass part for the accompanist, who had hitherto been required to improvise all accompaniments from either the full score or more frequently from a single bass part with numerals indicating those harmonies which were not immediately obvious. One can readily imagine the boon this change was to amateur organists.

In America, Novello's editions were introduced rather slowly, although a New York office of the firm was established in 1852. Not until 1894 when H. W. Gray—a publisher of church music in his own right—became American agent for Novello, did the full benefit of these cheap octavos sweep the country.[4]

Another approach to the problem of inexpensive music was through subscription series, or music periodicals. These were intended primarily for smaller church choirs, and they served a dual purpose: by the simple device of having each member subscribe to the periodical, the actual distribution of the music was achieved; by planning the contents in such a way as to supply seasonal demands, the less-trained choirmasters received the benefit of expert selection of repertory, thereby bringing to their attention outstanding works which might otherwise never have become known.[5]

The first and best of these magazines of church music was *The Parish Choir,* edited and published by the Reverend Charles L. Hutchins for the purpose of "providing a good class of Church Music at a price which would bring it within the reach of any choir desiring to use it."[6] The series began in 1874 as a 4-page, 12mo monthly. Beginning in 1878 it was enlarged to octavo size, and shortly thereafter became a semi-monthly. In 1887 it was changed to a weekly magazine, continuing as a weekly until it ceased publication in 1919.

The American Choir was inaugurated in 1896 by Charles S. Elliot, as a "fortnightly publication of New Church Music by the best Composers." In its first year, it offered a $100-prize for the best new anthem. It included works by N. H. Allen, J. Remington Fairlamb, Arthur Foote, W. W. Gilchrist, Charles H. Morse, S. B. Whitney and arrangements from Beethoven, Guilmant, and Mendelssohn. Unfortunately it survived through only three seasons and seventy-eight issues.

Another series of a similar nature is the group of magazines initiated by E. S. Lorenz. These differ from Hutchins' *Parish Choir* in that a considerable portion of their content consists of compositions by staff members who write in a rather stereotyped, popular style. This, while tending to lower the quality of the contents, has the advantage of consistency of style and difficulty, no small consideration for many amateur choirs. Lorenz began his publications with *The Choir Leader* in 1894. Three years later, he began *The Choir Herald* as a magazine containing easier and more popular anthems. In 1913 he began *The Volunteer Choir,* a third monthly magazine, containing material nearer the "gospel song" in mood and musical content. In 1936 the Lorenz Publishing Company began to issue a fourth serial, *The Quarterly Anthem Folio,* which included material for more professional choirs than any of their other magazines.

Today, with a dozen or more American publishers devoted almost exclusively to the issuance of old and new church music suited to all liturgies, there is a plethora of music available for use in our churches. The caliber of the selections made is dependent only on the tastes of the individual choirmasters.

CHAPTER IX

Quartet Choirs

OLD WAYS are changed but slowly, and often in a single church, a single community at a time. Fashionable Eastern churches made changes which were not reflected in smaller Western communities until many years later. Similarly, radical and conservative congregations varied in their practices within the same communities; indeed, all too often, congregations split up over controversies such as those observed in Chapter III.

The first Episcopal congregation to do without a clerk was St. James' Church, Philadelphia, where in 1815 William Augustus Muhlenberg, then a theological student, took over direction of the music. He removed the clerk's desk entirely, and thereafter Bishop White announced the Psalms. At St. Michael's, Charleston, the office of clerk was abolished in 1835, "the clergy having consented to give out the Psalms."[1] They were not eliminated in the various congregations of Trinity Parish, New York, until 1848.[2] In Presbyterian churches, clerks continued to be used generally until the period 1840-1860.

The growth of mixed choirs from the singing schools previously developed to reform the psalmody was mentioned in Chapter III. Frequently, upon the advent of the mixed choir, the clerk became its leader. In many Congregational churches he was called the chorister. For some time he was the only singer to receive remuneration for his services.

Lowell Mason[3] has described the condition of most choral groups at the time the Handel and Haydn Society of Boston was founded in 1815. There were still but few organs except in Episcopal churches.

The other congregations continued to use stringed and wind instruments. Pianos for rehearsals were completely unknown. Mason notes that

> The treble in the church choirs, as in the Handel and Haydn Society, was sung in whole or in part by men's voices, and the tenor was often sung by women's voices, thus inverting the order of nature and separating by two full octaves those who were made to go hand in hand.[4]

He further pointed out that the women could seldom carry their part independently, so that the sopranos were always led off and to a considerable degree sustained by tenor voices. The alto register of women's voices, universally used by 1850, was then unknown, and as seldom more than two or three men or a few boys attempted to sing the part, its effect was almost lost in the chorus.

These were still gallery choirs in most churches, located at the rear, where, with their accompanying instruments, they could be heard but not seen too much. As a result, the young people easily became restless during a long sermon or prayer. Thus, in 1826, four men had to be appointed to preserve order in the gallery of the First Presbyterian Church at Mendham, New Jersey.[5] In many Congregational churches, the people stood and faced the singers during the hymns, either to better view their efforts or perhaps to themselves follow the leader— a custom still observed in the mid-twentieth century in the North (Congregational) Church on Nantucket.

The infamous but popular "quartet choir" began to appear early in the nineteenth century. This term is descriptive of the volunteer chorus choir built around a quartet of strong solo voices which never blended with the ensemble, and for which frequent solo and duet passages were necessary, leaving a relatively small portion of the anthems for truly choral singing. Many churches, tiring of the struggle to maintain interest and discipline among the young people of their choirs, went so far as to use only the professional quartet for all their vocal music.

The type may possibly have been an outgrowth of the English verse-anthems or possibly the German chorale-cantatas. The latter are well known today from the many performances of those by Johann Sebastian Bach, but they were almost completely unknown here in the early nineteenth century. In a typical verse-anthem, such as Purcell's *Rejoice in the Lord alway,* a trio of solo voices—alto, tenor, and bass—alternate with passages by the full choir. But here again, it is most unlikely that many such anthems were known in America during the hey-day of the quartet choir.

Whatever their origins may have been, the quartet choirs, wherever they were maintained, soon degenerated into mere quartets of professional singers who were frequently more concerned with personal vainglory than with the worship of Almighty God. This fault became all the more apparent in liturgical churches, for the quartets could seldom achieve that impersonal association between music and liturgy which is the *sine qua non* of true worship.

The quartet choir exerted so great an influence that almost all of the sacred music composed in America during the nineteenth century consisted of solos or duos with concluding quartet. Yet as early as 1845 we find objections being raised; the following resolution from the *Proceedings of the American Musical Convention: held in the Broadway [New York] Tabernacle on the 8th, 9th, and 10th of October, 1845* is an example.

> Resolved: that all the advantages derivable from Quartette Choirs in churches can be combined in larger choirs, and that when larger choirs can be obtained it is not advisable to limit the number to four persons.

But resolutions, no matter how well worded, could not change the trend. At St. Michael's, Charleston, the traditional choir of boys and men gave way *ca.* 1840 to a paid quartet, which was not abolished until 1926. This date span is typical of church history across the country and in many denominations. Scanning local parish histories, one is confronted again and again with churches where congregational singing was led by a clerk-precentor, accompanied by a violoncello, until the 1840's when organs and quartet choirs were installed. The organs were replaced and enlarged each generation, but the quartet choir persisted in the majority of churches until after 1920. In fact, where a volunteer choir and reed organ or small pipe organ had been used in a rear gallery, the installation of a larger organ in the front of the church, behind the pulpit, was a universal incentive to eliminate the choir and have "finer" music from a professional quartet. Sad to relate, the conduct of various members of the choir during the church services was a common argument given for making the change.

Thus, for example, the First Presbyterian Church of Muncie, Indiana, founded in 1838, was served by a precentor for its first fifteen years, at the beginning of which period the hymns were still "lined out." Then for a time there was a volunteer choir with a small reed organ in the rear gallery. Later, when a two-manual Estey reed organ was purchased for $750, the gallery would not accommodate the new instrument, and a platform was built for organ and choir, to the right of the pulpit. In 1894, when a pipe organ was installed in their new building, the volunteer choir was replaced by a quartet. This in turn gave way in 1930 to a vested, full choir.[6]

Plate VIII shows the quartet choir of the First Presbyterian Church of Chicago in the characteristic setting of the 1890's—gas lights, costumes and all. The narrow choir loft is in the front of the church, six or eight feet above the wider platform where the clergy sat on chairs covered with black horse-hair behind a central pulpit. The velvet curtain is here drawn together at the center so that the organist could be included in the portrait; normally it would be drawn back to the sides whenever the quartet sang, then fully extended to conceal them during the sermon.

What may have been the extreme abuse of the quartet idea occurred in 1882 at St. Luke's Church, Marietta, Ohio. Aping the English cathedral choirs, there was installed a chancel choir with antiphonal singing by separate quartets for *decani* and *cantori*.[7]

As long as our churches laid their principal emphasis on the social gospel, with its liberal, almost secular focus, there was no true incentive for a less personal form of music than that offered by the quartet choir. Young people's need for fellowship found adequate expression in the musical side of the Sunday School and in occasional young people's choirs for the less-formal evening services. It remained for the liturgical movement of recent decades to demonstrate in a convincing manner how little of true worship there could be in the singing of a quartet. Curiously the Oxford Movement, which led the way for the revival of liturgical worship among Christians of many denominations, was in ferment in the years that saw the rise of the quartet choir in America.

[75]

CHAPTER X

The Oxford Movement and Boy Choirs

THE Tractarian, or Oxford, Movement was set in motion by the Reverend John Keble, at Oxford, in 1833, with a profound effect during the following decades on seminarians and younger clergy on both sides of the Atlantic. Many of our greatest English and American hymn writers were associated with its ideas: John Henry Hopkins, Jr., John Mason Neale, John Henry Newman, Frederick Oakeley, George Prynne, Clarence Walworth, and Isaac Williams, as well as Keble himself.

This movement in the Church of England, while essentially theological, found expression in a revival of many of the ancient rites and ceremonies of the Church. It soon came to exert a vast influence on church music and especially the music of the liturgy. It initiated the restoration of the mediaeval plainsong, or Gregorian, melodies, a work which was soon taken up by the Roman Catholic monks of the Benedictine abbey at Solesmes, France. It focused anew the aims and ideals of worship through music and as a result effected several distinct innovations, or rather renovations, in contemporary Anglican, Roman Catholic, and Protestant worship. These were the institution of boy choirs, the introduction of choral or "sung" services, the use of vestments, and processions.

Work with boy choristers had entirely lapsed in New York and Charleston by the time William Augustus Muhlenberg started his boys' choir at the Flushing Institute on Long Island in 1828.[1] Eight or nine years later, the Reverend Francis L. Hawkes introduced a vested choir into his school, St. Thomas' Hall, Flushing, Long Island. During the years 1831 to 1843, before the financial failure of the school, his boys frequently sang in New York churches in their white surplices with black ribbons.[2] By 1846, Muhlenberg had a permanent boy choir at the Church of the Holy Communion, New York.[3]

In 1844 two Episcopal parishes—the Church of the Advent, Boston, and the Church of the Holy Cross, Troy, New York—were established and endowed for the regular maintenance of the full offices of the Episcopal Church. They were pioneers of the Oxford Movement in this country. In both churches there were choral services within a short time; in the latter, under John Ireland Tucker, unaccompanied plainsong was regularly used by a choir of boys and girls almost from the start.[4]

Edward Hodges was brought to Trinity Parish, New York, in 1839, playing in St. John's Chapel until the new Trinity Church edifice was ready for service. He immediately took steps to bring Trinity's music as near as possible to the standards of the English cathedral service. At the consecration of the new church building on Ascension Day, 1846, special music was sung by a choir of fourteen boys and a double quartet. However, women were not completely dropped from the choir until Henry S. Cutler became organist and choirmaster in 1859.[5] He had already installed a choir of men and boys at Boston's Church of the Advent shortly before 1855.[6] About this same time a men's choir was also installed in St. Mark's Church, Philadelphia.[7]

By October 16, 1861 it was possible to have a choir festival in Trinity Church, New York, in which five choirs of men and boys participated, coming from Trinity, New York; Trinity, Hoboken; Trinity, Jersey City; St. George's, Flushing; and St. Andrew's, Providence. The program consisted of standard Anglican chant and Handel, with an anthem by Cutler.[8]

In the Middle West, the first attempt to establish a boy choir was made in 1862 at Racine College, in Wisconsin, by a Mr. Machlin, using college students and local school boys. He soon developed a choral service, using Helmore's *Psalter*. Unfortunately, financial difficulties at the college did not permit the work to continue for long.

In 1865 Bishop Whitehouse, the second Bishop of Illinois, established his *cathedra* in the Church of the Atonement, Chicago. His son, William Fitzhugh Whitehouse, began to train a group of boys for the choral service, using Cutler's *Trinity Psalter*. In 1867, he was joined by Canons John Harris Knowles and C. P. Dorset. Among the singing-men were several, including one alto, who had sung in English choirs. This pioneer work persisted for over a decade, with regular choral services—twice daily until the great fire of 1871—and trips to other churches for special services. Other Chicago churches soon began to follow this lead. The Church of the Ascension inaugurated a vested boy choir at Christmas, 1870; Calvary Church and St. James' Church did likewise in May, 1884; and St. Clement's did so in November, 1884.[9]

Apparently most of the singing by boys in these early days was done with the same coarse type of tone which is still found so often among the untrained ensembles in our public schools. No one prior to Cutler seems to have developed the higher "head tones" in their boys; no one, certainly, in the first half of the nineteenth century.*Whether the few eighteenth century boy-choir schools developed the head tones can not be determined. It is possible that they did, for the teachers in them were men of English cathedral background. At any rate, Cutler has been given credit for its later development. His boys had excellent top notes, but did not succeed in bringing the same type of tone into their lower registers. In 1873 the distinguished English organist and choirmaster James Kendrick Pyne came over from Chichester Cathedral for a two-year period at St. Mark's Church, Philadelphia, where James Pearce had instituted a boy choir six years earlier. Following the S. S. Wesley tradition, Pyne's choir at St. Mark's soon became known for the outstanding purity of its tone. His technique was carefully studied by George F. Le Jeune, who applied Pyne's methods during the following decade in his own choir at St. John's Chapel, New York, and who perpetuated them in this country through his teaching.[10]

The movement grew at such a rate that in 1895 *Nickerson's Illustrated Church Musical and School Directory of New York and Brooklyn* listed twenty boy choirs, all of them Episcopal. There were six others with boys, women, and men, while eleven Episcopal churches still had quartet choirs. One, the Church of the Beloved Disciple, had a quartet in addition to its choir of men and boys. The remaining

[78]

*Cutler's treble soloist at Trinity Church, perhaps the first "solo boy" in America, was William James Robjohn who used the pseudonym Caryl Florio.

churches listed—Baptist, Congregational, Presbyterian, Roman Catholic, and others—still used only quartet choirs.

Local parish histories show that the last decade of the nineteenth century marked the climax in the widespread development of the boy choir. There were few cities of any size which did not boast of several. In smaller communities where there was not sufficient talent available, boys were augmented by girls or women, oftentimes concealed behind a screen—such was the urge to emulate, in appearance at least, the larger city churches. Such was the case at St. Michael's Church, Bloomingdale, New York (now Amsterdam Avenue and 99th Street, New York City) where the children of the Leake and Watts Orphan Asylum served in the choir, the boys vested and seated in the chancel, the girls behind a curtain nearby.[11]

The next step was the founding of special choir schools—parochial schools, either for boarders or day students, where the boys could receive their schooling and at the same time have daily rehearsals and services integrated into their schedules. This was attempted *ca.* 1870 by Canon Knowles at the Cathedral of SS. Peter and Paul in Chicago, but the fire of the following year disrupted his plans.

The Boys' School of St. Paul's Parish, Baltimore, had been founded in 1849 as a day school, meeting at first in the Sunday School room of the church. When the Reverend J. S. B. Hodges became rector in 1870, he at once took steps to build a choir of men and boys. Scholarships were given in the School, which thus provided adequate scholastic background for the musical training of the twenty choirboys. From 1883 to 1923, when the school was located on East Franklin Street, the boys made an interesting picture as they marched in cassocks and caps to the church for the daily Evensong.[12] A distinguished succession of organist-choirmasters have trained the boys during the present century—Miles Farrow, 1894-1909, Alfred Madeley Richardson, 1909-1912, Alfred R. Willard, 1912-1921, and Edmund S. Ender since 1921.

Grace Church, New York, had been slow to give up its quartet choir, but when a boy choir was finally established no halfway measures were used. Choir and school were started by the Reverend William R. Huntington and his organist, James M. Helfenstein, in 1894. They moved into their own school building in 1899, with provision for sixteen boarders. The building was expanded in 1915, with playgrounds provided on the roof. Until 1922 it was run as a military school. That same year, Helfenstein was succeeded by Ernest Mitchell. The boarding department was discontinued in 1934 and the school reorganized as a twelve-grade day-school, continuing to provide an education for the church's choir boys.

Next in order was the choir school established at New York's Cathedral of St. John the Divine by Bishop H. C. Potter in 1901. It began as a day school only, but moved into its present building with full accommodations for forty boarders in 1913. Choirmaster-organists have been Walter Henry Hall (to 1909), Miles Farrow (1909-1931),[*] and Norman Coke-Jephcott (1931-1953).[†]

Bishop William White founded a parish day school at St. Peter's Church, Philadelphia, in 1834. This was reorganized in 1905 as a choir school with daytime accommodations for fifty boys. Since then, the organist-choirmasters have been Felix Potter (to 1912), George Daland (1912), Lewis A. Wadlow (1913-1915), and Harold W. Gilbert (since 1915).

The choir school of Washington Cathedral was established in 1909 as a day school. This has since expanded into a strong college preparatory school (St. Albans School) with both boarders and day students, where the thirty choir boys form a special group of day students on scholarships. The first organist-choirmaster was Edgar Priest; after his death in 1935, Robert Barrow served until the appointment of Paul Callaway in 1939.

St. Thomas' Church, New York, established its choir school in 1919 under the musical direction of T. Tertius Noble, who was succeeded in 1942 by T. Frederick H. Candlyn.

A still larger type of day school, St. Dunstan's, Providence, was established in 1929 by the Reverend Walter Williams. Here in one school were trained the choir boys for three different parishes of the city. This novel arrangement continued for over twenty years.

Where there have not been special schools, or scholarships in other private schools available for boys, the usual practice has been to pay them a small weekly fee as a reward for regular attendance, and to send

[80]

___

*Frederic Alexander Birmingham's *It Was Fun While It Lasted* (1960) has a chapter telling of life as a choir boy under Miles Farrow.
†d. 1962.

them to summer camp for several weeks every year. Grace Church, Newark, began this practice shortly before 1890. At first the boys were taken to various places in North Jersey, Midvale being popular for many years. The Reverend Elliot White started Camp Nejecho ("NEw JErsey CHOirs") in 1910, on the Metedeconk River near Adamston. He was succeeded by the Reverend Morton A. Barnes in 1913, who expanded the camp's facilities to serve choirs from other parishes in New Jersey and also from adjacent states, so that at times it accommodated as many as two hundred boys. Unfortunately the camp closed in 1946, due to Father Barnes' failing health.

Camp Wa-Li-Ro, directed since its inception in 1934 by Paul Allen Beymer, is located at Put-in-Bay, Ohio, on an island in Lake Erie. It has enrolled *ca.* 300 boys each summer from American and Canadian choirs. This combines choir-school work with the camp life, and includes an annual Choirmaster Conference.

A camp of another sort was founded at Camp Duncan, Bretton Woods, New Hampshire, *ca.* 1916 by Frank R. Hancock. This provides a summer home for twelve boys, chosen from various choirs along the East Coast, who sing during July and August at the Chapel of the Transfiguration, Bretton Woods, as well as at concerts in nearby summer communities.

In the past few decades there has been a marked decline in the number of boy choirs in the United States. This has been due first of all to the natural reversal in those parishes where the work with boys proved unfeasible economically and demographically. A further compelling factor has been the increased competition of the public schools for the leisure time of their pupils, through the many school-sponsored musical activities. Typical of their coming and passing has been the fate of the Massachusetts festivals. The Massachusetts Choir Festival Association was founded in 1876 for mixed choirs. In 1890, it became the Massachusetts Choir Guild, conducting an annual festival for boy choirs until 1918, when sufficient support could no longer be mustered.

On the other hand, full choral services have become increasingly popular. In 1927, acting under authorization of the General Conven-

[81]

tion of the Episcopal Church, the Joint Commission on Church Music published *The Choral Service,* followed in 1936 by *The American Psalter* and *The Plainsong Psalter,* thus providing Anglican and plainsong settings for both choir and congregational participation in "sung" services. By this action the Episcopal Church was given not only an authentic but an authorized setting of the choral services comparable to the Vatican-Solesmes edition of the Roman *Graduale.*

Choir vestments have been mentioned earlier, in connection with the eighteenth-century boys at St. Michael's, Charleston, South Carolina, and with St. Thomas' Hall, Flushing, Long Island, in the 1830's. The first Choral Eucharist was sung under the auspices of the Church Choral Society[13] at the Church of the Annunciation, New York, on June 8, 1852, with the Reverend John Ireland Tucker as celebrant, the Reverend John Henry Hopkins, Jr., as deacon, and a choir of surpliced clergy. The resultant scandal was considerable.[14] Cutler's choir at the Church of the Advent, Boston, was vested *ca.* 1856.[15] He vested the Trinity, New York, choir on October 7, 1860.[16]

> This matter, which had so long been agitating the minds of the vestry, congregation, and choir, was happily settled by the visit of the Prince of Wales. When His Royal Highness notified his intention of attending service at Trinity Church, it was deemed proper that the service should be carried out in a manner worthy of the occasion, which certainly called for the vestments as used in the Church of England. To prevent any possible awkwardness on the occasion, the choir wore their surplices on the previous Sunday.

At that service, during the second lesson, two gun reports were heard, and a musket ball fell into one of the pews. In another church the excitement of appearing for the first time in vestments was too much for the choir; it marched around in solemn procession without being able to sing a note!

In the Episcopal Church, these innovations coming from the Oxford Movement met bitter resistance over a period of years. At the General Convention of 1868, a group of New Jersey laymen proposed a Canon:

Of the manner of conducting Divine Worship.

SECTION I. No ministerial vestments shall be worn by any minister during Divine Worship, or when present at, or officiating in, any

Church of the Advent, Boston

PLATE VII.   Choir Boys at the Church of the Advent, Boston, *ca.* 1856

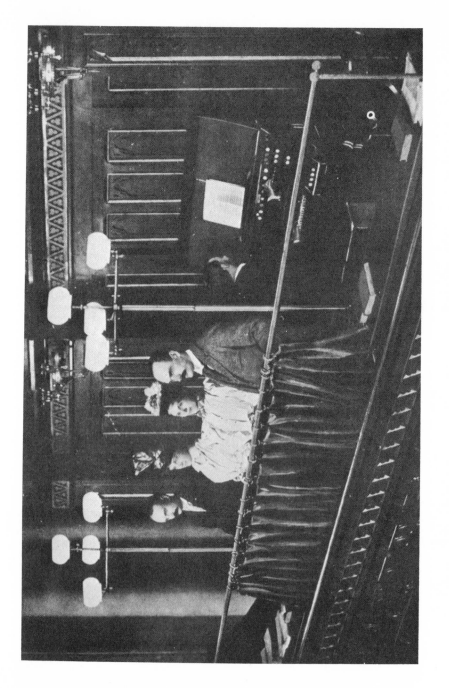

PLATE VIII. The Quartet Choir of the First Presbyterian Church, Chicago, in 1896

rite or ceremony of this Church, excepting surplice, stole, bands, or gown, which shall be used as heretofore accustomed on all regular occasions of worship, and, at the discretion of the minister, may be used at rites and ceremonies. And no Ecclesiastical vestment shall be worn on occasions of Divine Worship or Church ceremonies, by Choirs or other assistants therein: Provided this section shall not be construed to relate to episcopal vestments.

SECTION II.   Candlesticks, crucifixes, super-altars so called, made of wood, metal, or other substance, shall not be used or suffered to stand upon or hang over any communion table as part of the furniture or decorations thereof.

SECTION III.   Bowing at the name of Jesus, except in repeating the creeds, turning or bowing towards the Communion Table, except so far as enjoined by the rubric, making the sign of the Cross except in Baptism, the elevation of either of the elements during the Holy Communion, or of the Alms or oblations of communicants or others, processional singing in churches, except as provided by the rubrics, and the use of Incense in, and during, the conducting of Divine service, are all hereby declared unlawful.[17]

The proposal was referred to a Committee of Five Bishops who reported back to the General Convention of 1871, recommending

that certain acts in the administration of the Holy Communion, and on other occasions of public worship, hereinafter enumerated, be prohibited by canon, to wit:

(1) The use of incense.

(2) Placing or retaining a crucifix in any part of the church.

(3) Carrying a cross in procession in the church.

(4) The use of lights on or about the holy table, except when necessary.

(5) The elevation of the elements in the Holy Communion in such manner as to expose them to the view of the people as objects toward which adoration is to be made, in or after the prayer of consecration, or in the act of administering them, or in conveying them to or from the communicants.

* * *

They further recommend here:

(1) That no Rector of a Parish or other minister shall be allowed to introduce the Choral Service without the consenting vote of the Vestry, or contrary to the prohibition of the Bishop.

(2) That no surpliced choir shall be employed except under the same limitations; and when such choirs are employed, the only addition to their ordinary attire shall be a surplice reaching to the ankles.[18]

* * *

The report was signed by Bishops Alfred Lee of Delaware, John Williams of Connecticut, Thomas March Clark of Rhode Island, William H. Odenheimer of New Jersey, and John Barrett Kerfoot of Pittsburgh. There was a stormy session when it was presented but no official action was taken, then or subsequently.

That same year, Bishop McIlvaine of Ohio requested one of his clergy to disband a surpliced choir and to discontinue the practice of singing in procession. The priest refused and was brought to trial on the questionable grounds of having violated the doctrine and discipline of the Church, as well as breaking his ordination vow. Nevertheless, vested choirs continued to become more and more popular. By 1895, they were in such vogue that almost all the metropolitan choirs listed in *Nickerson's Directory,* cited above, were careful to specify that they were vested.

The one problem that remained was to find a satisfactory garb for the women in mixed choirs—a problem never fully solved. A musical ideal of the Oxford Movement was the restoration of the vested choir of men and boys to the chancel, in a location corresponding to the cathedral choir stalls. We have already noted some of the makeshifts which were employed to conceal the necessary use of women's voices where a sufficient number of boys and men were not obtainable. As Peter Lutkin expressed one viewpoint:

> It is against all tradition, precedent, or practice in all the historic churches to permit women to perform priestly functions, and the services of a chancel choir can only be looked upon as an adjunct to the priestly ministrations at the altar.[19]

The problem has been considerably complicated by the fact that so many non-historic churches have introduced processional singing by vested, mixed choirs as to confuse the thinking of music committees in the historic churches. In recent years, the matter has become partly

[84]

clarified, with the result that more and more mixed choirs are returning to their traditional places, either in side aisles, transepts, or in rear galleries.

In many churches, women singers have tried to wear adaptations of the men's cassocks and cottas, with caps varying from simple skull caps, Canterbury hats, to academic mortar-boards. Sometimes variations of academic gowns have been worn. None of these make sense, either liturgically or aesthetically. One solution, which has come to the fore in recent years, is a women's gown and cap patterned after the colonial Pilgrim habit.

The use of processional singing has been mentioned several times in this chapter. As long as choirs sang in the rear gallery, there was no occasion for a procession, nor could the choir mount to the gallery gracefully at the close of one should it be attempted. With the advent of chancel choirs, however, the procession was found to be a colorful and convenient way to move the choir from the vestibule to the chancel seats or stalls. It is almost unknown in England and on the continent, save for the processions associated with the major festivals and these are usually outdoor processions. In America, however, it has become a prominent feature in the ceremonial of many denominations. Like other Tractarian innovations, the choir procession was bitterly opposed in many places. Although now a bit of English legend, the following anecdote could easily have been told of many American bishops: The story goes that, at an episcopal visitation to an English parish which was much under the influence of the Oxford Movement, the bishop refused to begin the service until the choir laid aside their processional cross. They are said to have retaliated by "revising" the opening hymn to

> Onward, Christian soldiers,
> Marching as to war,
> With the cross of Jesus
> Left behind the door.

Trinity Church, New York, was well to the fore of the new trend, processional hymns being introduced there on All Saints' Day, 1866. St. Paul's Church, Buffalo, was more typical of the general trend in Episcopal churches; there the chancel was enlarged to accommodate the choir in 1890, and the cross first carried on Easter Sunday of that year.[20]

It is interesting to note how many of these practices which were fought so bitterly in the Episcopal Church a century ago are today the common property of many denominations. Boy choirs are no longer cultivated exclusively in the Episcopal Church. The use of choral prayers and responses in many Protestant churches has given their services an increased musical content approaching that of the choral service itself. Processions are used today without prejudice whenever the occasion and the church edifice permit. Most significant of all the changes, however, is the fact that today one will rarely find a church of any kind where the choir does not wear some form of vestment.

CHAPTER XI

The Growth of Choir Repertory

A FEW sixteenth century cathedrals of Latin America where, for a time, works by outstanding European composers were performed were noted in Chapter I. Within the confines of what is today the United States, church music throughout the seventeenth and much of the eighteenth century was limited to a few Psalm tunes or simple plainsongs. Although most of the tune-books contained a few anthems, there is little indication they were used to any extent in church services. Rather, they were employed more commonly as *pièces de résistance* in public concerts given by the singing schools and musical conventions. Only upon special occasions, in a few leading churches, were anthems performed during the eighteenth century.

Such an occasion was observed at Trinity Church, New York, in 1761, when William Tuckey composed and directed "an Anthem on the death of his late Sacred Majesty [George II]." In December of the following year, an anthem on Psalm XXXIV was performed at the conclusion of the "charity sermon," to the following text:

Solo by Mr. Leadbetter—
 I will give thanks unto the Lord,
 His praise shall be ever in my mouth.
 O praise the Lord with me.
Verse and Chorus—
 And let us magnify his name together.
Solo by Mr. Tuckey—
 Blessed is he that considereth the poor and needy, &c.
By Mr. Leadbetter (Recitatio and Air)—
 Lo the poor crieth and the Lord heareth him.
 Yea and saveth him, out of all his trouble.

Solo by Mr. Tuckey—
He is Father of the fatherless, and defendeth the cause of the Widow.
Verse (Three voices)—
Blessed be the Lord God of Israel, from everlasting to everlasting,
world without end, and let all the people say, Amen.
Chorus—
Amen. Hallelujah. Amen.[1]

Here was a small cantata, or verse anthem, similar in form to those of Purcell and other Restoration composers in England, but one within the capabilities of the boys from the Trinity charity school.

A few anthems have already been mentioned in Chapter VI. The only ones for which the circumstances of their performance are known are the Masonic Odes, or Odes for the Feast of St. John the Evangelist, as they are variously called. The Feast of St. John (December 27) was observed annually at Charleston, South Carolina, by a procession to one of the churches, where members of the Masonic Lodge listened to a sermon and an ode, usually written and composed for the occasion. None of this music is extant, but the texts of several odes have been preserved.[2] These display the contemporary cantata form—alternating recitatives, airs, and duets, with concluding chorus.

A program from the dedication of an organ in Zion Lutheran Church, Athens, New York, shows the same cantata form:

ORDER OF EXHIBITION . . .
Prelude on the organ.
Solo—
Praise thou, my soul, the most mighty and great King of Glory.
Duetto—
Whose wondrous Mercies increase every Moment before thee;
Chorus—
All hearts and tongues: raise your melodious Songs.
etc., etc.[3]

Benjamin Carr's *Masses, Vespers, Litanies* (1805), mentioned in Chapter V, appears to have been used quite widely by Roman Catholic churches, although its content did not represent a very high standard.

In 1809, the Reverend William Smith published *The Churchman's Choral Companion to his Prayer Book*. This collection, which was used at Trinity Church, New York, for nearly two decades, was dedicated to, and bore a note of recommendation by, the Right Reverend Benjamin Moore, Bishop of New York. It contained a curious mixture of said and sung verses and called for considerable intoning on the part of the minister. It consisted of contributions from the Philadelphia organist-composers Benjamin Carr and Raynor Taylor as well as chants by the English composers William Boyce and William Jones.

Jacob Eckhard,[4] during his first year (1809) at St. Michael's, Charleston, compiled a manuscript book for the use of his choir. It contained tunes, chants, canticles, and anthems which had been composed by his predecessors as well as some of his own compositions. Selections from this manuscript were published at Boston in 1816 by J. Loring with the title of *Choral Book*. The manuscript itself, still preserved by the church, is a fascinating summary of the creative musical activity at St. Michael's over several generations. Performed by its vested boy choir, this was unquestionably the finest music in any church in the country. Not only was this true in the matter of repertory and performance, but even more so in its liturgical correctness and taste. The entire establishment reflects the conscientious work of clergy, vestry, and musicians to a degree not observed elsewhere.

In the front of his manuscript, Eckhard faithfully copied down the instructions of the vestry cited in the previous chapter. Its music is divided into three sections, each scored for the boy trebles and figured bass. At several points the treble part divides briefly, and at other points there is a suggestion of an independent bass part. Thus there is a distinct possibility that the trebles may have divided and have been joined upon occasion by the adult voices of the clerk and organist, thus providing three parts comparable to those in Francis Hopkinson's anthem.

The first section of music in the manuscript consists of some one hundred Psalm- and hymn-tunes. Eckhard had been brought up in the Lutheran Church and had earlier served as organist at St. John's Lutheran Church in Charleston, so it is not surprising to see included among these tunes the chorales *"Kommt her zu mir spricht Gottes Sohn"* and *"Nun freut euch, lieben Christen g'mein."* The great English tunes are represented by *St. James, London New, Windsor, St. Anne's, Bedford, Irish,* and *Old Hundredth.* Tunes of more recent vogue are *Adeste fideles, Pleyel's Hymn,* and *Sicilian Mariners.* Even

[89]

more interesting are the tunes with local names: *Tradd Street, Church Street, St. Philip's New,* and *St. Michael's.* These are identified as compositions of Peter Valton,[5] Jarvis Henry Stevens (son of an early organist of St. Michael's who himself served as such in 1783) and the Reverend Dr. Henry Purcell (1742-1802), rector of St. Michael's from 1782 until his death, and an active supporter of its boy choir. There is no real evidence as yet, but one cannot help wondering if this Henry Purcell was not some connection of England's famous Henry Purcell.

The manuscript has an interesting sequence of tunes. Valton wrote one which he called *St. Michael's,* Dr. Purcell has a *St. Michael's New,* and Eckhard in compiling the manuscript added a *St. Michael's Newest.* From numerals given with some of the tunes, it has been determined that Eckhard's manuscript was used in conjunction with an edition of *The Book of Common Prayer and Selection of Psalms with Occasional Hymns* published in Charleston by W. P. Young in 1799, bearing a certificate signed jointly by Dr. Purcell and the Reverend Robert Smith, rector of St. Philip's Church, dated November 10, 1792.

The second section contains single- and double-chant settings of *Venite exultemus, Benedic anima, Jubilate Deo, Deus misereatur, Gloria Patri,* and *Gloria in excelsis.* Most of these are by Eckhard himself. They are noted in full with regular time values, rather than as simple tunes with pointed text beneath.

The final section contains five rather extensive anthems. The first two have texts dealing with benevolence and charity, and were composed by Eckhard for the concerts of the Orphan House in 1798 and 1806. Two Christmas anthems are by the composers Francis Linley (1771-1800) and Capel Bond (*d.* 1790). The manuscript is concluded by an anonymous anthem for services on Independence Day, based on Psalm CXLV.

Without in any way belittling this outstanding collection, one might note in passing that the *Te Deum, Kyrie,* and *Sanctus,* or *Trisagion,* are completely missing. Presumably local tradition did not include their use among the musical portions of the services. But such a condition was perhaps preferable to that prevailing at Trinity Church, New York, where William Jackson's *Te Deum* in F was sung weekly for over twenty years prior to 1839![6]

The following is the

ORDER OF MUSIC
At the Services Connected with
The Consecration of Trinity Church, New York
ON THE
FEAST OF ASCENSION,—May 21st, 1846

VOLUNTARY.—during the entrance of the Procession.
†ANTHEM.—'The Lord is in his holy temple,' &c.
VENITE, and proper Psalms, 84, 122, & 132   Chaunted
†TE DEUM.
†BENEDICTUS.
PSALM.—Selection XXI. v. 2 & 3. Tune   Bristol
†RESPONSES, at the Decalogue.
†GLORIA, at the giving out of the Gospel.
PSALM C (Selection LXXIX) Tune   Old 100th
ANTHEM.—'Surely I have built thee an house to dwell in,' &c.
VOLUNTARY, on the withdrawal of non-communicants.
TRISAGION.
HYMN XCV. Tune   St. Ann's
GLORIA IN EXCELSIS.

N.B.—As the Organ is in a very imperfect and incomplete state, there will be no concluding voluntary.

The pieces marked † have been composed for the occasion by Dr. Hodges.

This was the opening service in the present edifice. It included the Office of Consecration, Morning Prayer, Holy Communion and a sermon; it lasted from eleven in the morning till three in the afternoon.

There is preserved in the Library of Congress a manuscript collection of Trinity's service music, dated November, 1844, which was copied by a Samuel Maynard for Hodges' use. The only parts extant are those for two trebles and a bass; there is no indication as to whether there were originally others, or whether, like the Hopkinson and Eckhard manuscripts, these were all that were intended. The manuscript contains the following Morning Services:

Boyce in A & C	Jackson in E, E♭, & F	Nares in C
Gibbons in F	King in F & C	Rogers in C
Hodges in D, F, & C	Langdon in A	

and Evening Services by Hodges in C & F.

Whereas Hodges' own work at Trinity still reflected much of the Georgian era in English church music, the fresh spirit of the Oxford Movement was evidenced in the music for the consecration service in John Ireland Tucker's Church of the Holy Cross at Troy, New York (December 6, 1848):

Venite & Psalms	Lord Mornington in E
Te Deum & *Jubilate*	Mendelssohn in A
Anthem: *122nd Psalm*	Naumann
Communion Service	Hodges
with a *Kyrie* written for the occasion.	

From this point on, for nearly seventy-five years, there were two separate streams in the American repertory. One was predominantly that of the quartet choir, theatrical and colorful but with little regard for devotional dignity. The second struggled, with little success at first, to restore and still further develop the historic stream of liturgical music. To a large degree these two currents are but American reflections of the prevailing European tastes; there was this difference, however—the European music which became popular over here, gaudy and operatic though it was, had nevertheless been filtered out so that only the better works were used in America. Our own composers, without the breadth of background of their European counterparts, wrote much that was merely cheap imitation of that which they were incapable of understanding. Unfortunately, our nineteenth-century congregations were even less capable of understanding music which had dignity and true inspiration.

European works which became notoriously popular during the last half of the century were Haydn's *Imperial Mass*, Mozart's *First Mass in C*, Rossini's *Stabat Mater*, and Gounod's *St. Caecilia Mass.*[7] Although originally written for, and widely used in, Roman Catholic services, they were all adapted to English texts and either sung as service music in the liturgical churches or, with separate movements, used as anthems in other churches. Handel's *Messiah* and subsequent oratorios were also popular, and excerpts from them continue to be sung to the present time, although with less operatic effect than, for example, the "Inflammatus" from Rossini's *Stabat Mater*.

In worse taste were the adaptations made for church use of well-known secular works. While Samuel P. Warren was organist-choir-master at Grace Church, New York (1868-1894), "Jesus, Lover of my soul" was sung to the melody of "When the swallows homeward fly," and "A charge to keep have I" to the *Prima-Donna Waltz*. Similar atrocities were the adaptation published by Hart P. Danks of the *Benedictus* ("Blessed be the Lord God of Israel") to the march from Wagner's *Tannhauser*, and the arrangement of the familiar Sextet from Donizetti's *Lucia di Lammermoor* to the text "Guide me O thou great Jehovah." This form of musical sacrilege has largely disappeared from our church services *(Deo gratias!)* but excerpts from Wagner's *Lohengrin* and Mendelssohn's *Midsummer Night's Dream* are still used at all too many wedding ceremonies.[8]

An early example of the work of the maudlin school of American composers is the *Spanish Hymn arranged and composed for the Concerts of the Musical Fund Society of Philadelphia by Benjamin Carr. The air from an ancient Spanish Melody*. The tune is still found in many hymnals as *Spanish Chant*. Carr's extravaganza was first performed on December 29th, 1824, by the Musical Fund Society, then in its infancy. The first stanza, "Far, far o'er hill and dell," was scored for solo voice and organ or piano, the second for solo voices with the quartet singing a background of "Miserere mei, Deus," the third for solo with a quartet background of "Requiem aeterna," and the final stanza for full chorus. In similar style was his anthem *Triumphant Zion*, for solo and chorus, "as sung at St. Augustine's, Philadelphia, 1829, at the Jubilee Catholic emancipation."

Music libraries are replete with anthems and canticles turned out in quantity for the popular quartet choirs. The so-called organ parts in all of them are so pianistic as to make one suspect the piano was much more frequently used for accompaniments, as indeed it must have been in many parts of the country. Typical of those is Lucien H. South-hard's *Morning and Evening, a collection of pieces* [i.e., solos and quartets] *intended for use as voluntaries at the commencement or close of public worship* (1865).

The preceding title is significant, for it points to a common feature of the programs quoted in this chapter. In spite of singing schools, Lowell Mason's musical conventions, teachers' institutes, and so forth, there was little congregational singing in the nineteenth century. But one or two hymns are included in the majority of service programs, and an opening anthem by the choir appears to have been the common practice. For a time, beginning in 1887, the Trinity Church choir in New York, under Arthur H. Messiter, sang the opening anthem in procession.[9]

The Reverend Wilbur L. Caswell tells of two old men who often, during his tenure as assistant minister at St. Thomas' Church, New York (1910-1916), went into raptures over "the good old days" under Warren, when every Easter, Madame Grimm sang "Fill the font with roses." This was George W. Warren's *Second Easter Cantata,* published in 1878 to a text by the popular and prolific American sentimentalist Mrs. Lydia Sigourney. Marie Grimm was listed as Warren's soprano soloist as late as 1895. Like his *First Easter Cantata* ("The Singing of Birds"), "Fill the font" was written in a lilting six-eight rhythm. Most popular elsewhere of George Warren's compositions was *The Magdalene* (1877), "for one or two voices and quartette." It was arranged for many combinations, the most popular being as a solo for lacrimose contraltos.

Climax in the quartet style came with the compositions of Dudley Buck and Harry Rowe Shelley. The latter's songs and anthems are still in the repertory of many soloists and choirs. Dudley Buck, whose fertile genius seemed inexhaustible, long remained a popular favorite, especially with his settings for the *Te Deum.* Although his sympathetic treatment of the texts is worthy of the finest art-songs, they are simply too expressive for the meditative needs of most church services. (Plate X shows two pages from the manuscript of Buck's cantata *The Triumph of David.*)

The following program (typical in many ways save that it is a bit more elaborate than usual, due to the occasion) was sung at the dedication service of the new Broadway Tabernacle Church, New York, on March 5, 1905:

Salutation.
Doxology [presumably Thomas Ken's, sung to *Old Hundredth*]
Invocation.
Anthem: "Te Deum laudamus" in C, by Larkin.

Commandments.

Beatitudes.

Responsive Reading from the Psalter.

Apostles' Creed.

Old Testament lesson.

Hymn: "A mighty fortress is our God."

New Testament lesson.

Anthem: "Sanctus" from *Messe Solonelle* by Gounod.

Prayer.

Offertory solo: "Lord, thy glory fills the heavens" from *Stabat Mater* by Rossini.

Prayer.

Hymn: "O God, beneath thy guiding hand."

Sermon.

Service of dedication.

Hymn of dedication [written for the occasion]

Prayer and benediction.

Organ postlude: "Adoration" from *The Holy City* by Alfred R. Gaul.

In many of the larger churches of all denominations, orchestral instruments were used during the later half of the century in connection with the Haydn, Gounod, and Mozart masses, and excerpts from oratorios. These were used, not for basic accompaniment as were the few instruments of colonial psalmody, but to augment the organ in louder and more colorful volume of sound in a manner calculated to attract larger audiences. These audiences, it may be remarked, seldom resembled singing, worshipping congregations. The practice survives, even today, in the brass and tympani that some churches add on Easter Sunday to help entertain the throngs which join the fashion parades created by American advertising.

Two programs in the more conservative, devotional idiom have been cited earlier in this chapter. Except for a few works by Henry S. Cutler, most of the music suitable for liturgical purposes up to the time of Horatio Parker came from English sources.

The following are two significant programs from Canon Knowles' work in Chicago.[10] The music at his first choir festival in the cathedral, on November 30, 1870, consisted of

Cantate Domino & *Deus misereatur* in A	Bridgewater
Anthem: "Like as a Father"	Hatton

Gloria in excelsis from *12th Mass*	Mozart
Two solos and "Hallelujah" from *Messiah*	Handel

At a lecture on "Church Music" given February 16, 1879, Canon Knowles' choir sang

Plainsongs: 7th & 8th tones; "Pange lingua."
Anglican chants by Croft & Barnby.
Hymn tunes by Crüger & Dykes.

Anthems: "O where shall wisdom be found"	Boyce
"Hosannah in the highest"	Stainer
St. Cecilia Mass	Gounod

The program for Cutler's choir festival at Trinity Church in 1861 was cited on page 77. On November 19, 1885, the program for the thirteenth annual festival of the choirs of Trinity Parish, under the direction of Walter B. Gilbert, consisted of Choral Evensong and the following anthems:

Behold I bring you glad tidings	Giovanni Croce
O how amiable are thy dwellings	Vaughan Richardson
Blessing, Glory, Wisdom	J. S. Bach [!][11]
Distracted with care and anguish	Haydn
Judge me, O God	Mendelssohn
The earth is the Lord's	Spohr
A great multitude	W. B. Gilbert

On Christmas Eve, 1894, the following music was sung at Dr. Tucker's jubilee service at the Church of the Holy Cross, in Troy:

Magnificat & *Nunc dimittis*	E. J. Hopkins
(composed for the occasion)	
Festival *Te Deum*	Warren
"Comfort ye" & "And the glory of the Lord" from *The Messiah*	Handel
"All my heart this night rejoices"	Horatio Parker

Representative of the better parish music throughout the country at the end of the century is the following, sung at Grace Church, Baltimore, on Christmas morning, 1897:

Opening anthem: "For unto us a Child is born"	
from *The Messiah*	Handel
Venite	chant

[96]

Te Deum in E♭	Schumann
Benedictus	Barnby
Introit anthem: "Mercy and truth are met together"	Stainer
Communion Service in E♭	Stainer
Hymn 49	*Adeste fideles*
Offertory anthem: "Glory, honor, praise, and power"	Mozart
Hymn 60	*Regent Square*
Gloria in excelsis	old chant
Nunc dimittis	chant

During October, 1904, the General Convention of the Episcopal Church met in Boston, holding its principal services at Trinity Church where Wallace Goodrich was then organist and choirmaster. The anthems and service music sung by the Trinity Choir during that month were in marked contrast with quartet choir repertories such as that of the First Church in Boston six years later. Both are quoted in full in Appendix B at the rear of this book. There are more works by American composers listed in the First Church repertory, but all are in the theatrical, quartet idiom. The subsequent passage of a half-century of time has dimmed their lustre only to accentuate the more permanent values in the works found in the Trinity repertory.

With very few exceptions, music in the Roman Catholic churches in this country during the period from 1830 to 1920 was little different from that described above. Indicative of its paucity is the statement made in 1840 by Bishop Benedict J. Fenwick of Boston that in two-thirds of the Roman Catholic churches of America there was no singing at all.[12] The glorious heritage of mediaeval and Renaissance music was entirely unknown, due in large measure to the nature of the congregations, composed as they largely were of poor German, Irish, and Italian immigrants who had known little better music in their homelands. Without adequate background, it was only natural that, as they were able to afford music, they should turn to the more theatrical types as represented by the quartet choir, particularly when such a high percentage of operatic singers were Italian and Roman Catholic, and therefore available at little or no expense. The following program is typical of what has too often been the case when "special music" was desired:

[97]

At the Church of ———, West ——— Street, New York, on Sunday, April 21 [1903] Vespers will be celebrated at 8 o'clock, and a meeting of the Archconfraternity of Our Lady of Victories will be held. The musical programme will be as follows:

Prelude (organ and orchestra) *Pilgrim's March*	d'Archambaud
Dixit Dominus (quartette)	Barnby
Laudate pueri	Gregorian
Magnificat (quartette)	D. Giorza
Meditation (violin and organ)	Hauser
Unfold ye portals (chorus from the St. ——— Academy)	Gounod
Tantum ergo (chorus)	Rossi
Postlude, *Festival March*	Mendelssohn

The soloists are:

Soprano, Mrs. K———
Tenor, Signor O. M———
Alto, Miss M———
Basso, M. J. Jean ———

The orchestra from the St. ——— Academy, under the direction of Prof. ———, will supplement the organ, at which Mme. ——— will preside. The Rev. ——— will preach. A procession in honor of Our Lady of Lourdes will be held.[18]

One notable exception in the East was the Jesuit Church of St. Francis Xavier in New York City, where, under the Reverend John B. Young, S.J., a boy choir flourished *ca.* 1885.

Michael H. Cross[14] has traced the music used at St. Augustine's Church, Philadelphia, during much of the nineteenth century. For the first thirty years Benjamin Carr served as organist, using music from the collection he compiled for the purpose.[15] His successor, Benjamin Cross, introduced many of the Haydn and Mozart masses which had been published in mid-century by Vincent Novello,[16] the first four-part masses being sung during the 1840's. Other Roman Catholic churches in Philadelphia used a similar repertory, which may be regarded as typical of all the Eastern city churches.

Until the time of Bishop Kendrick (consecrated 1830), many English hymns and other pieces were sung at all services, including even the Mass.

Owing to the efforts of John B. Singenberger[17] with his Caecilian Society and its magazine, the dioceses of Chicago, Cincinnati, Milwau-

Edward Hodges
(1796-1867)

Henry Stephen Cutler
(1824-1902)

PLATE IX.

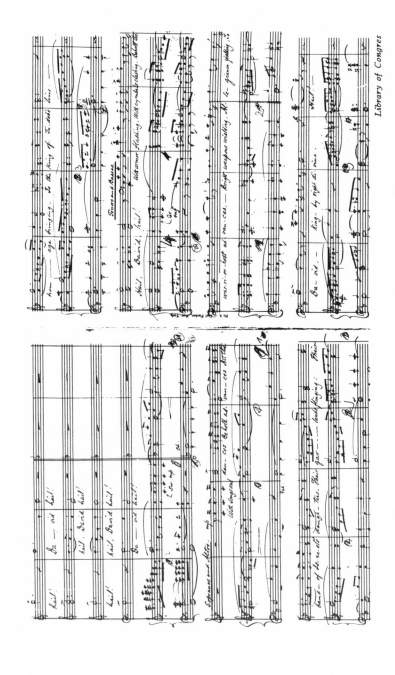

PLATE X. Pages from the Manuscript of Dudley Buck's Cantata *The Triumph of David*

Library of Congres

kee, Minnesota, Missouri, and Iowa were far ahead of the East in correcting such abuses. Apart from Archbishop Henni of Milwaukee, who gave much support to Singenberger, the American hierarchy did little during the nineteenth century to promote music.

St. John's (Benedictine) Abbey, Collegeville, Minnesota, was an exception among American religious houses and seminaries. Founded *ca.* 1850, by the early 1870's it was cultivating Gregorian chant and polyphonic masses. Nonetheless, in 1900 there were still more Lutheran and Episcopal than Roman Catholic churches using plainsong in their services. On the credit side, it should again be emphasized that here, as in Protestant church music, conditions between 1850 and 1900 were no worse than in corresponding European institutions.

With a few exceptions, the first real progress in liturgical music was due to the labors of men of German extraction who had been reared in the principles of Caecilian music. This movement, led by such men as Kaspar Ett, Karl Proske, and Franz Witt, culminated in the Ratisbon edition of the Church's plainsong in the 1860's, and in the formation of the Caecilian Society, whose aims were reforms in the use of the plainsong, the encouragement of congregational singing, the revival of polyphony, and the elimination of the orchestral masses of the Haydn, Mozart, and Gounod types. Their own compositions, patterned on the simplicity of the Palestrina *Missa Papae Marcelli,* were in a singable, homophonic style which readily lent itself to parish use.

In America the movement was headed by Singenberger, who founded the Caecilian Society in 1873, at St. Francis, Wisconsin. A first general meeting was held in Milwaukee on June 17, 1874, with one in Dayton, Ohio, the following year. Thereafter annual conventions, with demonstrations by massed choirs, were held in various cities, mostly in the Middle West, although a few were held in the East. It flourished principally among the German-American congregations, reaching a membership of over three thousand as early as 1878. Like the parent society in Germany, its interests lay in cultivating plainsong and polyphony, and in purging the services of cheap, sentimental music. At first using the Ratisbon edition of the plainsong, Singenberger and his pupils were using the more traditional rhythm in their classes as early as 1890, and were thus ready for the transition to the Vatican-Solesmes edition in 1908. The Society had prepared the ground in America for a favorable reception of the famous *Motu Proprio* of Pius X[18] and furnished the means for implementing many of its provisions. The influence of the Society thereafter began to decline, partly because the need for its pioneering had passed and partly because of its failure, save in a limited degree,[19] to reach other than German-speaking musicians.*

The Society's magazine, *Caecilia,* was founded by Singenberger in 1874. At first it was published by J. Fischer & Brother in Dayton; it subsequently moved to New York with that firm, and later to St. Francis, Wisconsin, where its editor was located. Until Singenberger's death in 1924, the magazine continued to be published in German with occasional articles in English, but even these were oriented toward the German Catholic parishes. After Singenberger died, it was edited by his son, Otto. In more recent years it has been published by McLaughlin & Reilly, in Boston.

Throughout its career—the longest of any music periodical in this country—*Caecilia,* like its parent society, worked for a restored plain-song, simpler choral services, and the German traditions of vernacular congregational singing.

*In 1964, the Society of St. Caecilia and its sister organization, the Society of St. Gregory, merged to form the Church Music Society.

CHAPTER XII

Shape-Notes and Gospel Songs

THE PRAISES of Almighty God have never been sung exclusively by well-ordered congregations and choirs within Georgian or Victorian-Gothic walls. Indeed, in no facet of American life has the cleavage, social or otherwise, been so sharply drawn as between those familiar with historical hymnody and those who know only the so-called "gospel songs." The latter songs form such a distinctive lore, and at the same time such a large segment of the field of religious music in this country, that some attempt should be made to describe them.

In Chapter III mention was made of the early singing schools and the spread of popular hymnody under the influence of the "Great Awakening." To the Baptists and Methodists of New England, and more especially of the rural South, in the period immediately following the Revolution, belong the credit for spreading the movement still further and more deeply into the religious-social life of the country in a seemingly radical manner, and yet one in which consequent conservatism has preserved many songs intact, but ever fresh, to the present time. Camp meetings—begun in the Kentucky Revival of 1800— the Shakers, and the Millennial enthusiasts were the natural breeders of what George Pullen Jackson calls the "revival spirituals."[1]

In his two collections *Spiritual Folk-Songs of Early America*[2] and *Down-East Spirituals,*[3] Jackson has published 550 tunes and texts which have been recorded from folk-singers and traced to their published sources. In tonality and rhythm, these are similar to the secular ballads of the times. Some are actually the identical secular tunes, for a common query of the song leaders was "Why should the devil have all the pretty tunes?" Many of the texts are lineal descendants of the Elizabethan ballad "Jerusalem, my happy home," now found in the most conservative hymnals.

In his earlier work, *White Spirituals in the Southern Uplands,*[4] Jackson traces the movement in its published forms from the early New England collections, through the Southern collections, and into the Middle West. Outstanding among these collections in both content and influence were Ananias Davisson's *Kentucky Harmony,* published shortly before 1816,*and Allen D. Carden's *Missouri Harmony* of 1820. Two collections which became the basis of annual mass-singing meetings—where hundreds would gather for an all-day sing in school, courthouse, or country meeting-house—were William Walker's *Southern Harmony* (1835), and *The Sacred Harp,* first compiled in 1844 by Benjamin F. White and E. J. King.[5] These collections went through many editions, copies of which are still used at rural singing-meetings in the South.

A generation or more ago it was thought that the Negro spiritual was a unique phenomenon, characteristic purely of the race and its nineteenth-century American environment. Today, thanks to Jackson's research, it has become apparent that the Negro spirituals differ but little from the earlier gospel songs.[6] These were taken up and adapted by the Negro in mid-century, at the very time they were beginning to go into eclipse in white circles. They were exploited by the Fiske University "Jubilee Singers" and others, beginning in 1871, for the purpose of raising money for the support of Negro educational institutions. This resulted in the curious circumstance that the Negro spiritual became better known in cultured musical circles than its white source and counterpart. Consequently but erroneously, music dictionaries have been wont to describe the spiritual as "the nearest approach to 'folk-music' in the United States."[7] Some of the spirituals have their own individual charm, and it is encouraging to note that they are being used today for their own merit, entirely apart from ulterior, sentimental considerations.

As is well known to students of the history of music, solfeggio, using

*The *Kentucky Harmony* was copyrighted in 1817.

the syllables *ut* (or *do*), *re*, *mi*, *fa*, *sol*, and *la*, may be traced to the teachings of Guido d'Arezzo (*ca.* 995-1050), who recognized that the sequence of initial pitches of successive phrases in the familiar plainsong hymn-tune "Ut queant laxis" was a ready aid to the tonal memory for purposes of sight-singing. All through the Middle Ages, the Guidonian hand and gamut were basic patterns for music instruction. Their role during the Elizabethan era is vividly described in the familiar opening scene of Thomas Morley's *Plaine and Easie Introduction to Practicall Musicke* (1597). Subsequent generations have modified the hexachords of the gamut to a single octave sequence—*do, re, mi, fa, sol, la, ti, do*—which remains the best known device for teaching singers to read music at sight. Among English and Welsh choral groups, through an interesting perversion, the educational method has become the main technique, so that their music is printed with these syllables above the text rather than with the standard musical notation.

In America, out of the efforts of the early singing-school teachers to apply solfeggio in their classes, there developed a perversion of the notation itself. Andrew Law[8] developed a four-shape notation which he published, without lines and spaces, in his *Music Primer* (4th edition, Cambridge, Massachusetts, 1803). Another four-shape notation was printed in the *Easy Instructor; or A New Method of teaching Sacred Harmony, containing the rudiments of music on an improved plan, wherein the naming and timing of the notes are familiarized to the weakest capacity* (Philadelphia, 1802) by William Little and William Smith. This is the basis of the system of "patent notes" which still permeates the Southern gospel song-books, and is the only music notation known to many thousands of rural singers to this day.[9] The system uses a right triangle for the first and fourth degrees of the octave scale, both called *fa*. The second and fifth degrees are called *sol* and use a round note. The third and sixth degrees are called *la* and use a square note, while the leading tone, or seventh degree, is called *mi* and is represented by a diamond-shaped note. These shape-notes, "patent notes," or "buck-wheat notes," as they are variously called, are used with a standard clef and key signature on regular lines and spaces, so that the music may be read by a trained musician as well as by one who can read only the patent notes.

[103]

fa　sol　la　fa　sol　la　mi　fa

Two pages from the first edition of Little and Smith's *Easy Instructor* are reproduced on Plate XI. Note that the melody is found on the third line, as in most tune-books of the period; the tenor is on the top line, while the alto part uses the *c* or alto clef. The famous fuging tune *Greenfield*[10] extends across both pages.

Jackson[11] lists thirty-eight different collections published in this notation prior to the year 1856. In the forties, a seven-shape system came into vogue, which uses a different shape for each degree of the scale, with the standard nomenclature of solfeggio:

do　re　mi　fa　sol　la　ti　do

This gradually superseded the older system throughout the South and has since spread westward.

Subsequent decades have seen a commercialization of the gospel song and a basic change in its inherent character, so that today it is the product of a veritable religious "tin-pan-alley." Arthur L. Stevenson[12] made an effort in 1930 to compile some accurate statistics of the publishing aspects of the gospel-song trade. While by no means complete, due to the natural reserve of private firms, one company reported total sales between 1909 and 1928 of 7,699,873 copies of 21 different collections, sales of which ran between 8,000 and 812,489 copies of individual collections. Another firm reported sales of over 1,000,000 copies for two titles and 500,000 copies for two other titles, the latest in 1908. In more recent years, competition has become so intense that sales of between 20,000 and 50,000 copies of a given collection are now considered good. Collections are published annually, on the cheapest paper, in order to assure a frequent market. In 1950 there were fifty titles received for copyright in the Library of Congress. Of these, approximately one-third, or all of those published south of the Mason-Dixon Line, employed shape-notes.

The singing schools, usually taught by the compilers themselves or by their agents, were to a considerable degree responsible for the volume of sales. These schools were still being held in urban communities throughout the country until after the Civil War. Today they are limited to the rural South and West.

The tune-books of Lowell Mason, Thomas Hastings, William B. Bradbury, and others in the first half of the nineteenth century were planned to serve the needs of all sides of religious life. They contained a medley of new and old Psalm-tunes, conservative adaptations of German chorales, chants, and new gospel songs.

In the latter half of the century, in the urban centers of the North, gospel songs received tremendous vogue through the activity of Ira Sankey (*cf.* page 232) the song leader long associated with the evangelist Dwight L. Moody. Other prominent leaders and composers of gospel songs were P. P. Bliss (1838-1876), Robert Lowry (1826-1899), George Coles Stebbins (1846-1945), and, in the present century, Homer Rodeheaver, the trombone-playing song leader for the evangelist Billy Sunday.

During the earlier periods, the music contained in the gospel songbooks had a character worthy of the studies which today help to preserve them. Some of the melodies have found their way into the standard hymnals of the various churches. In recent decades, however, the gospel songs have become but a weak echo—melodically, rhythmically, and harmonically—of the "popular songs" which are plugged so insistently on screen and radio. Indeed many of the texts themselves are scarcely distinguishable from the saccharine lyrics of their secular counterpart, and none of them deserve to survive the cheap wood-pulp on which they are printed.

CHAPTER XIII

Nineteenth Century Leaders

CONTINUING the survey of leading church musicians from
Chapter VI, one notes that many of these in both the eighteenth and nineteenth centuries were Englishmen who migrated to America in middle life, after a considerable career in their
native land. It would be interesting but difficult to explore the social
and economic considerations which prompted these moves.[1] One factor
is well recognized—the snobbishness of fashionable churches which
many times hired an inferior English organist in preference to a native
musician. This phenomenon had not become entirely extinct by the
end of the nineteenth century. (Indeed, it was not limited to musicians, for there has been the same prejudice in the appointment
of clergymen, especially toward Scottish ministers in Presbyterian
churches.) But the proportion of such appointments is not readily apparent, and only the better musicians are named below. Of Englishmen, only Edward Hodges and T. Tertius Noble attained pre-eminence
in this country. Two who did important work at the beginning of the
nineteenth century were George K. Jackson (*cf.* page 220) and
Benjamin Carr (1768-1831).

Carr studied as a boy in England under Samuel Arnold and Charles
Wesley. He was a soloist in the Ancient Concerts in London before
coming to the United States. His father, Joseph Carr, had been a
music publisher in London. The family first set up shop in Philadelphia in 1793. Later, Joseph, with another son, Thomas, set himself up as
a music publisher and dealer in Baltimore, while Benjamin started a
similar business in New York, retaining the Philadelphia shop. The

Carrs were leaders in printing patriotic music. Benjamin Carr published "Hail Columbia," at Philadelphia, in 1798. From the Carrs' Baltimore establishment came the first edition of "The Star Spangled Banner," Thomas Carr having set Francis Scott Key's text to the tune of *Anacreon in Heaven,* which his father published shortly after September 13, 1814.

Benjamin Carr became popular as a composer, especially of works such as the *Spanish Hymn* described on page 93. In addition to the *Masses, Vespers and Litanies* (1805),[2] he compiled a *Collection of Chants* (1816), the *Chorister* (1820), and edited the significant *Musical Journal.* He was one of the founders of the Musical Fund Society in Philadelphia (1820). At one time he was organist of St. Joseph's Roman Catholic Church, the church attended by Lafayette, Rochambeau, and other French officers. He was for a long time organist of St. Peter's Episcopal Church, and from 1801 until 1831 was in charge of the music at St. Augustine's Roman Catholic Church. He died in Philadelphia on May 24, 1831, and was buried in St. Peter's churchyard.[3] His portrait is at Plate IV.

Not all the foreign-born church musicians of the nineteenth century came from England. In the secular realm there was an increasing number of German musicians as the century progressed. Three Germans were outstanding in their influence in the field of sacred music, Jacob Eckhard (*cf.* pages 209-10) at Charleston, South Carolina, whose manuscript was described in Chapter XI, Louis H. Hast at Louisville, Kentucky (*cf.* pages 217-18) and John Baptist Singenberger (1848-1924) the outstanding Roman Catholic musician of the era.

Singenberger was born in Kirchberg, Switzerland, on May 25, 1848. He studied at the Jesuit college in Feldkirch, Austria, the University of Innsbruck, and the Munich Conservatory. A favorite pupil of Franz Xavier Witt, he was appointed director of the seminary choir at Chur in 1871. He was brought over to this country in 1873 to be the music instructor at the Catholic Normal School and Pio Nono College at St. Francis, Wisconsin. Within a few months he organized an American Society of St. Caecilia, patterned after the German society of the same name. In 1874 he founded, and for the remainder of his life edited, the monthly journal *Caecilia.*[4] An able teacher, but with a humble personality, he was a veritable Dr. Witt transplanted to American soil, a pioneer in the development of liturgical music in the American Roman Catholic Church. As expressed by a biographer,

> Against the confusion of thought, the lack of principle, and the compromise with worldliness prevailing round about us in matters of Catholic Church music, this man stood out for us like a central figure symbolic of definite purpose and program, and of unyielding adherence to sound principle.[5]

Many honors came to him—an LL.D. from the University of Notre Dame and, from the Vatican, the titles Knight of St. Gregory and Knight Commander of St. Sylvester. He died in St. Joseph's Hospital, Milwaukee, May 29, 1924. The July-August, 1924, issue of his magazine contains eulogies and a complete list of his compositions, arrangements, and editions. His portrait is at Plate XIII.

A number of eighteenth-century tune-book compilers were mentioned in Chapters III and IV. There are biographical notices of forty such men from the first half of the nineteenth century in Simeon Pease Cheney's *The American Singing Book* (Boston, White, Smith & Company, 1879). Especially in the second quarter was tune-book compiling carried into the field of "big business" and extensively commercialized.[6] In many ways this was unfortunate for, by the simple expedient of saturation at the level of most common usage, more substantial musical fare was crowded out and thwarted in what might otherwise have been a healthy growth.

Lowell Mason (*cf.* pages 224-25) did noble work in the introduction of singing classes into the public schools and in training teachers for such work, and his influence was greatly augmented by the many tune-books which he published. One of the most famous of these was the *Carmina Sacra* which went through thirteen editions between 1841 and 1860. It is estimated to have sold over 500,000 copies.[7] The full scope of his influence may be realized if we recall that America has been settled a little over three hundred years. During the first half of this time, there was relatively little musical development. But then for sixty full years Lowell Mason was a dominating factor in church and school music, and in the pedagogy and philosophy of music education. While he did much to stimulate interest in singing, he probably did more to depreciate its standards than any other person of his era. A reviewer of his *Sabbath Hymn & Tune Book* (*ca.* 1850), wrote:

> No one has done so much as he, in his day and generation, to extend the practice and lower the taste in sacred music. In the mechanism of getting up books of psalm and hymn tunes, and in making money out of them, he has been *facile princeps,* out of sight ahead of all competitors.[8]

Important colleagues of Mason were Thomas Hastings (*cf.* page 218) Henry Kemble Oliver (*cf.* page 229) and William Batchelder Bradbury (*cf.* page 203). The latter sets forth the following creed in a *Lecture on Music,* the manuscript of which is preserved in the Library of Congress. It is interesting as the ideal of a church musician in the mid-nineteenth century, but it is weak in that nothing is said about the appropriateness or quality of the music to be sung:

> I have for myself adopted the following articles of faith and practice with reference to this subject:
>
> 1st. I believe it the privilege and duty of *all* to unite in singing as an act of worship.
>
> 2nd. I believe that, from the congregation at large, a number possessing more musical talent than the rest should be organized into a separate body with a competent leader and occupy a place by themselves.
>
> 3rd. That this choir so organized should not only serve in the capacity of *leader to the congregation* but that a part of each service may and should be performed entirely and exclusively by themselves,—the congregation at such times being silent listeners. That in such services new and beautiful music appropriate to the occasion may be performed with as much taste and skill as by attentive study and practice they can command.
>
> 4th. and lastly, that for *Congregational Singing* only such tunes as are simple in their structure and very easy of execution should be introduced, and that these should consist chiefly of old and familiar tunes such as the congregation generally can sing; that in each service one such congregational tune should be selected, and when introduced by the choir, all the people should arise and sing it to the best of their ability, without reference to *art* or musical effect, but simply and solely as an act of worship before their Maker.

During the eighteenth century Trinity Church, New York, had already begun to exert considerable leadership in the religious life of the country. Stephen P. Dorsey[9] has shown how the Trinity Church edifice of 1789 influenced the building of Gothic Revival churches, especially in New England. With its "new" edifice of 1846, Trinity became the unofficial cathedral church for all America—its influence and its generosity widely felt. The mother church and chapels of the parish have been served by a succession of distinguished organists, a table of whom will be found in Appendix A, pages 187-89.

Edward Hodges (1796-1867), the first of the more distinguished Trinity organist-choirmasters, has been mentioned previously. He was born in Bristol, where he was organist of St. James' and St. Nicholas' churches before coming to America. In England he had already established himself as an inventor and an authority on the organ, being responsible for the introduction of the C-compass. He obtained the degree of Doctor of Music from Cambridge University in 1825. In 1838 he became organist of St. James' Cathedral, Toronto, but was induced to move to New York the following year. He served at St. John's Chapel until the opening of the new Trinity Church in 1846. Through a curious instance of unbridled exploitation on the part of the organ builder, Henry Erben, Hodges was not given full credit for his work in designing the new Trinity organ; indeed, he was not even included among those who first performed on it.[10] Nonetheless, he soon became nationally esteemed for his skill as a performer. In 1851 he was a leader in founding the short-lived but significant Church Choral Society.

Hodges composed some twenty-five anthems, seven services, and other shorter works for his choir, none of which have remained in the repertory. Most of these were very homophonic in style and with simple harmonic progressions. One anthem, more ambitious than others in its attempts at polyphonic writing, is a setting of Psalm CXXII, composed for the consecration of Trinity Chapel in 1855. The opening chorus has a solo passage and subsequent obligato on the words "I was glad when they said unto me," for a "clerical-baritone." The passage "O pray for the peace of Jerusalem" is an unaccompanied exhortation for three priests. "Peace be within thy walls" is set to sustained chords by the chorus with a steady pulse in the accompaniment;

it bears the note: "Peace is not a time of idleness and somnolence but more properly a period of steady occupation. E.H."

Hodges' work was interrupted by illness in 1858 and after an abortive attempt to resume his activity, he returned to Bristol in 1863, and died there in 1867. His biography was written by his daughter, Faustina,[11] who was a talented organist in her own right. A distinguished son, John Sebastian Bach Hodges, is discussed below. The bulk of his musical library was acquired by the Library of Congress in 1919. His portrait is reproduced at Plate IX.

His successor at Trinity, Henry Stephen Cutler (*cf.* pages 206-7) published a *Trinity Psalter* (1864), and in the following year a collection of twenty-two *Trinity Anthems* which he had composed for use there. His portrait is at Plate IX.

Other Trinity musicians of the period who were well known for their compositions and editions were William Henry Walter (*cf.* page 236), Walter Bond Gilbert (*cf.* pages 214-15), and Arthur Henry Messiter (*cf.* pages 227-28). Stubbs[12] has written of Messiter that during much of his regime from 1866 to 1897, Trinity was the only church in New York where the services were not marred by choral inconsistencies. During his final year of service, the Trinity choir sang twenty-two communion services (including seven adapted Latin masses), 11 morning and 14 evening services, together with 96 anthems. Of the latter, 28 were by German composers, 61 by English, and 7 by American composers.

Just as at St. Michael's, Charleston, in the eighteenth century, the combination of a clergyman-musician and a competent organist resulted in an outstanding musical establishment, so in all churches in modern times musically trained clergy are able to advance the quality of their musical services to a level unattainable by the organist-choirmaster alone, no matter how competent he may be. During the second half of the nineteenth century the choral music and ceremonial of the Episcopal Church was greatly enriched through the efforts of four clergymen who were also accomplished musicians.

John Ireland Tucker (1819-1895) was born to a prominent Brooklyn family on November 26, 1819. As a boy he sang in Muhlenberg's choir at the Flushing Institute. After graduation from Columbia College in

1837, and a "grand tour" of Europe and the Levant, he served for a time as organist of St. Thomas' Church, New York. He graduated from General Seminary in 1844 and was ordained to the diaconate by Bishop Onderdonk.

Mrs. Phebe Warren of Troy, New York, had, around 1812, begun a "Saturday Sewing-school," where neglected children of the neighborhood were taught the "Catechism and plain sewing." In 1839 her daughter-in-law, Mary Warren, converted it into a day school, meeting in rooms of St. Paul's Church. Music played an active role in the school from the start, and the children soon began to sing from the gallery during Sunday services. Jealousy of the professional quartet, coupled with Mrs. Warren's wide philanthropic interests, led her to build, in 1844, the Church of the Holy Cross, "as a house of prayer for all people without money and without price." To this new church on Christmas morning, Tucker came to sing the choral service and preach his first sermon. His church was visited, especially in its early years, by many clergymen who were keenly interested in the many innovations being practiced. For Tucker—pioneer exemplar of the ideals of the Oxford Movement in this country—not only sang the choral services daily, but celebrated the Eucharist on all days for which propers were provided. He preached in a surplice using colored stoles according to the season, introduced flowers in the sanctuary, and used the plainsong melodies for chanting. Years later, at the occasion of Holy Cross's Jubilee, Tucker noted that at the time they commenced using the full choral celebration of the Holy Communion, there was not a single cathedral in England which did so. In all this he was ably supported by his first organist, Nathan B. Warren, the talented son of his church's benefactor. In 1858 he received the degree of Doctor of Sacred Theology from General Theological Seminary. He was active in the Church Choral Society, but otherwise remained close to the confines of his own parish, turning down many offers from other parishes. His influence was enhanced on the national scene by the series of publications which he prepared. His *Service Book* (1873), with its plainsong and Merbecke, opened up a new world to American church musicians. His *Parish Hymnal* (1870) provided material for schools and special occasions. The first of his *Tunes Old and New, Adapted to the Hymnal* (1872), and the *Children's Hymnal* (1874) led the way from Lowell Mason's style. At the Church of the Holy Cross, the chancel was lengthened in 1889. Thereafter the girls continued to wear their red or white uniforms, but the choirmen were vested, and processions with a crucifer inaugurated. Christmas Day, 1894—the Jubilee of his ministry at Holy Cross—was the occasion of many honors. Death came from a stroke on August seventeenth of the following year.[13]

John Henry Hopkins, Jr. (*cf*. pages 219-20) became in 1855 the first instructor in church music at the General Theological Seminary. John Sebastian Bach Hodges (*cf*. page 219) was active in the work of the Episcopal Hymnal Commissions of 1874 and 1892. He composed over one hundred pieces of church music—hymn tunes and anthems, and compiled *The Book of Common Praise* (1868).[14]

The work of John Harris Knowles (*cf*. page 221) in Chicago was discussed on page 78. In his reminiscences, Knowles tells of a scene in Aurora, Illinois, shortly before 1867.

> I presume the first choral service in the West was held on one wet Sunday morning, when not a soul came to church but myself, the quartette choir, the sexton, and Mr. W. S. B. Mathews, the organist. He, ever eager for new knowledge, had got from me all the points of the choral service, so then and there we had a solemn function all by ourselves, the choir in the gallery, the parson in the chancel, the church empty (of all but angels) and the sexton looking wondering on.[15]

During the second half of the century, Boston was distinguished by a small group of church musicians who were not only outstanding in their own generation as leaders and recitalists, but also in the following generation because of their influence as teachers. And it is of interest to note that each was pre-eminent in the music of a separate liturgical tradition.

Benjamin Johnson Lang (*cf*. pages 221-22) served in Congregational churches during most of his life, following in the musical traditions of the early Psalmody and subsequent hymnody of Lowell Mason. James Cutler Dunn Parker (*cf*. page 229) was organist-choirmaster of Trinity Church, Boston, for twenty-seven years, serving under that leader of Evangelical or "Low Church" Episcopalians, Phillips Brooks. During the same years in Boston's Church of the Advent, Samuel

Brenton Whitney (*cf.* pages 238-39) advanced the "High Church" traditions, begun by Henry S. Cutler, with devotion and a keen insight into the true relation of church music to liturgical worship. The more mundane aspects of Roman Catholic music were exploited by George Elbridge Whiting (*cf.* page 238) at the Church of the Immaculate Conception, with elaborate "concert vespers" which attracted large congregations, or rather, audiences, over a period of many years.

The name which will always first come to mind whenever one speaks of our late-nineteenth-century, or Victorian, music is that of Dudley Buck (1839-1909), known today through compositions which, while no longer revered as they were two generations ago, are by no means forgotten. During his lifetime they were held in such regard that each new work was promptly reviewed in the *Atlantic Monthly* by the distinguished critic William F. Apthorp. His *"Te Deum* in B Minor" and the Easter anthem "As It Began to Dawn" were sincerely believed by many to be the highest expression of religious music.

Buck was born in Hartford on March 10, 1839. He studied in Leipzig during the years 1858-61 under Hauptmann, Richter, Plaidy, and Moscneles; he then spent a year in Paris. Returning to Hartford, he was organist at the Park Church from 1862 to 1868. In 1869 he became organist and choirmaster at St. James' Church, Chicago, losing his effects in the great fire of 1871. He then served at St. Paul's Church, Boston, until 1875 when he went to New York to become both assistant conductor under Theodore Thomas and organist at St. Anne's Church. His talent did not lie in the field of orchestral conducting, however, and commencing with 1877 he devoted himself entirely to church music, serving at Holy Trinity, Brooklyn, until 1901. His last year as an active musician was spent at Plymouth Church in that city. He retired in 1903 and died in Orange, New Jersey, on October 6, 1909.

Dudley Buck pioneered organ recitals in much the same way as Theodore Thomas had pioneered orchestral music in this country. He was one of the founders of the American Guild of Organists. He also compiled a *Dictionary of Musical Terms* and *Illustrations in Choir Accompaniment, with Hints on Registration* (1877). Many of his anthems and services appeared in the several series of *Episcopal Church Music, designed for either quartette or chorus choir.* He was com-

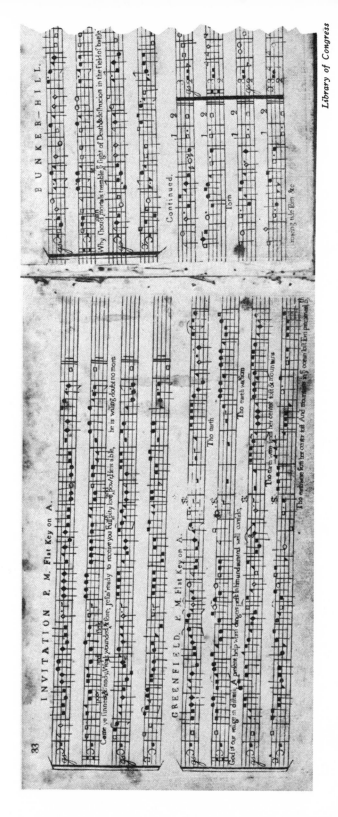

Library of Congress

PLATE XI. Shape-notes from Little and Smith's *Easy Instructor*, 1802

PLATE XII. A Page from Lowell Mason's *Carmina Sacra*, 1841

missioned by Theodore Thomas to compose works for the Philadelphia Exposition of 1876 and the Chicago Fair of 1893. In 1880 his cantata on Longfellow's *Golden Legend* won the one-thousand-dollar Cincinnati Festival prize. Our first successful composer of larger choral works, his compositions were also extensively performed in England and Germany during his lifetime. He had an excellent sense for texts, but due to popular demand he developed a more or less set formula which soon became overworked. Seen in perspective, his work shows a compromise between the public's taste and the composer's ideals. In spite of his predilection for quartet-choirs, he succeeded in raising the general level of public taste. Outstanding among his pupils were John Hyatt Brewer, Frederick Grant Gleason, Charles B. Hawley, Harry Rowe Shelley, and R. H. Woodman. His portrait is at Plate XIII, a page from his *Triumph of David* at Plate X.

These are but a few of those who labored in this country during the nineteenth century to perfect our praise of Almighty God with song and instrument. Skills and tastes have changed so that today much of their early work seems uncouth, their later work maudlin and super-saccharine. Yet in very few instances can their sincerity be questioned —for in the last analysis, their careers and their accomplishments must be interpreted against the full background of their era and its manifestations in the other fields of art and society. The pulpit itself has gone through a similar metamorphosis; Dudley Buck, after all, was much akin to Phillips Brooks.

CHAPTER XIV

Reed and Pipe Organs

IN CHAPTER VII were described the organs built or purchased in this country during the eighteenth century. Save for numbers and size, there was little change in the organ situation during the first half of the nineteenth century. Few organs were under expression —that is to say, with one or more sections enclosed in such a manner that the volume of sound could be regulated by adjustable shutters. Still fewer had pedal key-boards, and those few had no separate ranks of pipes for the pedals, it being necessary when performing upon them to "borrow" from the manuals by means of coupling.

Trinity Church, New York, used its Hall organ until the new building was erected. Plans for a new organ were initiated with the appointment of Dr. Hodges as organist in 1839; he was instructed at that time to draw up specifications for an instrument to cost no more than ten thousand dollars, exclusive of the case. The contract was awarded to Henry Erben, who had recently built an organ for St. John's Chapel of Trinity Parish. The Trinity Church organ was not completed until October 7, 1846. It contained 12 Great, 9 Swell, 2 Swell Bass, 6 Choir stops, and a single 32′ diapason Pedal stop, with a total of 2,169 pipes.[1] After Cutler's choir was moved into the chancel, a second chancel organ, with 7 Great, 6 Swell, and 2 Pedal stops, was built by Hall and Labagh, in 1864, to accompany the choir. From then until 1923 it was necessary to have separate organists for each instrument. On at least one occasion in playing for congregational singing, this resulted in the widely separated organists using different tunes for the same hymn.

Except for the Trinity organ, there were no others in the country large enough for recital purposes until the Boston Music Hall organ was installed in 1863. A possible exception was the Tremont Temple Organ in Boston, built in 1853 by Hook and Hastings, containing 70 stops and 3,096 pipes on 4 manuals.

Reed organs came into increasingly wide use in smaller churches during the nineteenth century. These melodeons or harmoniums, as they were called, began to be manufactured in France and in Bavaria shortly after 1800. In America the first instruments of this type were constructed *ca.* 1818, having a single bellows and never more than two sets of reeds.

In 1846 a new type of instrument, in which the air was sucked downward through the reed instead of being blown upward, as before, was patented by J. Carhart. Shortly after this the George A. Prince Company of Buffalo built an "organ-melodeon" with two manuals, four sets of reeds, and an independent pedal of 1½ octaves; it still retained the basic melodeon principle, however, and depended on a single bellows.

In 1850 one of their mechanics, Emmons Hamlin, perfected the voicing of the reeds and in 1855 joined Henry Mason in a new firm which developed an organ-harmonium with a double bellows and the new reeds. In 1861 these instruments were renamed "cabinet organs." The knee-swell was introduced in 1862.[2] Other firms, notably the Estey Organ Company of Brattleboro, Vermont, effected similar developments and increased production to a point where many homes and almost all churches possessed at least one reed organ. Various tone qualities were developed for the several ranks of reeds in imitation of the pipe-organ tones. Some of the larger instruments contained as many as twenty-four sets of reeds on two and three manuals, with full sets of pedals. A principal virtue of these instruments was that, unlike the piano or pipe organ, their pitch was seldom affected by variations in temperature and relative humidity; rarely did they need further tuning once they left the factory. So many of these American reed organs were built on the suction, or exhaust, principle that the type came to be known in Europe as the American Organ.

Only in the forties of the twentieth century was their use in American rural churches seriously challenged. And when one considers the relative tone qualities, initial expense and cost of upkeep of the electronic "organs" which are fast replacing them, there is little to commend the modern substitute. Indeed, the most satisfactory of the electronic instruments are those which use their vacuum tubes for amplification only and continue to use reeds for the basic sound production. The reed organ has always been looked down upon, and especially in our own time, but one may at least conjecture that the true reason for this is that so few people ever heard them played by competent organists—for almost always the churches which used reed organs had to depend on amateur players with little training and even less talent.

The swell box for pipe organs was invented by Abraham Jordan in 1712, and initially installed in St. Magnus' Church, London. The first octave couplers—the first known in England, at least—were embodied in the organ built by John Harris and John Byfield in 1726 for the Church of St. Mary Redcliffe, Bristol. The horizontal bellows was developed by Samuel Green in 1789. It was not until the invention of the pneumatic lever by Charles Barker, in 1832, however, that the limiting factors theretofore imposed by the tracker, or mechanical, action began to be overcome; and it was some time before his ideas could be successfully applied. Meanwhile, the electro-magnets invented by Sturgeon had been adapted to an organ by his friend Wilkinson, ca. 1826, but were far too cumbersome for efficient use. Dr. H. J. Gauntlett patented another electric action in 1852, but it was never applied to an organ. In 1861, however, Dr. Albert Péschard began work in France on a system of electric control associated with the Barker pneumatic system. This action was successfully installed in the organ in the Collegiate Church at Salon, near Marseilles.

In the United States, Hilbourne L. Roosevelt built a small electric-action organ in the Newport home of Ross R. Winan in 1876, and three years later he successfully installed an electric action for the remote divisions of the Garden City (Long Island) Cathedral organ.*Thereafter he employed combinations of tracker, pneumatic, and electric action, depending on the size of the organ under construction. This type of action was brought to its most efficient form by the English

[118]

*Sometime before 1886, Hilbourne L. Roosevelt built an electric-action organ for the Holy Communion Church, New York City. Then in 1869 he exhibited a second electric-action organ at the Industrial Exposition. He died on December 30, 1886.

organ technician Robert Hope-Jones in 1887, at St. John's Church, Birkenhead. In 1903, Hope-Jones came to America and for a decade was associated with various firms, effecting many improvements in mechanism and control.[3]

Another major change in organ construction came in 1895, when John Turnell Austin perfected the universal wind-chest. With this development, separate chests for each rank of pipes were no longer needed.

Hilbourne L. Roosevelt had served his apprenticeship under Hall and Labagh. He set up his own shop in 1872 in New York, employing many of the men who had formerly worked for Erben. During the next thirteen years he perfected a notable form of pneumatic action, worked at orchestral voicing, and strove to unite striking tonal features of the several European schools of organ design. After his death in 1885, his brother, Frank H. Roosevelt, carried on the business for another eight years.[4]

Elias and George G. Hook began to make organs in Salem, Massachusetts, in 1827, moving to Boston five years later. They had built 170 instruments by 1855, when Frank H. Hastings joined the firm. Between then and 1920, the firm of Hook and Hastings built over 2,500 organs. (Plate XVII shows the organ they installed in the Plymouth Church, Brooklyn, in 1866, with curtains drawn where the quartet choir sat until 1932. The flags and pulpit frontal are modern additions, but otherwise the church appears here much as it did in the days of Henry Ward Beecher and John Zundel.)

William Allen Johnson of Westfield, Massachusetts, built his first small organ in 1844, and had completed about three hundred by 1871, when his son William H. joined the firm. Their last instrument, No. 860, was built in 1898. Most of them modest in size, the voicing, balance, and tone quality of these Johnson organs excelled all other American instruments in their day. The pipework, produced by Edwin Hedges, was a beautiful example of the art. Much credit for the perfect voicing belongs to other Johnson workmen, such as Edward Chaffin, Thomas Dyson, and Charles Willet. John V. V. Elsworth has described 112 of these instruments which are still in use in New England and elsewhere.[5]

The nineteenth century saw the small classic-style organs developed into large instruments, which, during the first quarter of the twentieth century, became more and more orchestral in character. Church organs were influenced in many cases by the interest in large recital instruments and even by the eccentricities of the organs developed for moving-picture palaces, where not only were all the instruments of the band, symphony, and jazz orchestras imitated, but even the sounds of the barnyard. Fortunately, we have now moved beyond this era and are witnessing a return to earlier concepts of purity of tone.

During the first three decades of the twentieth century, American organ builders excelled in the development of pneumatic and electric actions, as well as in new types of pipework. They built elaborate, completely-detached consoles which could be located at any convenient point in the church or auditorium without regard to the location of the organ pipes. But during these same years, and especially during the period from 1915 to 1930, builders neglected and impoverished their tonal schemes. Standards of chorus work which had been set by Hilbourne Roosevelt were largely forgotten, especially by those who followed Hope-Jones' leadership in developing unit chests from which each rank of pipes could be played at several pitches from any manual.

The Cassavant Brothers of St. Hyacinthe, Quebec, have built many fine instruments since the beginning of the twentieth century. These have excellent mixture-work and full harmonic development in their chorus reeds, with powerful basses. Ernest Skinner and W. E. Haskell have made notable contributions in new solo voices. Skinner's frenchhorn and erzähler, a type of gemshorn, have been widely adopted. Haskell, working for the Estey Organ Company, has made interesting innovations in flue pipes. Especially significant is his success in doubling the larger flues back within the pipe, thereby saving considerable space within the organ.

With the rise of musicological studies during the second quarter of the present century, especially in American colleges and universities, the merit of the classical organ literature was largely discovered anew. As a consequence of this, an accompanying counter-revolution has taken place in the organ-building world; in the ensuing revival of taste, the short-lived ascendancy of Hope-Jones and the theater-organ school has, it appears, been successfully terminated.

Holtkamp of Cleveland has built a number of modern versions of the small seventeenth-century German baroque instruments. G. Donald Harrison, formerly with Willis, in England, and now with Aeolian-Skinner, in Boston, has developed a fine type of modern instrument. This combines the best of French and German characteristics into a unique ensemble with excellent balance and blend between flues and reeds, and with ingeniously contrived mixture and mutation stops for coloring foundations and building tonal pyramids without high wind pressures.

During the Second World War the organ-building industry suffered greatly from material restrictions, and in many instances they turned from the manufacture of musical instruments to making the instruments of war. Subsequently they returned to organ building only to find their market seriously challenged by the electronic imitation organs. Under the stimulus of this competition, and with the support of the many churches whose needs could not be met earlier, organ makers are today producing the finest instruments in American history. This is true not only of the larger organs but also of the small and medium-sized organs which directly compete with the electronic instruments.

CHAPTER XV

Organ Repertory

THERE are few indications that the organ was used independently either within or outside of the church service throughout the eighteenth and during the first part of the nineteenth centuries. Gradually, however, voluntaries and interludes between the stanzas of the Psalms and hymns became a prominent feature of the service music. Gould's mention of interludes played on a violoncello was cited on page 24. The practice became so common that around 1850, John Zundel, the organist of Henry Ward Beecher's Plymouth Church, Brooklyn,[1] published a collection of *444 New Interludes and Voluntaries.* This is but one of a considerable number of such collections published from mid-century on. James Cox Beckel in his *Amateur's Organ School* gives the details, with full musical examples, of "The Manner of Performing the Service in the Clinton Street Presbyterian Church, Philadelphia":

Opening Voluntary in Fa [48 measures long]   Max Tzorr
Anthem by Choir [not given save by this caption]
Hymn after Reading of the Scriptures introduced by short prelude according to the organist's fancy:
Prelude in Do [8 measures]
The Hymn Tune is then played by the organ, solo, generally on the Swell, but may be varied at the option of the player. This is commonly called 'Giving out the tune':
Hymn No. 37 from the Psalter: 'Who is this that comes from Edom.'
When joined by the Choir, the accompaniment should consist of 2 Diapasons to which Principal may be added when necessary. At the close of each verse an interlude is played by the organist adapted to the nature of the hymn, in general 4 measures in length:

[4 specimen interludes to the above hymn]

After Prayer by the Pastor, follows another hymn in like manner. The Sermon being over, another hymn is sung, the Benediction pronounced, the congregation dismissed, the organist plays his concluding Voluntary or Postludium.

When a Voluntary is played during the Collection, it should correspond with the nature of the hymns to be sung, as these are indicative of the character of the discourse to be delivered, making thus an harmonious whole, or unity in the Service.[2]

During the latter part of the nineteenth century, and in the early part of the twentieth, skillful organists were also expected to add elaborate furbelows to their hymn accompaniments. Patterned after operatic arias, many of these instrumental descants were so embellished with trills and turns that they came to be known as "bird song" accompaniments. These are seldom heard today, but the custom of playing interludes before at least the last stanza of each hymn is still observed in some places.

Prior to the coming of Hodges to New York in 1839, there is no evidence of any use being made of the organ works of J. S. Bach or any of the other eighteenth-century continental masters. They may have been known in some of the Moravian and Lutheran congregations, but their use by them failed to influence in any way the music of other denominations.

The program of 1792, cited on page 88, called for a "prelude on the organ," but the common indication for the use of the organ independently was the "voluntary." Two such voluntaries were listed on the program for the consecration of Trinity Church, New York, in 1846, a program which concluded with a note to the effect that the concluding voluntary would be dispensed with, due to the incomplete state of the organ.

This organ was the one Erben constructed to specifications drawn up by Hodges, the organist of Trinity Church. There was considerable friction between the two men, and when the installation was finally completed in October of 1846, the builder arranged an exhibition inviting practically every prominent organist in the country to play on it with the notable exception of Hodges himself. The newspapers were most critical of the affair; the New York *Express* of October 9th commented as follows:

> Here now is Trinity Church, open seven days in the week. . . . Here is an organ in the Church, which every Sunday is played upon magnificently by one of the best organists in the country. Here are a dozen, more or less, organists, most of them residents of this city, and every seventh day playing organs in the different churches from Bloomingdale to Bowling Green. Two days are named when this church shall be opened, and this organ shall be played, and all these organists shall play it, and such a continuous procession down Broadway, and such a suffocating jam at the gates of the church, and such a rush, when they are opened, into the body of the church, and such a buzz and a chatter, and a running about, up the pulpit stairs, into the vestry, and over the barriers of the chancel, were never seen before. . . . The solemn aisles and the high-arched nave of that beautiful temple have been resounding with noisy, boisterous laughter, and idle jesting; while, upon the glorious organ, that sublime achievement of genius . . . have been performed arias from "Robert le Diable," marches from the military bands, and waltzes from the ballroom. These were interspersed with chromatic improvisations, and complicated fantasias, and voluntary variations on popular airs, or perhaps, here and there, A Kyrie from a Mass or a fugue from an opera.

Hodges played a private recital a few months later to demonstrate the organ to members of the vestry. His daughter tells of his playing Bach fugues daily in their home, so his repertory must have been somewhat better than the type of works listed by the *Express*. The latter were, however, the common fare of the day for both concert audiences and church congregations.

Recital programs are not an entirely accurate indication of the music used in church services, but they do reflect the taste of their soloists, and that same taste was reflected in their choice of service music. George Washbourne Morgan (1822-1892) came to New York from England in 1853. He served for a year at St. Thomas' Church and then at Grace Church for thirteen years. Later he played at St. Anne's Roman Catholic Church and finally at Dr. Talmadge's Broadway Tabernacle. The first outstanding concert organist in this country, he was also the first to play Bach and Mendelssohn in recital; his masterpiece, however, was Rossini's "William Tell Overture"!

The program at the opening of the (Boston) Music Hall organ on November 2, 1863, was somewhat more dignified than at Trinity Church two decades earlier, but there was the same effort to have many organists participate in the exercises:

PART I

1. Ode, recited by Miss Charlotte Cushman
2. Opening of the organ by Herr Friedrich Walcker [the builder]
3. a. Grand Toccata in F   Bach
   b. Trio Sonata in E flat   Bach
   John Knowles Paine, organist of the West Church, Boston,
   and Professor of Music at Harvard University
4. Grand Fugue in G minor   Bach
   W. Eugene Thayer of Worcester, Massachusetts

PART II

1. Two choruses from *Israel in Egypt*   Handel
   George W. Morgan, organist of Grace Church, New York
2. Grand Sonata in A, no. 3   Mendelssohn
   Benjamin J. Lang, organist of the Old South Church
   and of the Boston Handel and Haydn Society
3. a. Lamentation in Parasceve   Palestrina
   b. *Kyrie* and *Sanctus from a Mass*   Palestrina
   c. Movement from the anthem *O Give Thanks*   Purcell
   Dr. S. P. Tuckerman, organist of St. Paul's Church
4. Offertoire in G   Lefébure-Wiley
   John H. Willcox, organist of the Church of the
   Immaculate Conception
5. Hallelujah Chorus from *The Messiah*   Handel
   G. W. Morgan[3]

Willcox was one of Morgan's principal competitors for honors as an organ virtuoso, but neither contributed to the development of a serious repertory for the organ. Dudley Buck, however, exerted a wide influence, both by the content of his programs and by his restrained style of playing. His *Illustrations in Choir Accompaniment, with Hints on Registration,* 1877, did much to improve service playing throughout the country.

Plate XVIII shows the organ installed in the First Congregational Church of Washington, D. C., by J. H. & C. S. Odell in 1873. It contained 37 stops, with 2,266 pipes, on 3 manuals and pedals, using pneumatic action. The exhibition concert on November 25, 1873, featured George W. Morgan and Henry E. Browne of New York, and they played the following program:

Overture to *Masaniello*	Auber
Browne	
Prelude & Fugue in D minor	Bach
Morgan	
"Rest in the Lord" from *Elijah*	Mendelssohn
Miss Adelaide Phillips	
March	Wely
Adagio & Finale from the First Sonata	Mendelssohn
J. P. Caulfield	
Overture to *William Tell*	Rossini
Morgan	
Fantasia, *Martha*	H. E. Browne
Browne	
Aria from *The Prophet*	Meyerbeer
Miss Phillips	
Impromptu	Morgan
Morgan	
Hallelujah Chorus from *The Messiah*	Handel
Philharmonic Society	
Variations on American National Airs	H. E. Browne
Browne	

The present photograph was taken on Easter Day, 1896, with the blind organist, John W. Bischoff, at the console.

Another two decades passed and the transcriptions of choral and orchestral works appeared more popular than ever. At the same time, more European organ compositions were being played, as evidenced by the following New York programs of 1885.[4] At Chickering Hall, on Tuesday, October 20, at 3:30 p.m., the first of ten recitals by S. N. Penfield:

Concerto No. 2, in B flat	Handel
Morceau de Concert	A. Guilmant
William Tell Overture	Rossini
Fugue in E flat (St. Ann's)	Bach

At Grace Church, on Thursday, October 22, at 4:00 p.m., the forty-first of Samuel P. Warren's weekly recitals:

Prelude and Fugue in B minor (Bk. II, no. 10)	Bach
Andante in A	Henry Smart
Sonata in C minor (Op. 56, no. 3)	A. Guilmant
Offertorio in B flat	F. Capocci
Scherzo in D	F. Capocci
Two transcriptions by W. T. Best:	
Air du Dauphin	J. L. Rockel
"Splendente te Deus" from the *Motet in C*	Mozart

At Chickering Hall, on Monday, December 7, Frederic Archer's fifty-eighth recital:

Homage à Handel	Moscheles
Rhapsodie Hongroise	Küchenmeister
Andante and Variations	Schubert
Fugue in G minor	Bach
Overture to *Fra Diavolo*	Auber
Coronation March from *Le Prophète*	Myerbeer

At Chickering Hall on Thursday, March 18, of the following year was played the first of a series of five organ and harp matinées by George W. Morgan and his daughter Maud. Morgan's numbers were

Prelude and Variations in B flat	Handel
Rhapsody No. 2	Saint-Saëns
Air and Variations	Onslow-Morgan
William Tell Overture	Rossini

The files of the *Church Music Review* (later called the *New Music Review*), which was published from 1901 through 1935, graphically portray the decline of the transcriptions. The following two programs are taken from the December, 1901, issue. Harry Rowe Shelley, playing in the Union Church, Worcester, Massachusetts:

Passacaglia and Fugue	Bach
Finale from *Symphonie Pathetique*	Tschaikowski
Prelude to *Parsifal*	Wagner
Concert Satz	Thiele

Will C. Macfarlane, playing in St. Thomas' Church, New York:

Prelude and Fugue in E flat (St. Ann's)	Bach
Piéce legère, Scherzo, Communion	Loret
Christmas Sonata	Dienel

The Seraph's Strain, Le carillon	Wolstenholme
Grand Choeur Dialogue	Gigout

From the February, 1902, issue, the following program played at St. Bartholomew's Church, New York, by Samuel A. Baldwin:

Fantasia and Fugue in G minor	Bach
Etude symphonique	Bossi
Pastorale in E	Cesar Franck
Lamentation	Guilmant
Scherzo from the Fifth Sonata	Guilmant
Cantabile	Loret
The Question, The Answer	Wolstenholme
Fugue on the chorale "Ad nos ad salutarem undam"	Liszt

The following program played by W. H. Donley, organist of the First Presbyterian Church of Indianapolis, on the St. Louis Exposition organ, October 27, 1904, has its transcription, but it also includes two compositions by American composers:

Epithalamium	Woodman
Scherzo	Dethier
Magic Fire Scene *(Die Walküre)*	Wagner
Toccata in E flat	Capocci
Elevation—"Sursum Corda"	Elgar
Concert Variations on "The Star-Spangled Banner"	Buck
Fantasie Rustique	Wolstenholme

Since 1935 the columns of *The Diapason* listing organ programs show no trace of many of the composers named above. The transcriptions are likewise completely missing. Instead, there is a wide variety of new compositions being played, together with an equally-wide selection from the old masters, a selection no longer limited to a few works of Bach and Handel.

Much of this reform can be traced to the example and teaching of a few men like Buck and Farnam. A large share of the credit also belongs to the American Guild of Organists.[5]

Today's organ recitals, and the organ music used in connection with church services, include not only the classic preludes and fugues and organ sonatas of past centuries, but also works of the modern French and American schools. They also contain a considerable number of chorale preludes, both old and new, based on the familiar chorale and other hymn melodies.

The first American composers who wrote any considerable amount of organ music were men of Dudley Buck's generation—B. J. Lang, J. C. D. Parker, S. B. Whitney, G. E. Whiting, and Buck himself. None of their works have shown permanent merit.

More significant were the works of Buck's pupils: John H. Brewer, Frederick G. Gleason, Harry Rowe Shelley, R. H. Woodman, and others of their generation, including Clarence Dickinson, Arthur Foote, Harvey Gaul, H. A. Matthews, T. Tertius Noble, Horatio Parker, and James H. Rogers. Of this second generation of American composers for the organ, there are still but few works which show any degree of originality and style.

Outstanding among the present generation of organ composers are Edward Shippen Barnes, Seth Bingham, Joseph Clokey, Garth Edmundson, Philip James, Leo Sowerby, Everett Titcomb, the Canadian Healey Willan, and the late Pietro Yon.[6] Of these men, Sowerby and Willan, at least, have achieved in their work stature and individuality of style which places them on a par with the leading modern European composers for the organ.

Part Three

THE CONTEMPORARY SCENE

Be filled with the Spirit,
Addressing one another in Psalms and hymns and spiritual songs,
Singing and making melody to the Lord with all your heart.
—EPHESIANS 5:18-19.

CHAPTER XVI

Changing Repertory

CHAPTER XI detailed the development of choir repertory during the nineteenth century from little more than simple fuging tunes printed as "anthems" in the back of the tune books through excerpts from oratorios and arrangements from popular works of a secular character. By the beginning of the twentieth century, churches throughout the country were seeking more dignity and worship in their music, and were becoming less interested in entertainment of the concert-hall variety. To be sure, there were many churches whose taste still reflected that of the eighteen seventies, but these were in the back-wash rather than the main current of the stream. Now, at mid-century, thanks to the radio and easier transportation, there are few churches, even in small, remote communities, where standards of music have not shown a discernible improvement. This is not to suggest that small, volunteer choirs are able to use the elaborate service-music of professional cathedral choirs; it is evident, however, that they are more and more using music of liturgic and esthetic worth, even though simpler.

Archibald T. Davison[1] has admirably summarized the attitudes and conditions affecting our church music. If music be given adequate recognition in the over-all program of the church, it must be adequately supported financially; further, it must be kept in its proper role, consecrated to the worship of Almighty God, and never diverted to less worthy, secular ends. One should also add that it must be directed by an individual with a solid foundation in repertory as well as in the technique of performance.

It is possible, of course, to paint entirely too optimistic a picture. In a recent work of uneven content,[2] the author surveyed the field of American church music by sending out 189 questionnaires, of which 96 were answered. The following were named as favorite anthems:

Hallelujah (Messiah)	Handel
Festival *Te Deum*	Dudley Buck
Psalm 150	César Franck
Beautiful Saviour	Christiansen
Hark, Hark My Soul	Shelley
Open Our Eyes	Macfarlane

Four out of the six are by American composers, but three of these, or half, are works for quartet choirs. If a cantata had been included in the list, it certainly would have been Stainer's *Crucifixion*.

Charles N. Boyd, in an article entitled "Choir Development since 1876,"[3] pointed out that *ca.* 1875, choirs were using material like Adolph Baumbach's *Sacred Quartetts* and Harrison Millard's *Selections . . . for Quartette and Chorus Choirs,* with Dudley Buck's compositions beginning to come into use. By the end of the century, anthems by Caryl Florio (W J. Robjohn), George W. Marston, Eduardo Marzo, George W. Chadwick, Arthur Foote, W. W. Gilchrist, P. A. Schnecker, Harry Rowe Shelley, J. B. Singenberger, and Arthur Whiting had become popular. From the point of quality, this list does not compare at all favorably with the music of Trinity Church, Boston, in 1904, or with that of the First Church, Boston, in 1910 (see Appendix B).

In 1923 Harold W. Thompson conducted a survey of "what anthems our leading choirmasters find most useful."[4] Summarizing his replies from 104 directors from all parts of the country, Thompson found that 1,040 anthems by 229 different composers were listed. Counting each anthem mentioned as a single vote, the poll by composers was as follows:

Horatio Parker	61	Gounod	20
George C. Martin	59	J. H. Rogers	19
T. Tertius Noble	56	Stevenson	19
John E. West	23	Philip James	18
César Franck	22	Dickinson	18
Stainer	22	Shelley	18

Sullivan	18	Goss	14
Gretchaninoff	17	Palestrina	12
Brahms	16	Chadwick	12
Myles B. Foster	16	Woodward	12
Mendelssohn	15	Rachmaninoff	11
Spicker	14	D. D. Wood	10
Foote	14		

It should be observed that over half of these are American composers. In this respect American church music is far ahead of its secular counterpart, where, in 1935, only the Boston and Chicago Symphony Orchestras could show an average of between four and six works by American composers in their annual repertory.[5]

Of those answering Thompson's questionnaire, 43 served in Episcopal churches; the rest were divided among Protestant bodies, with a preponderance toward the Presbyterians and Congregationalists. Thirty-two used adult, mixed choirs, 22 used quartet and mixed choirs, 18 used quartets only, and 22 used choirs of boys and men.

The following anthems received the largest number of votes:

Souls of the Righteous—Noble	29
Ho, Everyone that Thirsteth—Martin	22
Hail, Gladd'ning Light—Martin	21
Fierce Was the Wild Billow—Noble	17
How Lovely is Thy Dwelling-Place (Requiem)—Brahms	13
Psalm 150—César Franck	13
In Heavenly Love Abiding—Parker	13
The Lord is My Light—Parker	12
Fear Not Ye, O Israel—Spicker	12
Still, Still with Thee—Foote	11
Cherubic Hymn—Gretchaninoff	10

Note that six of these are works by American composers.

In a less favorable vein, Edward Shippen Barnes commented in 1928 that

> The public as a whole—and even the rank and file of choirmasters—lag woefully behind the composers. The following still hold their own as national favorites:
>
> | | |
> |---|---|
> | Hark, Hark My Soul | Shelley |
> | Consider and Hear Me | Pflueger |

O Pray for the Peace of Jerusalem	Knox
Tarry with Me	Baldwin
O Come to my Heart, Lord Jesus	Ambrose

and even such monstrosities as:

| I'm a Pilgrim | Marston |
| Even Me | John C. Warren[6] |

In 1945 the new editor of *The Musical Quarterly,* Paul Henry Lang, published a long editorial deploring the decadent state of church music, both in this country and abroad.[7] Had this been published one or two decades earlier, his statements would have been far more accurate, for the condition of our musical repertory as conditioned by the quartet choirs certainly merited condemnation. However, several factors began, as early as the second decade of this century, to broaden the scope of the repertory available for use by alert choirmasters, thereby enriching our music by the elimination of less worthy works and by stimulating fresh composition for the church.

Interest here in Johann Sebastian Bach's organ works grew fairly steadily from the mid-nineteenth century, but relatively little was known of his choral writing until J. F. Wolle inaugurated the annual Bach Festivals in 1912 with his now-famous Bethlehem Bach Choir. From Wolle's pioneering, the Bach cult in America has grown until today there are few choirs indeed which do not use Bach chorales, choruses, or cantatas.

Similarly, a Palestrina cult was advanced considerably by the work of Montani's Palestrina Choir in Philadelphia. This cult was broadened to include the entire rich field of sixteenth-century polyphony by the work of Archibald T. Davison in the nineteen tens and twenties with the Harvard and Radcliffe glee clubs. Many works which he first edited and published for these college groups are today enriching the repertory of better choirs throughout the country.

After the First World War, American knowledge of, and interest in, Russian church music was enhanced by the concerts of Serge Jaroff's Don Cossack Choir. Much of this literature was made available for church choirs through the editions of Lindsay Norden, Kurt Schindler, and Winfred Douglas.

As interest in the polyphonic era grew, a number of Spanish works were edited in the late nineteen twenties by Schindler and Walter Williams. Editions of the works of the Tudor musicians Byrd, Gibbons, Tallis, and others, prepared in England by Fellowes and Terry in this same period, have become equally popular. The exploitation by school and college choral groups of this great literature from the past has aided church music in two ways: it has trained young people in these varied styles of music, and it has taught congregations to appreciate and understand their beauty.

A still different type of church music has come to the fore in recent years. This is congregational unison singing supported by the choir. In part it probably dates from the time of the Oxford Movement. It also owes much to Lutheran traditions, and it grew in this country simultaneously with the wider knowledge of, and interest in, the Lutheran Church, as their language barriers were finally overcome. One notices the trend in the number of new hymn-tunes for unison singing which have been taken into more recent hymnals. There have also been a growing number of unison settings of canticles and service music for the liturgical churches, composed for this purpose by outstanding composers. Thus, for example, the Episcopal *Hymnal 1940* includes, in a section devoted to service music, three unison communion services, which are sung by the entire congregation in many churches. In others, where a well balanced choir is often difficult to maintain, the new unison works provide an ideal solution to the problem of suitable repertory.

We have already noted the relatively small number of works by American composers performed in the past by American symphony orchestras. Mueller, in his book *The American Symphony Orchestra,*[8] points out that in the decade from 1935 to 1945 the lot of American composers improved, probably due to patriotic considerations during the war years. Even so, there were still performed more works by contemporary foreigners than by Americans.

The following lists show the results of a fresh tabulation of the repertories of 37 leading choirs in this country, choirs chosen for their geographical diversity as well as for the quality of their work. Each choir reported the anthems and service music used during some one season between 1949 and 1953. Twenty-four were from Episcopal churches, 4 Presbyterian, 3 Church of England in Canada, 2 Roman Catholic, 2 Lutheran, one Methodist, and one from a Moravian church. Denominational differences evidently had little effect on repertory, many of the Protestant churches singing the same motets which were used by Roman Catholics. Only in the service music was the preponderance of Episcopal churches noted.

The first startling difference between this tabulation and that of Thompson[9] is that although Thompson's replies came from nearly three times as many churches, the present lists show much wider repertories than those of thirty years ago. These 37 choirs used 2,761 anthems by 480 composers, considerably less than half of them being American; but this change is because of the addition of many earlier rather than contemporary foreign composers. As in Thompson's list, each anthem mentioned in each repertory was counted as a single vote for the popularity of the composers.

J. S. Bach	123	Gounod	29
Healey Willan	114	Mozart	28
T. Tertius Noble	70	Ireland	26
Handel	63	Dickinson	25
Mendelssohn	60	Martin Shaw	25
Sowerby	50	Stainer	25
Stanford	46	Clokey	20
David McK. Williams	45	Goss	20
Palestrina	44	Joseph Haydn	20
Thiman	44	Tallis	20
Titcomb	39	Merbecke	18[10]
Byrd	38	Mrs. H. H. A. Beach	17
Holst	38	Gretchaninoff	17
Purcell	35	Gordon Jacob	16[10]
S. S. Wesley	35	H. Alexander Matthews	16
Bairstow	34	Rachmaninoff	16
Brahms	33	Elgar	15
César Franck	33	George C. Martin	15
Victoria	33	John E. West	15
Horatio Parker	32	Bortniansky	14
Charles Wood	32	Jacob Handl	14
Walford Davies	31	Philip James	14
Tschaikowsky	31	Weelkes	14
Candlyn	30	Attwood	13

Beethoven	13	Macfarlane	11
Farrant	13	Vulpius	11
Harvey Gaul	13	Crotch	10
Orlando Gibbons	13	Darke	10
Franz Schubert	13	Friedell	10
Chesnokov	13	Hilton	10^{10}
Lotti	12	Jennings	10
Oldroyd	12	Silby	10
Geoffrey Shaw	12	Whitehead	10
Stokowski	12		

The following anthems and selections of service music received the largest number of votes:

Communion Service—Merbecke	18
God be in My Head—W. Davies	17
Greater Love hath no Man—Ireland	17
Jesu, Joy of Man's Desiring—J. S. Bach	16
The Lord is My Shepherd (Brother James' Air)—Jacobs, arr.	16
There shall a Star (Christus)—Mendelssohn	15
With a Voice of Singing—M. Shaw	15
How Lovely is Thy Dwelling-place (Requiem)—Brahms	14
Te Deum in B flat—Stanford	14
God so Loved the World (Crucifixion)—Stainer	12
O Saviour of the World—Goss	11
Hallelujah (Messiah)—Handel	11
Benedicite in F—Stokowski	11
Lead Me, Lord—S. S. Wesley	11
Psalm CL—César Franck	10
And the Glory of the Lord (Messiah)—Handel	10
Lord for Thy Tender Mercies' Sake—John Hilton (falsely attributed to Farrant)	10
Benedictus es, Domine in A flat—H. A. Matthews	10
Rejoice in the Lord alway—Purcell	10
Benedictus es, Domine in E flat—Willan	10

Only two works on Thompson's list have remained popular, although most of the others still receive a few votes. The same is true of the proportion of works by American composers; save for the three canticles named, popular American composers still received fewer than ten votes for individual compositions.

In Roman Catholic churches, as the Caecilian Society declined in influence, the work of reform was continued by a new organization, the Society of St. Gregory. Formation of the Society was projected by Nicola A. Montani at a meeting in June, 1913, at Baltimore, attended by the Very Reverend Leo P. Manzetti, the Reverend Dr. M. Petter, and Montani. A first convention was held later that summer at the Catholic Summer School of America in Cliff Haven, New York. A constitution was adopted which enunciated the Society's aims

> to foster fraternal assistance and encouragement among the members thereof, in their endeavor to promote the cause of Sacred Music Reform according to the provisions of the *Motu Proprio* of the late Holy Father, Pius X.

Summer schools of sacred music were sponsored, a quarterly bulletin, *The Catholic Choirmaster,* was started, and a Bureau of Information was established. A hymnal of such devotional and artistic character that it could be officially recommended for use throughout the Church was projected. Biennial conventions in various cities throughout the country have born witness to the growth and work of the Society.

One of the most effective devices of the Society in its work towards higher standards in church music has been the *White List*. This is an extensive list of recommended service music, designed

> to afford the Catholic Choir Director a choice of compositions for his choir that he may feel safe in securing for church use.

Inaugurated in the July, 1919, issue of *The Catholic Choirmaster,* it took on such significance that it was published in book form in 1928. A fourth edition appeared in 1947. Its antithesis in the form of a *Black List* was first published in the October, 1922, issue of *The Catholic Choirmaster.*

In 1920 the Society's convention was also an International Gregorian Congress. When one of the outstanding leaders of the Gregorian renaissance, Dom André Mocquereau, was told that he was to conduct five thousand children from various Eastern cities in the singing of the chants, he was appalled, but later commented:[11]

> At the first rehearsal with them, my fears were changed to enthusiasm and I realized that my dream had come true and that through the

medium of the children of America the great heritage of congregational singing will be restored to the Church.

Remarkable strides have been made in teaching plainsong to the children through the parochial school system, particularly through the materials prepared by Justine Ward. This is equally true in many of the convents and other houses for women. On the other hand, to quote Father Finn:

> Many of the choirs of men in seminaries, colleges, and monasteries concur to hinder progress. One of the most trying experiences is to listen to such choirs struggling with Gregorian chant. The torture of their high notes and the murkey meaninglessness of their low grunts![12]

Notable exceptions to this have been Father Finn's own Paulist choirs in Chicago and New York;[13] St. Mary's Seminary, Baltimore; St. John's Abbey, Collegeville, Minnesota; and St. Benoit du Lac, Canada.[14]

Unfortunately, little of this has been reflected at the parish level, where still too few priests are willing to support the work necessary to maintain good liturgical music. The choirs of J. Alfred Schehl at St. Lawrence's Church, Cincinnati, Edgar Bowman at the Church of the Sacred Heart, Pittsburgh, and Warren Foley at the Church of the Blessed Sacrament, New York, are three which have well demonstrated what can be accomplished when clergy and musicians work together for the best in church music.

In order to provide a clear concept of what the complete repertory of a modern church choir includes, there is listed in Appendix B a summary of all the anthems and service music used by the Washington Cathedral Choir during the decade between 1941 and 1951. While this is a professional choir of men and boys,[15] its repertory includes many works which are used effectively by smaller parish choirs. Thus, for example, over half the works sung by the choir of St. Andrew's Church, New Orleans, during the 1950-51 season are included in this repertory, as are half of those sung at St. Paul's Cathedral, Boston. At Washington Cathedral, all masses and canticles are sung in English, but many anthems, motets, and carols are sung in their original languages.

To be a living progressive art, there needs to be a constant stream of new, original work coming from the younger generations. The size of the group of mid-century American works listed on pages 198-99 is therefore most encouraging. So too is the response to the various prize competitions, and individual commissions. In past years, larger choral works have frequently been commissioned by various music festivals, but there have been almost no steps in this direction suitable for church use. It is heartening to learn in recent years of works such as Sowerby's *Come Holy Ghost,* commissioned by Washington Cathedral for the four hundredth anniversary, in 1949, of The Book of Common Prayer.

The American Guild of Organists[16] sponsors a biennial prize-anthem competition. Another significant competition was inaugurated in 1947 by the Church of the Ascension, New York, under the direction of its rector, the Reverend Roscoe Thornton Foust, and its organist-choirmaster, Vernon de Tar. Each year a different type of composition is specified, but each one is designed to fit into the services of the annual patronal festival of the parish. The following were the winning compositions of the first five years of the award:

1948—Praise to the Risen Lord (cantata) . . . . Louie White
1949—The Earth is the Lord's . . . . Clair Leonard of Bard College
1950—Blessed are the Poor in Spirit . . . . Ronald Arnatt,
    organist-choirmaster, Church of the Ascension and St. Agnes,
    Washington, D. C.
1951—*Te Deum* . . . . Roger Hannahs,
    organist-choirmaster, St. John's Church, Ithaca, New York.
1952—This Son so Young (solo cantata for tenor) . . . . Louie White
1953—(no award)

On the local level, parish churches should continue on an even wider scale than in the past to encourage the composers living in their respective communities. This does not mean that all attempts at composition no matter how unskillful should be given indescriminate hearing, but rather that local composers of competence should be stimulated to prepare works for special occasions for their own people. A steady volume of such works, written for a specific occasion of interest both to the composer and the organist or choir interpreting the works, would go far toward the continued development of our art and would help to counterbalance the plethora of arrangements which still fill too many publishers' catalogs. It was heartening to note that of the thirty-seven choirmasters whose repertory has been analyzed above, thirteen reported compositions of their own in the repertory.

Due to the increasing and proper emphasis on the role of church music in aiding and stimulating congregational worship it becomes correspondingly difficult to introduce *avant garde* contemporary music into the church service, especially works of an experimental character. This has resulted in a paucity of such works of a sacred character and more interest by composers in works for secular performance. The few sacred works of this type now being composed are usually of a sort which may be used in the secular concert hall until audiences become sufficiently familiar with their style to permit their use as vehicles for worship. Recent noteworthy examples include:

Let down the Bars, O Death	Samuel Barber
Canticle of the Sun	Leo Sowerby
Mass	Igor Stravinsky
Alleluia	Randall Thompson

CHAPTER XVII

Schools, Conferences, Commissions

MUSIC education has always been one of the most neglected aspects of church work in this country. The need for formal seminary training on the part of their clergy was realized at an early date in the New England communities, a need which led to the founding of Harvard College in 1636. Congregations, today, in need of a clergyman do not turn to some person in their midst who can read intelligibly and ask him, without further preparation, to assume the duties of a pastor. Yet constantly throughout our history have congregations blithely asked anyone who could play or sing fairly well to become their organist or choirmaster with no expectation that any further specialized training would be sought. More than any other single cause, it has been the blind efforts of such congregations, no matter how well intentioned, which have kept church music in low repute. Nor will this condition be improved until individual congregations come to realize that the ministry of music requires intensive and specialized study.

Colonial efforts at music education were described in Chapter III. In the eighteenth century these efforts were directed at the entire congregation. The general level of musical training had dropped so low that the singing schools for many decades were concerned with teaching suitable numbers of persons to sing the Psalm-tunes, in order to assure the simplest use of music in divine worship. The efforts of the teachers named in Chapters III, VI, XIII were directly concerned with congregational singing. Not until Lowell Mason's teacher-training class at the Boston Academy of Music in 1834 was there any specific training provided for leadership in church music. Save for these classes and the various teacher's institutes which he sponsored, there was no advanced training available except as a sincere, talented musician placed himself under a competent teacher either in this country or abroad. Reading the biographical sketches in Appendix C, one soon notes that most of our leading church musicians went abroad for their professional study until very recent times.

Only during the past generation have we seen church musicians developing from former choir boys, for the simple reason that American choir schools are, for the most part, but two generations old. Today, there are not a few leaders who were choir boys until their voices changed, who then studied the organ either under their former choirmaster or in a conservatory, and who now serve with a maturity bred of long experience.

Secular conservatories and music schools, which achieved mature stature in this country during the last quarter of the nineteenth century, have for the most part ignored the needs of the church. Organ study has been concentrated more on recital playing than on service playing; choral training, aside from experience in the large school-chorus and individual voice-training, has been limited to the most elemental instruction in conducting. Instruction in liturgy and choir repertory has been completely ignored.

There have been two notable exceptions. At Northwestern University, soon after he founded the School of Music in 1896, Peter Christian Lutkin established a Department of Church Music which has exerted a strong influence throughout the Middle West. A decade later, at the New England Conservatory, Wallace Goodrich, although he did not organize a specific department for church music, was able to orient the work in organ and choral classes toward the needs of the church to a degree not followed elsewhere.

The first independent conservatory for church music to be established in this country was the Trinity School of Church Music, organized by Felix Lamond in 1912, with a faculty drawn from the outstanding musicians employed by Trinity Parish in New York. The school offered "a three-year course of daily training in the liturgy and music of the Episcopal Church." The faculty consisted of the following:

[145]

Organ—Felix Lamond, R. J. Winterbottom, F. T. Harrat, and Moritz E. Schwarz.

Choirboy training—George E. Stubbs.

Mixed-choir training—Edmund Jaques.

Theory—A. Madeley Richardson.

Vocal training—John Carrington.

Composition—Mark Andrews.

The school was discontinued when Lamond left New York in 1918.

The same year that Trinity School of Church Music was established, Clarence Dickinson was appointed Professor of Music at the Union Theological Seminary in New York. There, in 1928, he established a School of Sacred Music which has, in subsequent years, turned out a large number of well-grounded organists and choirmasters. A balanced academic and music curriculum leads to the award of both undergraduate and graduate degrees in sacred music. Dickinson was succeeded as director by Hugh Porter in 1945.[1]

The Westminster Choir College was founded in 1926 by John Finley Williamson, an outgrowth of his work with the choir of the Westminster Presbyterian Church of Dayton, Ohio. At first offering only a three-year diploma course, the college moved in 1929 to Ithaca, New York, where its curriculum was expanded to a four-year course leading to the Bachelor of Music degree. In 1932 it moved to its own campus on the outskirts of Princeton, New Jersey, and since then its curriculum has been enlarged to include graduate courses.

The music department of St. Olaf's College at Northfield, Minnesota, until 1944 under the direction of F. Melius Christiansen, has trained many Lutheran musicians; in recent years a summer school at Lake Forest, Illinois, has extended the influence of Christiansen's work.

The Roman Catholic Church in this country has similarly suffered from want of trained organist-choirmasters. Most of the earlier music education, like that of Singenberger at St. Francis, Wisconsin, was aimed primarily at preparing music teachers for the parochial schools. This was in line with the pronouncement of the Second Council of Baltimore in 1866:

> We consider it very desirable that the elements of Gregorian Chant be taught and exercised in the parochial schools.[2]

Dudley Buck
(1839-1909)

John Baptist Singenberger
(1848-1924)

PLATE XIII.

F. Melius Christiansen
(1871-1955)

Horatio Parker
(1863-1919)

PLATE XIV.

This still constitutes a large phase of the activity of Roman Catholic music education.

In 1918, the Pius X School of Liturgical Music was founded at the Manhattanville College of the Sacred Heart, in New York, by two devoted women, Mother Georgia Stevens and Mrs. Justine Bayard Ward. Here was a school established with the explicit purpose of furthering the aims of the *Motu Proprio* of Pius X, by training choir leaders who could effect its aims on the parish-church level. While in later years their successful teaching was extended to include the training of school music supervisors and teachers, the Pius X School continues to devote its primary attention to the training of church musicians.

A second school devoted exclusively to the training of musicians for the Roman Catholic Church is the Gregorian Institute of America, founded in 1941 by Clifford A. Bennett. This is not a resident school but rather combines the use of correspondence courses with summer sessions in various parts of the country. In 1949, it conducted twenty-eight such sessions in as many communities.

Summer conferences for church musicians, running from five days to three weeks, are playing an increasingly important role not so much in basic training for organists and choirmasters as in renewing ideals, providing fellowship with others who speak the same musical language, and furnishing an opportunity to learn new repertory. In the Episcopal Church, the first of these was organized at Episcopal Theological School, Cambridge, Massachusetts, in June, 1915, by Richard G. Appel. Dean Hodges lectured on the Prayer Book, the Reverend Harvey Officer, O.H.C., on plainsong, Peter Lutkin on *a cappella* music and hymnology, Walter A. Spalding on church music from the layman's point of view, and Walter Clemson on the business side of choir management. From this beginning, there developed the Wellesley Conference which has met each year in late June on the campus of Wellesley College.

A similar music conference was begun at Evergreen, Colorado, in 1923 by Canon Winfred Douglas. This has grown into a three-week summer school combining lectures with "laboratory work"; its dean since 1940 has been the Reverend Walter Williams. Since 1949, the Evergreen Conferences have also sponsored the Little Music School, lasting but one week, and devoted to the problems of musicians working in smaller mission churches.

At Camp Wa-Li-Ro, on Put-in-Bay in Lake Erie, there is an annual choirmasters' conference where all phases of boy-choir work are studied. The camp itself is a choir school and camp for boys, under the direction of Paul Allen Beymer, which provides experienced boys for demonstration purposes at the conference.

In recent years, several university music schools have sponsored summer institutes devoted to church music. In a few cases the success of the institutes has led to the formation of special departments of church music in the schools themselves.

The Board of Christian Education of the Presbyterian Church in the U.S.A. has sponsored occasional music conferences each summer since 1946 in connection with its Leadership Training Schools. There were four of these in the summer of 1951.

The American Baptist Board of Education and Publication sponsored a ten-day conference on religious music and drama at Green Lake, Wisconsin, in 1951. There were also two regional conferences of a single week's duration sponsored by the National Institute of Church Music.

At an early stage in the history of Singenberger's St. Caecilia Society, it was realized that occasional conferences, no matter how well attended, did not reach deeply enough into the life of the church to have permanent effects without other support. Consequently there was soon a considerable agitation for the establishment of music commissions on the diocesan and archdiocesan levels. At first little progress was made due to the lack of interest on the part of the hierachy, but the demand has gradually made itself felt. The first to form diocesan commissions with powers of censorship were Archbishop Elder of Cincinnati in 1898 and Bishop Richter of Grand Rapids in 1903.[3] By 1950, there were fifty-five official diocesan commissions to rule on acceptable music, authorize hymnals, and sponsor music conferences.

Few of the Protestant denominations are organized in such a way as to make it an easy matter to establish regional commissions. Many of them have, however, through their national organizations, appointed temporary commissions from time to time, to prepare official hymnals for nationwide use. In this respect they have been able to move further than has the Roman Catholic Church.*

An attempt was made in 1925 to organize a Commission on Music and Worship by the General Assembly of the Presbyterian Church in the U.S.A. An executive committee was appointed which served until 1929, cooperated with the editors of their new hymnal, but was unable to form a permanent commission. In 1934, the Board of Christian Education of this same body set up an advisory committee on music with plans for a full department of music. These did not materialize beyond the appointment of Calvin W. Laufer as editor of musical publications and consultant on church music. He was succeeded in 1938 by W. Lawrence Curry. In 1944, John Milton Kelly was appointed director of music for the Board of Christian Education. Among other activities, he supervised the preparation of a number of works on various aspects of church music for free distribution to organists and choirmasters throughout the church.

Joint Commissions on the Revision of the Hymnal have been appointed by the General Conventions of the Episcopal Church from time to time as its Hymnal has required revision.[4] Until 1916, their work was concerned only with the texts. When the commission of that year had completed its work, a standing Joint Commission on Church Music was created by the General Convention of 1919. During the two subsequent decades this commission prepared an official *American Psalter, Choral Service* book, and several issues of *A List of Texts of Anthems Approved by the General Conventions . . . of the Protestant Episcopal Church*. While not exactly comparable to the *White List* issued by the Society of St. Gregory for the advice of choirmasters in the Roman Catholic Church, the *List of Texts* has served a two-fold purpose: it has provided a means of approval for the use in Episcopal services of certain worthy texts not found in Holy Scripture or Prayer Book, and it has indirectly indicated approval of certain specific compositions. In recent years a growing number of music commissions have been appointed in local dioceses of the Episcopal Church. These have

[149]

*Morgan F. Simmons has made *A Survey of the Denominational Musical Programs of Sixteen Protestant Church Bodies* (Union Theological Seminary thesis, 1953).

sponsored festival services, symposiums, and hymn-sings as means of stimulating interest in the general improvement of church music.

The American Guild of Organists is a professional organization of organists and choirmasters drawn from all denominations. It was founded in 1896, largely through the efforts of Gerrit Smith (1859-1912), organist-choirmaster of the South (Dutch Reformed) Church of New York. The call for the first meeting on February 3, 1896, was signed by thirty-four leading clergymen and organists, including Bishop Potter of New York, Dudley Buck, H. N. Bartlett, Chester, Shelley, Warren, Whiting, and Woodman. Smith was elected the first Warden.[5]

There were many difficulties at first, some caused by professional jealousies, others by lack of understanding and appreciation on the part of clergy and musicians. But gradually the program of the Guild developed, until in 1946 its surviving founders could look back on a half-century of significant achievements. Chief among these was the marked change in professional standing which the choirmaster and organist has gained, both among his fellow musicians and in the community at large. Symbolic of this improved status is the title which many Protestant churches employ, "Minister of Music." Another significant Guild activity has been its work toward the standardization of organ consoles.

The Guild has awarded many medals and prizes to competitors in various pertinent fields. In more recent years there has been an annual prize offered for new compositions, which are published under the Guild's auspices—alternating each year between organ compositions and choral works.

Professional standards have been raised to a marked degree by the program of examinations offered annually by the Guild. This program was inaugurated in 1902 and has grown steadily since that time. Examinations are given in organ playing, theory, and general musical knowledge. More specifically, the organ-playing examination calls for performance, before a regional examiner, of certain specified organ works, of sight reading with the various music clefs, and of transposition. The theory examinations are written and cover harmonization of figured and un-figured basses as well as work in strict counterpoint. A third examination covers music history and literature. Three sets of examinations are given: satisfactory work in the first earns the degree of Associate of the American Guild of Organists (A.A.G.O.); in the second, the degree of Fellow of the American Guild of Organists (F.A.G.O.); in the third, the degree of Choir Master (Ch.M.). While there has been some criticism of the conservative character of these examinations, there has never been any suggestion that the degrees were not well earned. They have afforded adquate academic recognition to a number of talented church musicians who have preferred to study under an outstanding teacher rather than at a college or university. By 1952, 1,109 had earned the Associate's certificate, 350 the Fellow's, and 71 the Choirmaster's certificate. Over two hundred state and local chapters in every state in the Union, Hawaii, and the Canal Zone embrace a membership of twelve thousand active musicians. These chapters each sponsor recitals, forums, model services, and choral programs.

A somewhat similar organization was the National Association of Organists, formed at Ocean Grove, New Jersey, in 1908, by Tali Esen Morgan. The first president was Will C. Macfarlane. It held annual summer conventions at Ocean Grove until 1915 and thereafter at various cities until, in 1935, it merged with the American Guild of Organists.

Like the immortal J. S. Bach, the Guild early adopted the motto "Soli Deo Gloria." The following "Declaration of the Religious Principles of the American Guild of Organists" was formulated at its inception:

> For the greater glory of God, and for the good of his Holy Church in this land, we, being severally members of the American Guild of Organists, do declare our mind and intention in the things following:
>
> We believe that the office of music in Christian Worship is a Sacred Oblation before the Most High.
>
> We believe that they who are set as Choirmasters and as Organists in the House of God ought themselves to be persons of devout conduct, teaching the ways of earnestness to the Choirs committed to their charge.
>
> We believe that the unity of purpose and fellowship of life between Ministers and Choirs should be everywhere established and maintained.

We believe that at all times and in all places it is meet, right, and our bounden duty to work and to pray for the advancement of Christian Worship in the holy gifts of strength and nobleness; to the end that the Church may be purged of her blemishes, that the minds of men may be instructed, that the honor of God's House may be guarded in our time and in the time to come.

Wherefore we do give ourselves with reverence and humility to these endeavors, offering up our works and our persons, in the Name of him, without whom nothing is strong, nothing is holy. Amen.

CHAPTER XVIII

Outstanding Musicians of the Twentieth Century[1]

WHEREAS most of the nineteenth century leaders were either European born or at least trained on the continent, there was a significant group born after 1850, and active at the beginning of the twentieth century, who were not only native-born but who received all of their training from American teachers. Possibly because of this fact, these men were among the first American church musicians to achieve recognition in England and on the Continent.

The composers of this generation wrote either in a modified quartet style or in the more conservative choral style of liturgical music, depending on their background and the traditions of the church where they worked. They were well-rounded church musicians in the traditional sense, composing steadily, but also achieving distinction as organists and as choral conductors.

As was only natural, outstanding among those who continued to compose for the quartet choir were the men who had studied under Dudley Buck. Like their teacher, they used their soloists or full quartet as contrasting media against a background of chorus work; not for them was the obtrusive solo with concluding chorus of the mid-nineteenth century. At the same time, they continued to exploit and glamourize the solo voices in a way which gave many of their compositions a momentary popularity only to disappear with the passage of time. Leading composers in this style were John Hyatt Brewer (*cf.* pages 203-4), Arthur William Foote (*cf.* page 212), James Hotchkiss Rogers (*cf.* page 231), Raymond Huntington Woodman (*cf.* page 241), and Harry Rowe Shelley (1858-1947).

Of these, Shelley's music had the widest vogue. His career was typical: born in New Haven, Connecticut, on June 8, 1858, he studied at Yale under Stoeckel and then in New York with Buck and Dvořák. He began playing the organ in the New Haven Center Church at the age of fourteen. He was organist at the Church of the Pilgrims, Brooklyn, from 1878 to 1881, and again from 1887 to 1899 following an interim in Plymouth Church. From 1899 to 1914 he played at the Fifth Avenue Baptist Church in New York, and thereafter, until his retirement in 1936, at the Central Congregational Church, Brooklyn. He was one of the founders of the American Guild of Organists. He composed many anthems and cantatas in a singable, facile style, always with the quartet choir in mind. The two cantatas *Vexilla regis* and *Death and Life* are among his more significant works. He compiled *The Modern Organist, Gems for the Organ,* and several other useful selections. He died on the twelfth of September, 1947, at a convalescent home in Short Beach, Connecticut.

Horatio William Parker (1863-1919) while not exclusively a composer of church music, nonetheless ranks as the outstanding American composer of choral music prior to the present generation. He was born in Auburndale, Massachusetts, on September 15, 1863. Apart from music, his only education was at a private school in Newton. At the age of sixteen he became organist of a small church in Dedham, and afterwards of St. John's Church, Roxbury. From 1882 to 1885 he studied under Rheinberger and Abel in Munich. Returning to the United States, he taught music at the Cathedral School, Garden City, Long Island, and at the National Conservatory in New York. He served at St. Luke's, Brooklyn, St. Andrew's, Harlem, and Holy Trinity, New York, before becoming organist-choirmaster of Trinity Church, Boston, in 1893. In the following year he became professor of music at Yale University, becoming dean of its School of Music in 1904. In 1900 he resigned from Trinity Church, Boston, to become organist of New York's Collegiate Church of St. Nicholas. He conducted the New Haven Symphony Orchestra as well as various choral groups in New Haven, New York, and Philadelphia. He was a founder of the American Guild of Organists, and in 1905 became a member of the American Academy of Arts and Letters. Plate XIV portrays Parker as he received an honorary Doctor of Music degree from Cambridge University in 1902.

His musical edition of the Episcopal Hymnal (1903) is regarded by many as the best of the five musical settings of that book. He was a member of the Episcopal Hymnal Commission of 1916. He composed extensively for choir, chorus, orchestra, and organ. His oratorio *Hora Novissima* (1893), on the text by Bernard of Cluny, won him commissions for the *Wanderer's Psalm* for the Hereford Festival (1900), and *Star Song* for the Norwich Festival (1902). His choral works have been as popular in England as in his own country. He died in Cedarhurst, New York, on December 18, 1919.[2]

Others of the same and subsequent generations to Parker who, like him, have composed with the liturgy rather than the quartet in mind are T. Frederick H. Candlyn, Joseph Waddell Clokey, Eric Delamarter, Roland Diggle, Harvey B. Gaul, William Wallace Gilchrist, Philip James, Hugh A. Mackinnon, H. Alexander Matthews, and H. Everett Titcomb. Biographical sketches of these composers will be found in Appendix C.

The following group of six men served during the past generation in as many different churches in New York City. They composed, directed, and played the organ, but more especially they taught, through precept and example, in a way which advanced church music more than it had advanced in any other generation in our history.

George Edward Stubbs (1857-1937) was the son of the Reverend Alfred Stubbs, rector of Christ Church, New Brunswick, New Jersey. He graduated from Rutgers College and played in several Connecticut churches before settling in New York. There he served at the Church of the Heavenly Rest, Calvary Church, and St. James' Church. In 1892 he entered upon forty-five years of service at St. Agnes' Chapel, the longest tenure of any organist in the history of Trinity Parish. For thirteen years he was also music instructor at the General Theological Seminary. He was a founder of the American Guild of Organists, and received the Doctor of Music degree from the University of the South in 1906. His choir service book of 1902 was the first truly adequate book of its kind in this country, well printed and easy to follow. The second edition (1906) included 272 hymns, in a format which exerted considerable influence on subsequent American hymnals. His *Practical Hints on the Training of Choir Boys* (1888), was used extensively on both sides of the Atlantic. He also contributed regularly to the *New Music Review*. He died in New York, December 26, 1937.

Walter Henry Hall (1862-1935) was born in London on April 25, 1862. While still a student at the Royal Academy of Music, he conducted two choral societies and trained a boy choir. Coming to America in 1883, he was first organist-choirmaster of St. Luke's Church, Germantown, Pennsylvania, then from 1890-1896 at St. Peter's Church, Albany, New York. Moving to New York City in 1896, he served at St. James' Church, St. Matthew and St. Timothy's, and the recently-established Cathedral of St. John the Divine. In 1913 he became professor of choral music and director of the chapel choir at Columbia University. He also conducted the Musurgia Society and the Mozart Society. In 1893 he founded the Brooklyn Oratorio Society, which he conducted until his death. He was also a founder and warden of the American Guild of Organists. He composed considerable music for the Episcopal Church, including a festival *Te Deum* and a *Communion Service in G*. He wrote many reviews and articles, especially for the *New Music Review*. His *Essentials of Choir-Boy Training* appeared in 1907. He was a member of the Episcopal Joint Commission on Church Music, and of the Hymnal Commission. He died December 11, 1935.

Felix Lamond (1864-1940) was born in London and came to the United States as a young man. He succeeded Walter B. Gilbert as organist-choirmaster at Trinity Chapel, New York, in 1897. He taught organ and music literature at Columbia University from 1902 to 1907, and was music critic for the *New York Herald* from 1905 to 1915. An absolute perfectionist in style and taste, he was regarded as one of the outstanding teachers of his day. In 1912 he founded the Trinity School of Church Music for Episcopal Church musicians. During the First World War, he served in the American Red Cross. In 1918 he resigned from his post at Trinity Chapel to set up a Department of Musical Composition at the American Academy in Rome (Leo Sowerby[3] being the first to receive their Rome Prize, with its three-year fellowship for study in Italy). Lamond served as director of the department, giving untold assistance to many young American composers, until shortly before his death, which occurred in New York on March 16, 1940. He was made an honorary member of the Academy of St. Caecilia, at Rome, in 1923, and two years later was decorated with the Order of the Crown of Italy.

Thomas Tertius Noble (1867-1953) was born in Bath, England, on May 5, 1867, where he made his first public appearance at the age of eleven. In 1881 he went to Colchester under the tutelage of the Reverend Charles Everitt, who saw to his general education and for whom he served as organist in All Saints' Church. In 1886 he won a scholarship at the Royal College of Music, where he studied under Parratt, Bridge, and Stanford. From 1890 to 1892 he was the latter's assistant at Trinity College, Cambridge, leaving that post to become organist and choirmaster of Ely Cathedral. In 1898 he moved to a similar post at York Minster, where he founded a symphony orchestra, directed the York Musical Society, and in 1912 revived the York Musical Festival after a lapse of seventy-five years. He became a fellow of the Royal College of Organists in 1905. In 1913, he was brought to St. Thomas' Church, New York, to succeed Will C. Macfarlane. In 1919 he established its choir school, where he developed a fine boy choir in the best cathedral tradition. Many young musicians flocked to study under him, among the more notable of whom were Paul Callaway, organist-choirmaster of Washington Cathedral, Grove Oberle, organist-choirmaster of Emmanuel Church, Boston, Andrew Tietjen, late associate organist of Trinity Church, New York, and Searle Wright, organist-choirmaster at St. Paul's Chapel, Columbia University.

Columbia awarded Noble an honorary Master of Arts degree in 1918, and Trinity College a Doctor of Music degree in 1926. In 1932 the Archbishop of Canterbury conferred on him the Lambeth Doctor of Music degree. That same year a memorial window was unveiled at St. Thomas' Church to commemorate his fiftieth year as a church

[157]

musician. He was a member of the Episcopal Hymnal Commission of 1916, and of the Joint Commission on Church Music until his retirement in 1943 at the age of seventy-five.

Noble composed many anthems, services, and organ works, among the best known being his anthems *Fierce was the Wild Billow, O Wisdom, Spirit of the Living God,* and *Souls of the Righteous.* He published several useful collections of free organ accompaniments to familiar hymns, and, in 1943, a monograph, *The Training of the Boy Chorister.* He died at his home in Rockport, Massachusetts, on May 4, 1953. His portrait is at Plate XV.

(James) Miles Farrow (1871-1953) was born in Charleston, South Carolina, on October 13, 1871. He attended the Baltimore public schools, and Johns Hopkins University as a special student in the class of 1893. In music he was largely self-taught except for a few organ lessons from Harold Randolph at the Peabody Conservatory. He began playing the organ at the Roman Catholic cathedral in Baltimore. In 1894 he became organist-choirmaster at St. Paul's Episcopal Church, where with the Reverend J. S. B. Hodges, he built up an outstanding choir of men and boys. With this group, he presented many cantatas and smaller oratorios to overflowing congregations. In 1909 he moved to the Cathedral of St. John the Divine in New York, where, by the time the choir and crossing were consecrated, he had again built up a magnificent choir.

Columbia University honored him with the Doctor of Music degree in 1926. Ill health forced him to retire in 1931 after twenty-two years of service. He died at Catonsville, Maryland, on July 17, 1953. He composed little, but wrote *About the Training of Boys' Voices* (1898). His service playing and improvisations were generally admired by church musicians, and his devotion to his work and his choristers was an inspiration to "a noble army, men and boys," who remember him with affection.

David McK. Williams (1887-) was born in Carnarvonshire, Wales, on February 20, 1887. When three months old he was brought to Denver, where he sang as a boy under Henry Houseley at the Cathedral of St. John-in-the-Wilderness. At the age of thirteen, he became organist-choirmaster of St. Peter's Church, Denver. In 1908 he went to New York as organist of Grace Church Chapel, and studied under Clement Gale. From 1911 to 1914 he studied at the Schola Cantorum, Paris, under D'Indy, Vierne, and Widor. Returning to New York, he became a fellow of the American Guild of Organists in 1915, served at the Church of the Holy Communion (1914-16), and then went overseas with the 10th Siege Battery of the Royal Canadian Artillery. Returning in 1920 to the Church of the Holy Communion, he remained for only six months, and then began twenty-six years of service at St. Bartholomew's Church, where he developed one of the outstanding musical programs in the country.

Until his retirement in 1947, he was head of the organ department at the Juilliard School, on the staff of the music department of Union Theological Seminary, and a member of the Episcopal Joint Commission on Church Music and of the Hymnal Commission. He received the Doctor of Music degree from King's College, Halifax, in 1928. He has composed many services and anthems, of which his setting of the text *In the Year that King Uzziah Died* is outstanding. His *Thirty-four Hymn Descants* (1948) are very useful.

A principal musical phenomenon of the twentieth century has been the concert organ, the history of which was outlined in an earlier chapter. The men who excelled in its performance were Samuel Atkinson Baldwin, Seth Bingham, William C. Carl, and Clarence Dickinson; their biographies will be found in Appendix C. However, the one individual who, more than any other, led in the restoration of the organ to a place of dignity in the services of the church as well as in recitals was W. Lynnwood Farnam (1885-1930).*

Farnam was born in Sutton, Quebec, on January 13, 1885. He studied with his mother and local teachers until 1900, when he won the Strathcona Scholarship of Montreal for study at the Royal College of Music. In 1904 he became an associate of the Royal College of Organists. Returning to Montreal, he was organist-choirmaster of St. James' (Methodist) Church (1904-5), St. James the Apostle's (1905-8), and Christ Church Cathedral (1908-13). From 1913 to 1918 he served at Em-

[159]

*See also the biography by H. William Hawke, "Lynwood Farnam; His Life," *The American Organist* XLVII/7 (July 1964), 12–22.

manuel Church, Boston, after which he spent a year in the Canadian Army. Moving to New York City, he was at the Fifth Avenue Presbyterian Church during 1919 and 1920, and then at the Church of the Holy Communion until his death from cancer on November 23, 1930. His playing first attracted national attention at the San Francisco Exposition of 1915. His exceptional ability as a recitalist and as a teacher made him easily the outstanding organist of his generation, despite his relatively brief career. This was fittingly climaxed during the 1928-29 season by his series of recitals covering the entire organ literature of J. S. Bach.

Some of the most effective work for the improvement of church music has been accomplished by men whose time was spent in the classroom, at editorial desks, and in commission meetings, rather than more exclusively at the organ console. Such a man had been Singenberger in the nineteenth century. In the present century similar leadership has come from Waldo Seldon Pratt at the Hartford Theological Seminary, Peter Christian Lutkin at Northwestern University, Wallace Goodrich at the New England Conservatory, Robert Guy McCutchan and his successor at DePauw University, Van Denman Thompson. Biographies of these men will also be found in Appendix C.

The teacher who picked up the reins of Tucker and Hopkins in furthering the ideals of the Oxford Movement, especially in the development of the use of plainsong among Protestant churches, was Winfred Douglas.

(Charles) Winfred Douglas (1867-1944) was born in Oswego, New York, on February 15, 1867. He graduated from Syracuse University in 1891, and for a year was organist-choirmaster at the Church of Zion and St. Timothy, New York. Severe lung trouble, which plagued him throughout his life, necessitated his removal to Colorado, where he was ordained to the priesthood in 1899. From 1903 until 1906 he studied church music abroad, especially with the Solesmes monks on the Isle of Wight. Returning to this country, he became director of music for the Community of St. Mary, Peekskill, New York, where he applied his studies of the rhythmic and melodic principles of plainsong in many adaptations for English use. From 1907 on, he was canon of St. Paul's Cathedral, Fond du Lac, Wisconsin, and in 1934 he was appointed canon of St. John's Cathedral, Denver. From 1937 on, he also served as vicar of the Mission of the Transfiguration, Evergreen, Colorado.

He was president of the American Plainsong Society, a fellow of the American Ecclesiological Society, and a trustee of many Episcopal institutions. In 1917 he received the honorary Doctor of Music degree from Nashotah House Seminary. For many years he was an active member of the Episcopal Joint Commission on Church Music and the Hymnal Commission. For the former, he helped prepare *The Choral Service* (1927), *The American Psalter* (1929), and *The Plainsong Psalter* (1932). For the Hymnal Commission he prepared manuscript for the Hymnals of 1916 and 1940. He was also music editor of the first edition of *The American Missal*. His years of research into liturgics and plainsong made the final production of the *Monastic Diurnal,* in 1932, a definitive work. At the time of his death (January 18, 1944), he had nearly completed the musical edition of the *Diurnal.*[4] His concern for congregational worship through The Book of Common Prayer led to many adaptations of plainsong masses and to special hymn collections. His *Church Music in History and Practice* first appeared in 1937.

Throughout his life Canon Douglas lectured frequently on church music in general, and plainsong in particular. After 1923, when he founded the Evergreen Conference, much of his teaching was centered at its annual School of Church Music. His extensive library is now at Washington Cathedral. His portrait is at Plate XV.

Church musicians who have achieved fame through their choral directing are F. Melius Christiansen, William Joseph Finn, and John Frederick Wolle—a Lutheran, a Roman Catholic, and a Moravian. Biographies of Finn and Wolle will be found in Appendix C.

F. Melius Christiansen (1871-†) was born in Eidsvold, Norway, on April 1, 1871. As a boy he played in his father's band. Coming to the United States in 1888, he led the Scandinavian Band in Marinette, Wisconsin, for four years, then entered Augsburg College and the Northwestern Conservatory of Music, where he graduated in 1894. For a

†1955.

time he served as organist-choirmaster of Trinity Lutheran Church, Minneapolis, and directed the Augsburg College Chorus. In 1897 he went to Leipzig for two years study at the Conservatory under Gustav Schreck, cantor of the Thomasschule. Returning to this country, he served at Bethany Lutheran Church, Minneapolis, until his removal to Northfield, Minnesota, in 1903, where he became head of the music department of St. Olaf's College and organist-choirmaster of St. John's Lutheran Church. From the latter church choir he developed his famous St. Olaf's Lutheran Choir, which has toured the country annually since 1911, with a reportory largely composed of his own editions of music drawn from the Lutheran tradition. He retired in 1944, and in April, 1951, Minnesota held a statewide observance of his eightieth birthday. His portrait is at Plate XIV. There is a biography by Leola M. Bergmann, *Music Master of the Middle West* (University of Minnesota Press, 1944).

The twentieth century has seen the strenuous activity of a number of men working for the improvement of music in the Roman Catholic Church. Outstanding among them are Becket Gibbs, J. Alfred Schehl, Nicola Aloysius Montani, Carlo Rossini, and Pietro A. Yon; representatives, respectively, of English, German, and Italian traditions. Their biographies are also in Appendix C. It is an interesting fact that the only women who have achieved national distinction in the field of church music have been two religious and a lay woman of the Roman Catholic Church. Biographies of Sister Mary Cherubim and of Justine Ward are in Appendix C.

Georgia Stevens, R.S.C.J. (1870-1946), was born in Boston on May 8, 1870. She early showed a marked musical talent, and studied the violin intensively, first in Boston then at the conservatory in Frankfurt-am-Main. Returning to Boston, she studied under Loeffler. She entered the Roman Catholic Church in 1895 and a few years later became a religious of the Sacred Heart, serving her novitiate at Kenwood, in Albany, and at Roehampton, England. She made her profession at Ixelles, Belgium, in 1914, returning to America shortly after the outbreak of the First World War to find her life work at the Manhattanville College of the Sacred Heart. There in 1918, with Justine

Winfred Douglas
(1867-1944)

T. Tertius Noble
(1867-1953)

Plate XV.

Clarence Dickenson
(1873-1969)

Blackstone Studios

Leo Sowerby
(1895-1968)

Blackstone Studios

PLATE XVI.

Ward, she founded the Pius X School of Liturgical Music, which soon became a national center for teaching the principles of plainsong as enunciated by the monks of Solesmes. Since 1932 her choirs have given annual concerts of high repute. In later years her teaching was extended to work in the elementary parochial schools through her six-volume *Tone and Rhythm Series*. Mother Stevens died on March 28, 1946, but the vivid impression of her striking personality will long continue to radiate itself wherever musicians and religious gather.[5]

This period has seen three Canadian church musicians of such stature that their work has become well known in the United States—Healey Willan, Alfred Ernest Whitehead, and Graham George. (Biographies of Whitehead and George will be found in Appendix C.)

Healey Willan (1880-†) was born in London on October 12, 1880. He was a boy chorister at the resident choir school of St. Saviour's, Eastbourne. Later, he served as organist-choirmaster in Christ Church, Wanstead, Essex, and at the Church of St. John the Baptist, Kensington. In 1913 he came to Toronto to head the theory department of Toronto Conservatory, also serving as vice-principal from 1920 to 1936. For fifteen years he was professor of music at the University of Toronto. From 1913 to 1921 he was organist-choirmaster at St. Paul's Church, and since then at the Church of St. Mary Magdalene, where his use of plainsong and polyphony have become famous.[6]

A fellow of the Royal College of Organists, he received the Doctor of Music degree from the University of Toronto in 1921. His compositions include two symphonies, incidental music for fourteen plays, three operas, and a number of cantatas, organ pieces, chamber works, anthems, and songs. Probably the best known of all these is his simple unison *Missa de Sancta Maria Magdalena* (1928). He has the distinction of being the only composer from overseas to be commissioned to write an anthem for the coronation of Queen Elizabeth II.

Prior to the advent of radio and television it was perhaps only natural—insofar as church music is concerned—that outstanding New York musicians should be the best known nationally. It is to be regretted all the more, then, that in a survey of this nature, more attention cannot be given to the many local leaders who served with

†1968.

[163]

distinction during the past century. Among these, the following have become rather widely known—not as recitalists, lecturers, or composers, but rather by virtue of their local influence, due, in turn to the high quality of their work over a long period of time: Caroline Beardsley in Bridgeport, Connecticut; Charles Edwin Clemens in Cleveland; Edmund S. Ender in Baltimore; William C. Hammond in Holyoke, Massachusetts; blind Charles F. Hansen in Indianapolis; Ernest Arthur Simon in Louisville; and Harrison Wild in Chicago. (Short biographical sketches of these musicians will be found in Appendix C.)

Today there is more emphasis on choirmastership and composition for the church than ever before in our history. Skillful organists are always in demand, but are now taken more for granted than they were even one or two generations ago. Indicative of this maturity of musical development is the fact that few of our musicians are now foreign born. (Biographies of Paul Callaway, Vernon de Tar, Harold Einecke, Channing Lefebvre, George Mead, Richard Purvis, Barrett Spach, and Walter Williams are in Appendix C.)

The ranking composer of church music at mid-century is Leo Sowerby (1895-†). He was born in Grand Rapids, Michigan, on May 1, 1895, and studied at the American Conservatory of Music in Chicago, receiving the Master of Music degree in 1918. During the First World War he served overseas as bandmaster of the 332nd Field Artillery Regiment. In 1921 he won the first Rome Prize, the three-year fellowship for study in Italy offered by the American Academy in Rome under Felix Lamond. In 1923 he participated in the Salzburg Festival of Contemporary Music. Since his return to this country, he has taught at the American Conservatory, where he currently heads the theory and composition department. He has also served as organist-choirmaster of St. James' Church, Chicago, since 1927. He has been a member of the Hymnal Commission of the Episcopal Church and now serves on its Joint Commission on Church Music. He was awarded the honorary Doctor of Music degree by the Eastman School of Music, University of Rochester, in 1936.

His compositions have been widely performed, both at home and abroad, since his first violin concerto was heard in 1913. His sym-

†1968. [164]

phonies and other orchestral works have frequently been given first performances by the Chicago and Boston Symphony orchestras. His organ works, anthems, and services, many of which have been composed for specific occasions, have been used in numerous festival services. He has received a number of commissions and awards from organizations such as the Society for the Publication of American Music and the Columbia Broadcasting System. In 1946 he won the Pulitzer Prize for his oratorio *The Canticle of the. Sun,* using for the text the famous poem of St. Francis of Assisi. His *Forsaken of Man* (1940) is a significant setting of the Passion narrative.[7] A fluent yet craftsmanlike composer, his works are fully developed in his mind before being put to paper, and seldom changed thereafter. His portrait is at Plate XVI.

These men and women are being followed by a notable generation of younger choirmasters, organists, and composers—devoted and talented musicians who bid fair to lead our church music into still worthier expressions of worship, both as composers and as organist-choirmasters.

This survey of church musicians should not conclude without mention of a group of composers whose work has been predominantly secular, but who, none the less, have each made several notable additions to the repertory of American church music. This group includes Samuel Barber, Mrs. H. H. A. Beach, Mabel Daniels, Cecil Effinger, Robert L. Sanders, Arthur Shepherd, Randall Thompson, and Virgil Thomson.

CHAPTER XIX

The Hymnal of Today: A Merger of Many Traditions

THE TERM "church music" to most people means the anthems sung by the choir, and perhaps the organ music which they hear. But the music which reaches the greatest number of churchgoers is the music found in the hymnals.

Church music in the Colonies consisted of Psalms and hymns exclusively. As the choral music of the service has since become more elaborate in each denomination, so too have the contents of their hymnals, the degree varying only in accordance with their peculiar tastes and traditions.

Chapter XVI showed how the modern choral repertory has developed not only with the addition of new works but also with the cultivation of older classics. A similar development has taken place both textually and musically in almost all our hymnals. Indeed, the contents of the modern hymnal reflect the entire span of this book, with tunes ranging from mediaeval plainsong melodies like *Vexilla Regis*,[1] which the French sang when first they landed on the site of Detroit, to such modern tunes as Winfred Douglas' *St. Dunstan's* and David McK. Williams' *Non nobis Domine*.

In point of chronology the time span is even greater, for the modern hymnal contains plainsong melodies which can be traced to at least the sixth century, if not still earlier to the time of our Lord, as well as tunes drawn from each subsequent decade and century.[2] Similarly, the hymn texts range all the way from certain of the pre-Christian

Psalms to such contemporary lines as John W. Norris' "Give peace, O God, the nations cry."

Chapter II pointed out how impoverished musically were the seventeenth-century congregations; it was noted that the first music edition of *The Bay Psalm Book* contained but twelve tunes. Nearly a century later, the first Episcopal hymnal included only eighteen tunes. On the other hand, by 1809 the Eckhard manuscript[3] in musical Charleston, South Carolina, included around a hundred tunes, and today the average congregation knows about one hundred and fifty tunes from hymnals containing between three hundred and eight hundred tunes.

The Colonists sang their few tunes to many texts. *Old Hundredth* served equally well for William Kethe's "All people that on earth do dwell," Isaac Watts' "From all that dwell below the skies," or any other Long Metre poem. Even modern hymnals indicate the metres of all tunes in order to facilitate such interchanging of texts and tunes.[4] However, for most congregations today, each hymn-text is firmly wedded to a given tune—but only within a given area or denomination. Most hymnals have a choice of tunes for a considerable percentage of the texts because of geographical or denominational preferences for one tune or another. Quite often these preferences are based solely upon a divergence of tradition that began generations ago. Thus, "How firm a foundation" is sung to *Lyons* by most Episcopalians, but to *Adeste fideles* by the Congregationalists. Indeed, a few texts have never "settled"; neither Charles Wesley's "Jesus, Lover of my Soul" nor the anonymous American carol "Away in a manger" have ever been universally associated with a single tune, and both continue to vacillate between several popular tunes. But for most hymns there is today a single tune, in a well fitted, hand-and-glove relationship. Obvious examples of this close affiliation—in which the tunes themselves are often known by the first line of text—are Baring-Gould's "Onward, Christian soldiers" with *St. Gertrude,* Watts' "O God our help in ages past" with *St. Anne,* and Faber's "Faith of our fathers" with *St. Catherine.*

The inconsistencies of human nature are such that a tune popular in England with a given text is frequently unknown in this country, although the same text is equally popular here with another tune—

oftentimes one of English origin! Such a text is Charles Wesley's "Lo! he comes, with clouds descending," sung in England to *Helmsley,* but in America to J. F. Wade's *St. Thomas.* Another is Charlotte Elliott's "Just as I am, without one plea," sung in England to Elvey's *St. Crispin* but in America to Bradbury's *Woodworth.* The converse is equally true, for Sear's "It came upon the midnight clear" is known in England only to Sullivan's tune *Noel.*

To properly appreciate the hymnal musically, one should clearly recognize the various styles of tunes it contains, as well as their sources. The easiest style to identify is that of the plainsong hymns. But even here, imitations are often difficult to detect. Most people, for example, readily perceive the plainsong style in such a tunes as *Pange lingua,* "Sing, my tongue, the glorious battle," but fail to recognize Helmore's *Veni Emmanuel* as a nineteenth-century melody deliberately composed in the same style.

The chorales in the Lutheran and Moravian traditions are generally recognizable by the broad sweep of their lines, especially as in *Passion chorale,* "O sacred head, sore wounded," *Wachet auf,* "Wake, awake, for night is flying," and *Vom Himmel hoch,* "From heaven high." Others, such as *Nun danket,* "Now thank we all our God," are frequently sung too fast to permit their recognition as chorales.

Psalm-tunes which were popular in Colonial times and are still found in modern hymnals include *Bedford, Old Hundredth, Windsor, Hanover, St. James,* and *St. Matthew,* to mention but a few of the best-known ones. Unfortunately, over-zealous editors and organists have too often succeeded—by such devices as altered rhythms and omitted "gathering notes"—in disguising the old Psalm-tunes as stereotyped Victorian hymn melodies. Today the Psalm-tunes are thought of as the peculiar heritage of Scottish Presbyterians, for the simple reason that their exclusive use persisted longer in the Presbyterian Church.

Another style is the Methodist hymnody of the late eighteenth century, exemplified by such tunes as *Easter Hymn (Salisbury), Savannah,* and *Moscow.* As a type, they are much more florid than the earlier tunes, with a wider range, more harmonic outline, and less diatonic movement.

Next in order are the truly Victorian tunes, composed by men such as John Bacchus Dykes, Samuel Sebastian Wesley, and Joseph Barnby. These too are equally characteristic of their period and are as distinctive in style as are the plainsongs, chorales, and Psalm-tunes of other times. Many of these Victorian tunes, such as Dykes' *Dominus regit me* and Barnby's *Laudes Domini,* are so blended with the harmonizations given them by their respective composers as to be veritable part-songs. Whereas all tunes of the earlier periods, and most of those more recently composed, are better sung in unison, these Victorian part-songs suffer unless they are sung in full harmony. The reason for this lies in the fact that earlier tunes were composed and sung solely in unison, their composers but vaguely conscious of a possible harmonic background. The Victorians, however, thought in terms of full harmonies, and seldom of melody only.

The *English Hymnal* of 1906, aided by the folklorist-composer Ralph Vaughan Williams, pioneered in the use of folk songs as modern, unison hymn-tunes. This movement was taken up in America by the Episcopal Hymnal of 1916 and by several of the school hymnals; more recently it has been broadened to include Negro and white spirituals. In this same category fall some of the revived folk tunes from the early shape-note collections.[5] Among the loveliest of these revivals are the tunes *Land of rest* for "Jerusalem, my happy home," and *Kedron* for "Sunset to sunrise changes now."

Not all of the modern tunes are composed for unison singing, although as a class they lend themselves better to that style. T. Tertius Noble's unison *Ora labora* for Jane Borthwick's "Come, labor on," is now a generation old, and increasingly popular. Outstanding unison tunes of more recent date are Graham George's *The King's majesty* for "Ride on! Ride on in majesty!" and David McK. Williams' *Malabar* for "Strengthen for service, Lord." Both of these tunes are splendid examples of the use of modern rhythmic and harmonic combinations that are striking yet not disconcerting to a worshipping congregation.

These, then, are the various styles and periods represented in the modern hymnal. As noted in the beginning of this chapter, the hymnals of the several denominations differ for the most part in the musical emphasis inherent in their particular traditions. Apart from special texts emphasizing particular matters of dogma stressed by a given church, the contrast lies mostly in the larger or smaller number of "gospel songs" and Lowell Mason tunes employed. In the present-day Episcopal Hymnal, many nineteenth-century tunes of the Mason and Victorian genre have been eliminated in favor of plainsongs, Psalm-tunes, and chorales; on the other hand, some Presbyterian and Lutheran hymnals have deleted many of their own traditional Psalm-tunes and chorales while increasing proportionately the number of Victorian melodies.

However, there is a considerable body of tunes of almost every type and period common to all hymnals—even to the cheaper gospel song-books. Such is the catholicity of church music. Our theologians cannot always agree on matters of dogma or polity, but our congregations, to a considerable degree, praise God with identical words and melody. Theirs is the unconscious response to the tutoring of the Holy Spirit, which has melted the separate inspirations of many races and classes into a single, ecumenical body of song. To quote a recent work:

> The authors of the texts include all sorts and conditions of men. Some, though by no means all, of the great poets are here—Milton, Pope, Tennyson. There is also Mary Duncan known only for her lovely children's hymn "Jesus, tender Shepherd, hear me." There are leaders of great spiritual movements—St. Francis of Assisi, Luther, and John Wesley. There is the little isolated group of Malabar Christians in India. There are great Christian statesmen like St. Ambrose and scholars like St. Thomas Aquinas. There is the unknown Negro slave who wrote "Were you there when they crucified my Lord." There are Bunyan the Baptist tinker, Newman the Roman cardinal, and many a simple unknown Christian.
>
> Many lands have made their contribution. The hymns of America and Great Britain needed no translation. We have also the Dutch "We gather together;" the Danish "Through the night of doubt and sorrow;" the German "Now thank we all our God;" the Austrian "Silent night;" the Italian "Come down, O Love divine;" hymns in the Latin tongue, Greek hymns by John of Damascus and Clement of Alexandria, the Jewish Psalms; "Strengthen for service, Lord" from India, and "Jesus, Son of Mary" from Africa.[6]

Texts such as these have made the hymnal a veritable layman's manual of theology, for its lines comes closer to his every-day thought than all else in his religious life.

More and more the older hymnals brought out by a single editor have given way to co-operative efforts. Although the Episcopal Church from the time of its reorganization after the American Revolution has always controlled the texts appearing in its hymnals, it did not bring out an official collection of tunes until 1918; other bodies have been even less strict in the past. But today, each denomination, as it feels the need for a revised hymnal, is more and more approaching the work on a co-operative, nation-wide scale, in a few instances even stepping beyond denominational barriers.

Chapter VIII described some of the changes in hymnal format which have taken place in the four centuries and more since the advent of printing. Many churches still use volumes of texts only, or texts with melody only, in their pews. These are useful for congregational singing and for reading devotionally. The choir editions of today are printed with as much clarity as possible, in a rather standard size and format. The music is now on two staves only—treble and bass—much as though it were written for performance on a keyboard instrument, as, in part, it is. Several, if not all, of the stanzas in each hymn are printed between the staves, with each syllable or word of text carefully aligned with its proper notes. As a rule, larger note values (half-note units) are used for the earlier Psalm-tunes and chorales, quarter-note units for nineteenth- and twentieth-century tunes, and eighth-notes for the mediaeval plainsongs.

Hymnals tend to be revised once in each generation. There is, and should be, a constant addition of new material as well as a revaluation of the old. An age centered around research in nuclear physics needs hymns such as Howard Chandler Robbins'

> And have the bright immensities
> Received our risen Lord,
> Where light-years frame the Pleiades
> And point Orion's sword?[7]

CHAPTER XX

Matters Liturgical

THE SUBJECT of liturgy, its history and its reform, is far broader than the scope of church music alone, and yet there are many aspects of the latter which are controlled by the former. It may be profitable, therefore, to review some of the changes which have taken place in the liturgical practices of various American churches and to note their effect on church music.

Parts I and II of this work contain many allusions to liturgical usages of the eighteenth and nineteenth centuries. In Chapter V, some details were given of the order of worship in the Episcopal and the Roman Catholic Churches. In Chapter X, the growth of choral services was described.

Chapter XI noted the improvement in repertory and standards of performance in the music of the Roman Catholic Church, first under the efforts of Singenberger and his Caecilian Society, and later (Chapter XVI) under the stimulation of the *Motu Proprio* and the various organizations founded since 1910 to further and support its ideals. Since the basic form of the liturgy remains as it was after the revisions of the sixteenth century, changes which have come about in Roman Catholic church music have been largely limited to such improvements in the repertory and its rendition.

Certain modern needs in the shape of the liturgy have been met by services such as the Novena and the Benediction of the Blessed Sacrament. The liturgy of Benediction of the Blessed Sacrament consists of selected verses from the Psalms and of canticles borrowed from other offices and from the Mass itself. It has not, as yet, stimulated any creative effort on the part of composers. The Novena is a simple devotional service of no fixed liturgy whatever, its music being limited to simple hymns in English which frequently approach in style the gospel songs of Protestantism. The musical Vespers, described on page 98, have disappeared completely.

The modern Liturgical Movement is being felt in the Roman Catholic Church no less than in many Protestant denominations. Central altars, the Mass tied more closely to daily occupations and contemporary life, the wide use of Latin-English people's missals, token Offertory processions in which parishioners bring the Communion elements forward to the altar, dialogue Masses—all these things point toward an increasing emphasis on active congregational participation. If the hierarchy were to permit the use of English for singing, such permission would give hope for larger congregational participation and for better work on the part of volunteer choirs. It is interesting to note that resolutions pointed in this direction were expressed at the annual meeting of the Vernacular Society which met in Cleveland during August, 1952, in conjunction with the thirteenth National Liturgical Conference.

Changes made in The Book of Common Prayer by the Episcopal Church in 1892 added the full text of the *Benedictus* to Morning Prayer, and both the *Magnificat* and the *Nunc dimittis* to Evening Prayer. In 1928 the canticle *Benedictus es, Domine* was added as a permissible substitute for the *Te Deum* in Morning Prayer. Since then, American composers have produced a number of outstanding musical settings for these canticles.

The service of Holy Communion has undergone no comparable change in its contents, but the manner of its music has changed greatly. No longer, for example, are miniature anthems composed and sung on the *Gloria tibi* ("Glory be to thee, O Lord") which follows the announcement of the Holy Gospel. With the increasing popularity of the "family Eucharist"—a Communion Service around nine o'clock on Sunday mornings at which the entire family worships together—simpler unison services, sung not by a choir but by the entire congregation, have come to the fore.[1]

The Greek, Russian, and other branches of Eastern Orthodoxy in America do not, as yet, have a sufficiently long tradition here to have shown much evolution musically. They have profited in many ways by this very lack, for they have succeeded more, possibly, than any other of the liturgical churches, in keeping their music close to their people. Cantors and choirs sing well and without ostentation, entirely unaccompanied, even in relatively small churches, and with little or no financial support.

In the Lutheran Church, the morning service has always been some form of Ante-Communion, its music being the traditional Communion chorales. In recent years, however, there has been a marked revival in the use of plainsong, especially for the introits, graduals, and other propers of the liturgy. This movement has profited considerably by the earlier Episcopalian editions of plainsong with English texts. It has also revived the plainsong of Luther's German Mass,[2] a work comparable to Merbecke's Communion Service of 1550.

For many years Lutheran services in this country were conducted only in German. Gradually, extra sermons in English were given for the benefit of the young people, until finally the knowledge of German became so slight that the German services were generally discontinued. During the early years of the twentieth century, however, when the principal service was still in German, a form of Matins similar to the Episcopal office of Morning Prayer developed around the English sermon. This office of Matins has continued as a liturgical form wherever there is an early service preceding the regular Ante-Communion, but has remained a simple chorale service musically, with no distinctive canticles.

Although the liturgy of the Methodist Church uses large portions of The Book of Common Prayer, it has never cultivated the choral settings of the liturgy, and even today the music of Methodist worship is limited to hymns and anthems, with a few sung responses.

Otherwise within Protestantism, and especially in the Congregational and Presbyterian Churches, the influence of the Liturgical Movement may be seen in an increasing use of fragments of the traditional liturgies, chiefly excerpts or adaptations from The Book of Common Prayer. Instead of a single Scripture reading, there frequently are paired lessons from the Old and New Testament, each followed by appropriate anthems, if not by a traditional canticle. Versicles and responses, the suffrages, and the *Gloria Patri* are employed more and more, and are actually sung in churches where there is a strong musical establishment.

A curious offshoot of these movements is a trend back to gallery choirs in the latter churches, while in the Baptist, Congregational, and Presbyterian Churches there is still a trend toward chancel choirs. In churches where a central altar has been installed, the choir is placed beyond or behind the altar.

All of these trends—in Roman Catholic, Eastern Orthodox, Episcopal, and Protestant Churches—point in a single direction: more participation in the worship of the Church by the people, who themselves are the Church, the Body of Christ.

CHAPTER XXI

Full Flower

AFTER three centuries of development, the music in many of our churches has, in terms of comparison with both its European and its secular counterparts, reached a stage where the term that heads this chapter may be used without exaggeration. Admittedly there are those churches where—due to geographical isolation or congregational decadence—efforts toward worship through music have been few and feeble. But wherever there has been a will to provide the necessary financial support, there are adequate instruments, competent organists, and music worthy of the praise of Almighty God.

Characteristic of our American civilization, there is no single norm. No two churches are alike, just as no two communities are alike. Consequently, rather than describe the musical establishment of some non-existent "average" church, this chapter will consider the music in three quite-different churches—churches chosen not because they necessarily stand head-and-shoulders above all others in their respective types of musical activity, but because each is a brilliant, though conservative, example of a particular type of musical activity. The first church to be described emphasizes its congregational singing; there is a good choir, but its role in the music of the church is deliberately subordinated. The second is a "multiple choir" church, with musical activities in which all persons above the age of five may participate. The third is a professional choir of men and boys. The fact that they are, respectively, Lutheran, Methodist, and Episcopal churches is purely incidental. Similar musical establishments can be found in almost any denomination.

Trinity Evangelical Lutheran Church has been located in the down-town section of Indianapolis for over seventy-five years.[1] From its in-ception, the church has maintained a parochial school where, in the Lutheran tradition, the children of the parish have learned the chorales of the church along with their academic subjects. The mixed choirs and the organ are located in a rear gallery where they sing choral responses and the anthem for each service. They are but faintly heard, though, when the congregation takes up the strains of a chorale. Nor is there any hesitation on the part of the congregation. So familiar are they—through childhood study and congregational rehearsals—with each chorale in their hymnal, that when the organist, Berniece Fee Mozingo, has concluded the opening chorale-prelude, the congregation begins to sing with the first note of the chorale, without further intro-duction by the organ. The music of the liturgy is also sung by the congregation, and with equal skill and devotion.

The First Methodist Church of Santa Barbara, California, maintains five separate choirs under the direction of C. Harold Einecke.[2] These are not competing groups, but are rather parts of an integrated Choral Union system, divided purely on the basis of age. In no sense are they social organizations; members are accepted only on the basis of simple vocal auditions and are dismissed when three unexcused ab-sences occur. Each choir rehearses and sings in church services on a regular schedule.

The work begins with a probationers' choir composed of children between the ages of five and nine who rehearse one afternoon each week. They learn simple chorales and anthems by rote, taking home copies of the texts to be learned as prayers and recited each day. They serve about once every six weeks in the regular church service, singing the responses with the congregation as well as a simple unison anthem.

When nine years of age, those who show talent are advanced into either the girls' choir or the boys' choir, both of which rehearse once each week. At this age the girls are beginning to read music, and learn not only unison anthems but also two and three-part arrangements of works by prominent composers. At boys' choir rehearsals, the mem-bers receive regular training as boy choristers. They sing unison and two-part anthems and are occasionally joined by the men for four-part

[177]

anthems. Where a solo boy shows promise, he is given every opportunity to develop musically.

At the age of fourteen, the boys and girls are combined into a chapel
choir for their high school years. This group also rehearses once a
week, and sings each Sunday morning at the chapel service for young
people. Once in each month it also sings the responses and an anthem
at a regular Sunday service.

The chancel choir is the adult group into which all of the younger
groups feed. Where this multiple-choir system has been in effect over
a period of years it may result in an adult choir of well-nigh professional standards. The chancel choir forms the back-bone of the choral
music at all regular and special services; it rehearses for a two-hour
period each week. The younger groups seldom rehearse longer than
a single hour at a time.

Massed choirs of the church, known as the Choral Union and including all save the probationers, are used for antiphonal singing, and
for the larger choral works in special concerts, or on festival occasions.
As its name implies, the chancel choir sits in regular choir stalls on
both sides of the chancel; the other choirs sit in side and rear galleries.
An acolytes guild of teen-age boys and a full staff of librarians facilitate rehearsals and provide colorful but smooth-flowing details of the
service. A choir guild of mothers and fathers furnishes loyal support
in maintaining vestments, rehearsal room equipment, choir awards,
and the like.

Such a program represents the ideal for a parish church using volunteer, amateur musicians. There are sufficient singers to present the
larger choral works from time to time, and there is a constant flow of
trained young people into the adult choir. There is the one danger,
however, that all of the singing members of the congregation may be
drawn into the choirs, with a resulting decline in congregational
singing.

Quite different is the situation at Washington Cathedral, where Paul
Callaway has been organist and choirmaster since 1939. Here there is
no parish congregation but rather a constantly changing audience of
tourists who come to the cathedral services to see the beautiful edifice,
and to listen rather than to take an active part in its worship. There is

a professional choir of men and boys who are able to use many devices in chants and hymns which could not be employed to the same degree in a parish church. New tunes, descants, free accompaniments on the organ, alternation between unison singing and four-part harmony, singing in canon—all these devices may be employed without fear of disturbing a non-existent congregational participation. Similarly, more choral settings of the canticles may be employed in place of chants. Such is the true role of cathedral music. It cannot, and should not, be the goal of the parish church.

The Cathedral Church of Saint Peter and Saint Paul—to use the full title of the Episcopal cathedral in the national capital—maintains a choir of thirty boys and eighteen men, the latter equally divided between altos (countertenors), tenors, and basses. They rehearse in the choir cloister and sit during the services in the "great choir," divided into two balanced groups, with the first choir, or *decani,* on the right and the second choir, or *cantori,* on the left as one faces the high altar.

The average life of a choir boy is from five to six years. New boys are selected each year from a junior, or training, choir on a competitive basis, after voice and general intelligence tests have been given. The junior choir, under the direction of Richard Dirksen, the associate organist-choirmaster, rehearses two afternoons each week. After rehearsal, they sing Evensong in one of the chapels of the cathedral; on Sundays, after a short rehearsal, they sing at one of the early Communion services. They are each paid a small fee to foster incentive and regularity.

Each boy selected for the main choir is given a day scholarship in St. Albans School, the boy's preparatory school on the cathedral close. There the daily schedule is planned in such a way that the choir boys are able to rehearse in the choir cloister for an hour at the end of each forenoon. On the days that the junior choir does not meet, they return in late afternoon to sing Evensong. On Friday evenings they rehearse for two hours with the men of the choir.

The men are all on a graduated salary schedule, with provision for annual and sick leave. They rehearse with the boys on Friday evenings and then remain for another hour of additional rehearsal by themselves. Boys and men rehearse again for nearly an hour before each service in which they participate. During the summer months, while the boys are on vacation, the men's choir is increased to include twenty voices.

The normal Sunday throughout the winter finds the junior choir assembling at 9:00 a.m. and singing a Communion service half an hour later. The choir of men and boys assembles at 10:15 (the boys are warmed up ten minutes earlier) and sings for either a Morning Prayer or Communion service at 11:00 a.m. They reassemble at 3:15 p.m. and sing Evensong at 4:00. On the last Sunday of each month, in place of the sermon at Evensong, they sing a cantata or special group of anthems. The choir uses both Anglican and plainsong chant, and a wide repertory of services and anthems dating from the fifteenth to the mid-twentieth century, with particular emphasis on the Anglican tradition. Works used during the decade 1941-51 are listed in Appendix B. Plate XIX shows the choir singing in their regular stalls at a special service in 1951 when the British ambassador presented the cathedral with an altar cross and candle-sticks from the late King George VI.

Washington Cathedral has three Skinner organs. A small two-manual instrument in the Chapel of St. Joseph of Arimathea is a memorial to Edgar Priest, organist-choirmaster from 1910 to 1935. Another organ, with fifteen stops on two manuals, is located in Bethlehem Chapel. The great organ of the cathedral was dedicated on November 10, 1939. It contains 8,354 pipes on 125 stops. In addition to special recitals, there is a program of organ music following Evensong on the first Sunday of each month, played by visiting organists.[3]

CHAPTER XXII

"Praise God from Whom All Blessings Flow"

THESE familiar words, the opening line of the Doxology which Thomas Ken wrote as the conclusion to the "Three Hymns for Morning, Evening, and Midnight" in the *Manual of Prayers* for his school boys at Winchester College, England, in 1695, have long been used as the focal point of worship in our American churches—whether small country congregations meeting in a plain, frame building, or crowded city congregations within Gothic walls of seried stone. They give simple, straight-forward expression to the basic urge of our religious life—worship.

Mere intonation of the words, however, is not enough. They must be the heartfelt expression of the devotion of the congregation. One of the principal reasons for the superficiality of so much of our church music has been the identical shallowness in the worship life of our congregations. Too few of our clergy of today realize that worshipful music results from, and requires, a corresponding atmosphere in which it can live and work. Yet the lack of spirituality on the part of their congregations probably reflects their own spiritual poverty more than anything else. This is not the fault of our seminaries; rather it is an individual problem.

The seminaries are at fault, however, in not providing our future clergy with an adequate grounding in church music. For how can our clergy guide what they know not of? In recent years there has been some improvement in this respect among the seminaries of several denominations. A seminary program of music education must be very carefully handled, however, for a mere smattering of knowledge is a dangerous thing indeed when it comes to guiding church music. Happy the clergyman who knows how to select a competent musician, and then knows how to work sympathetically with him!

On the side of training the church musician himself, much needs to be done. How can we expect to have a music program which truly praises God when again and again music committees hire youngsters with but a half-dozen organ lessons because they are more amenable to the committee's personal tastes than their older, more exacting teachers?

Our music schools teach organ-recital repertory, but fail to teach how to accompany an anthem adequately or how to play hymns in a manner which will encourage rather than hinder congregational singing. They teach students to beat time, but give them no preparation for the multiple problems of choir training, to say nothing of choral repertory and interpretation.

That our churches at large are aware of these problems is evidenced by the rising interest in summer conferences to help correct deficiencies in music education, and in commissions to guide long-range programs through published lists, manuals, and pamphlets. The real problem is how to translate this work to the parish level.

It is an interesting phenomenon that the tourist of today can still find many traces of nineteenth-century America in the manners and customs of our people. Unfortunately this is also true of our church music. There are many churches, even in modern communities, at which all the abuses and faults described in earlier chapters persist unabated. Yet the fact that this is so need not be disheartening, for annually the improvement is considerable. A steady program of music education reaching to the individual parish level can accomplish wonders within the next generation.

Given an intelligent clergyman and a competent musician, through the medium of congregational "sings," or rehearsals, after certain services, in conjunction with parish dinners on week nights, and in the regular meetings of the various parish organizations, any church can revolutionize its worship-through-music in a few months.

There remains a needed word of caution to the individual church musician, be he chorister or choirmaster, cleric or layman. Music is by no means essential to worship; a "said service," totally devoid of music, can be far more worshipful than one where inappropriate or overly-difficult music is attempted. But if music be used in a manner which well fits the liturgy for which it is intended, it imparts a noble enrichment to the worship which it embodies.

What, then, constitutes proper church music? Differences of opinion inevitably arise; tastes unconsciously and reasonably differ. In spite of these variations, the following factors must always be held paramount:

1. The music should be a fitting expression of the words; the words matter most.
2. It should be good, as music.
3. The music should be in keeping with the spirit of the liturgy.
4. It should be chosen to fit the conditions existing in the church for which it is intended [i.e., the music must at all times be within the range of competence of choir and organist to perform adequately].[1]

Beyond these, the personality of the individual performer must always be sublimated to a corporate spirit of worship. Only under such conditions can we truly "praise God from whom all blessings flow."

APPENDICES

A. The Organists of Trinity Parish, New York City.

B. Selected Music Lists.

C. Biographies of American Church Musicians.

D. Notes and Bibliography.

APPENDIX A

The Organists of Trinity Parish, New York City

TRINITY CHURCH (1697–)

Organists			Assistant Organists		
1741–	1744	John Clemm, Jr.			
1744–	1761	John Rice			
1761–	1764	Thomas Harison			
1764–	1765	James Leadbetter			
1765–	1795	John Rice			
1795–	1804	William Müller			
1804–	1820	Charles Wilson			
1820–	1839	Peter Erben			
1839–	1859	Edward Hodges			
1859–	1865	Henry S. Cutler	(?) –	1863	W. J. Robjohn
			1864–	1865	W. A. M. Diller
1865–	1866	W. A. M. Diller			
1866–	1897	Arthur H. Messiter	1866–	1867	W. A. M. Diller
			1867–	1868	E. M. Bowman
			1868–	1873	John P. Morgan†
			1873–	1879	Henry Carter†
			1879–	1880	F. E. Lucy-Barnes
			1880–	1885	F. W. Thursch
			1885–	1897	Victor Baier
1897–	1921	Victor Baier	1897–	1901	Henry Hans Wetzler
			1901–	1904	R. J. Winterbottom
			1904–	1925	Moritz E. Schwarz
1922–	1941	Channing Lefebvre			
			1925–	1935	George Mead
			1935–	1941	Frank Cleveland
1941–		George Mead	1941–	1942	Clinton Reed
			1942–	1953	Andrew Tietjen†
			1953–		Robert Arnold

† Associate Organist.

ST. PAUL'S CHAPEL (1766–)

1776– 1790	John Rice	
1802– 1806	Henry Rausch	
1806– 1826	Thomas S. Brown	
c1826– 1834	William Blondell	
1834– 1843	Samuel P. Taylor	
1843– 1845	George Hodges	
1845– 1846	Henry Huntington	
1846– 1848	Henry W. Greatorex	
1849– 1855	William H. Walter	

1855– 1868	Michael Erben	
1869– 1877	John H. Cornell	
1877– 1901	Leo Kofler	
1901– 1929	Edmund Jaques	
1929– 1938	Herbert R. Ward	
1938– 1950	Marta Klein	
1950– 1951	Joseph T. Elliott	
1951– 1953	Paul Sifler	
1953–	Joseph T. Elliott	

ST. JOHN'S CHAPEL (1807–1909)

1813– 1820	Peter Erben
(?)– 1876	Charles E. Horsley
1876– 1904	George F. Le Jeune
1905– 1909	R. J. Winterbottom

TRINITY CHAPEL (1855–1943)

1855	S. Parker Tuckerman
1855–c1870	William H. Walter
c1870– 1897	Walter B. Gilbert
1897– 1918	Felix Lamond
1918– 1943	W. H. Beckwith

CHAPEL OF ST. CORNELIUS THE CENTURION (1868–)

c1878– 1886	Mrs. Winfield Scott Hancock
1886– (?)	Julia Gillis
(?)– 1905	Mrs. David Robertson
1906– 1925	Arthur F. Halpin
1926– 1944	Oscar F. Comstock
1945– 1952	Gladys Shailer
1953–	Albert F. Robinson

ST. CHRYSOSTOM'S CHAPEL (1869–1924)

c1880– 1883	John D. Prince
1883– 1895	Wenzel A. Raboch
1897– (?)	Alfred J. McGrath
1913– 1914	R. Burns Eglinton
1915– 1924	George Fowler

ST. AUGUSTINE'S CHAPEL (1877–)

(?)– 1884	Richard Horner
1886– (?)	Alfred J. McGrath
1894– 1895	Victor Nicholson
1895– 1902	Arthur L. Brown
1902– 1907	Theodore G. Leach
1907– 1908	William J. Rathgeber
1908– 1909	H. Leslie Goss
1909– 1919	Harry Fletcher
1919– 1953	Jennie Dobbins (Megerlin)
1953–	Andrew Donaldson

ORGANISTS OF TRINITY PARISH, NEW YORK

ST. LUKE'S CHAPEL (1892–)

1894– 1907	Frank P. Hoffman		1943– 1946	Walter Rye
1908– 1909	Jessie Belden		1946– 1949	Harry W. Cosgrove
1909– 1926	R. J. Winterbottom		1949–	Clifford L. Clark
1926– 1943	William Pollak			

ST. AGNES' CHAPEL (1892–1943)

1893– 1937	George W. Stubbs		1938– 1943	Kenneth White

CHAPEL OF THE INTERCESSION (1908–)

1908– 1941	Frank T. Harrat		1942–	Clinton Reed
1941– 1942	Andrew Tietjen			

APPENDIX B

Selected Music Lists

The following is a summary of the music sung at Trinity Church, Boston, under the direction of Wallace Goodrich, during October, 1904:

Te Deum & Benedictus:

King Hall in Bb

Martin in C

Stanford in Bb

Tours in F

Arthur Whiting in A

Magnificat & Nunc dimittis:

Barnby in Eb

Cruickshank in G

King Hall in Bb

Horatio Parker in E and Eb

Stanford in Bb

Kyrie: Goodrich

Sanctus: Eyre in Eb

Gloria in excelsis: Old chant

Anthems:

Brahms—How lovely is thy dwelling place *(Requiem)*

César Franck—Come, gracious Spirit

King Hall—The Light hath shined

Jadassohn—O God, be merciful

Martin—Hail, Gladdening Light

Mendelssohn—Grant us thy peace

　　　　　—O come, let us worship

Horatio Parker—I will set his dominion in the sea

Stainer—Awake, awake, put on thy strength

　　　　—I saw the Lord

Sullivan—I will mention the loving kindness of the Lord

The quartet choir at the First Church in Boston, under John P. Marshall, sang the following repertory during the season of October 2, 1910 to June 18, 1911. Repetitions during the season are indicated following the titles:

Barnby—The grace of God
    —O Lord, how manifold
Buck—As it began to dawn
    —Sing Alleluia forth
Chadwick—Art thou weary
      —O God, be merciful
Emerson—There were shepherds
Gadsby—O Lord, our governor (2)
Gounod—Lovely appear (2)
Hollins—O worship the Lord (2)
King—Break forth into joy (2)
Marsh—The Lord is my light
Maunder—Praise the Lord
Mendelssohn—O for the wings of a dove (Hear my prayer)
Olds—I sought the Lord
Roberts—I will lift up mine eyes
     —The path of the just
Shelley—Christians the morn (2)
    —God is love
    —Hark, hark my soul
    —King of love
Simper—Come unto me
Smart—The Lord is my shepherd
Stainer—I am Alpha
Sullivan—Who is like unto thee
Warren—The Lord is my shepherd
West—Like as the hart
    —The Lord is exalted (2)
    —"The Woods," etc.
Woodward—Comes at times
Composer not known—Be ye all of one mind (2)
          —I will always give thanks
          —It shall come to pass
          —Ye shall go out

As described in Chapter XVI, the music list of Washington Cathedral for the decade 1941-51 embodies a summary of the better music being used in American churches today. As listed below, no distinction is made as to works limited to trebles only, men only, or unison works, since the purpose of the list is primarily to show the breadth of musical literature possible in a well-planned repertory. Works marked with a dagger (†) were composed or edited by cathedral organists or choir members, works starred (*) were given first performance at Washington Cathedral. Pairs of canticles for either Morning or Evening Prayer are referred to as Services rather than by the first line of the canticles; thus a setting of the *Magnificat* and *Nunc*

[191]

dimittis is consistently called an Evening Service. The list is broken up into groups corresponding roughly with various chapters in this book.

MEDIAEVAL PLAINSONG

Canticles, with fauxbourdons
The Massacre of the Holy Innocents†
Missa de Angelis
Missa Marialis
Psalms

EARLY POLYPHONY, ETC. (15th to 17th centuries)

ENGLISH WORKS:

William Byrd—*Ave verum corpus*
    —Evening Service (fauxbourdon)
    —*Haec dies*
    —*Lumen ad revelationem*
    —I will not leave you
    —*Justorum animae*
    —Mass in 4 parts
    —*Miserere mei*
    —*Rorate coeli*
    —*Senex puerum portabat*
    —Sing joyfully unto God
    —*Vigilate*
    —When Israel came out of Egypt
Richard Dering—*Quem vidistis pastores*
Orlando Gibbons—Evening Service in Ab
    —O Lord, increase my faith
    —This is the record of John
John Hilton—Lord for thy tender mercy's sake
John Merbecke—Communion Service
Thomas Morley—Evening Service (fauxbourdon)
Peter Philips—*Ascendit Deus*
Henry Purcell—Glory and worship are before him
    —*Jehova, quam multi sunt hostes mei*
    —Let my prayer come up
    —Evening Service in G minor
    —Remember not, Lord
    —Thou knowest, Lord
    —Thy way, O God, is holy
Thomas Tallis—*Audivi vocem de caelo*
    —*Benedictus* (fauxbourdon)
    —Choral Service
    —Evening Service (fauxbourdon)
    —If ye love me

Tye—I will exalt thee
Weelkes—Hosanna to the Son of David
Whitbroke—Evening Service (fauxbourdon)

CONTINENTAL WORKS:

Allegri—*Miserere*
Anerio—*Christus factus est*
Arcadelt—*Ave Maria*
Jacques Clement—*Adoramus te*
Bartolomeo Cordans—*Jesu, Salvator noster*
Giovanni della Croce—When I was poor
Josquin DesPres—*Ave verum corpus*
Melchior Franck—Father, thy Holy Spirit send
Gabrieli—*In ecclesiis*
Jacob Handl—All they from Saba
        —*Canite tuba*
        —I ascend unto my father
        —*O magnum mysterium*
        —Resonet in laudibus
Hassler—*Cantate Domino*
Orlando di Lasso—*Inimici autem*
          —*Libera me*
Volckmar Leisring—*O filii et filiae*
Nanino—*Diffusa est gratia*
Palestrina—*Adoramus te*
      —*Exaltabo te*
      —*Exultate Deo*
      —In divers tongues
      —*Missa Aeterna Christi munera*
      —*O bone Jesu*
      —*Sicut cervus*
      —This is the day
Praetorius—Lo, how a rose
Vincenzo Ruffo—Evening Service (fauxbourdon)
Heinrich Schütz—Four Psalms
        —Give ear, O Lord
        —Seven Last Words
Sweelinck—Psalm 134
      —Born today *(Hodie nobis)*
      —Sing unto God
Viadana—*O sacrum convivium*
Victoria—Behold I bring you
    —*Jesu, dulcis memoria*
    —*O magnum mysterium*
    —*O vos omnes*
Johann Walther—St. Matthew Passion†

EIGHTEENTH CENTURY

ENGLISH WORKS:

Attwood—Turn thy face from my sins
Clarke-Whitfeld—Evening Service in F
Crotch—Lo, star-led chiefs
Handel—Let their celestial concerts
    —The Messiah
    —Round about the starry throne
    —Thanks be to thee
    —Your voices raise
Travers—Ascribe unto the Lord

CONTINENTAL WORKS:

J. S. Bach—Bide with us (Cantata no. 6)
    —Come thou, O come
    —Flocks in pastures
    —From depths of woe (Cantata no. 38)
    —God is a sun and shield (Cantata no. 79)
    —God's time is best (Cantata no. 106)
    —Jesus, joy of man's desiring
    —The Lord will not suffer
    —Now praise we great and famous men
    —O light everlasting (Cantata no. 34)
    —St. John Passion
    —Subdue us through thy kindness
Cherubini—The righteous live
Haydn—As waves of a storm swept ocean
Martini—*In Monte Oliveti*
Mozart—*Adoramus te*
    —*Ave verum corpus*
    —O God, when thou appearest

NINETEENTH CENTURY

ENGLISH WORKS:

Percy Fletcher—Ring out, wild bells
George Garrett—Prepare ye the way of the Lord
John Goss—O Saviour of the world
    —The wilderness
Macfarren—The Lord is my shepherd
George C. Martin—Hail, gladdening light
    —Ho, everyone that thirsteth
    —Let my prayer be set forth
Ouseley—O Saviour of the world
Stainer—Evening Service in Bb

Plymouth Church of the Pilgrims, Brooklyn

PLATE XVII. The Hook & Hastings Organ, Plymouth Church of the Pilgrims, Brooklyn, New York

First Congregational Church, Washington, D. C.

PLATE XVIII.   The Odell Organ, First Congregational Church, Washington, D. C.,
Easter Day, 1896

Walmisley—Evening Service in D minor
S. S. Wesley—Evening Service (arr. by Ley)
　　　　　—Lead me Lord
　　　　　—Thou wilt keep him
　　　　　—To my request
　　　　　—Wash me throughly
C. Lee Williams—Cast me not away
　　　　　—When the Son of Man shall come

CONTINENTAL WORKS:

Beethoven—Hallelujah (Mount of Olives)
　　　　　—The heavens are telling
Brahms—German Requiem
　　　　　—Lord, we leave thy servant sleeping
　　　　　—The white dove
Dvořák—Blessed Jesu
César Franck—Bow down thine ear *(Domine non secundum)*
　　　　　—Praise the Lord *(Dextera Domini)*
　　　　　—O Lord, most holy *(Panis angelicus)*
Gounod—Unfold ye portals
Grieg—Jesu, friend of sinners *(Ave maris stella)*
Liszt—The Resurrection
Mendelssohn—Hear my prayer
　　　　　—How lovely are the messengers
　　　　　—There shall a star
Reger—Christmas carol
Schubert—Great is Jehovah

EARLY TWENTIETH CENTURY

American music now takes the place of English music as the basic repertory. Continental music is represented only by two French works—Lili Boulanger's setting of Psalm XXIV and the Fauré *Requiem*. Canadian and Russian works are listed separately below.

AMERICAN WORKS:

Mabel Daniels—The Christ Child
Dickinson—Angels o'er the fields
Harvey Gaul—*Benedictus es, Domine*
Mary Howe—Song of Ruth
W. C. Macfarlane—Christ, our passover
J. S. Matthews—*Benedictus es, Domine*
T. T. Noble—*Benedicite*
　　　　　—*Benedictus es, Domine* in G minor
　　　　　—By the rivers of Babylon
　　　　　—Communion Service in B minor
　　　　　—Easter Alleluia

—Evening Service in A minor
—Evening Service in B minor
—Grieve not the Holy Spirit of God
—Lord of the worlds above*
—O hear thou from heaven
—O wisdom
—Souls of the righteous
—*Te Deum* in F
—That Easter morn
—When I survey the wondrous cross
Horatio Parker—Evening Service in E
—In heavenly love abiding
—Lights glittering morn
—Now sinks the sun *(Jam sol recedit)*
Edgar Priest—*Benedictus es, Domine*†
L. Stokowski—*Benedicite*
Titcomb—Communion Service
—Victory *Te Deum*
A. Torovsky—Softly the stars were shining
David McK. Williams—*Benedicite*
—*Cantate Domino*
—Communion Service
—*Deus misereatur*
—Evening Service in A minor
—In the year that King Uzziah died
—The stork
—To Bethlehem

ENGLISH WORKS:

J. H. Arnold—An easy modal *Te Deum*
—Evening Service
Bairstow—Communion Service in E♭
—I sat down under his shadow
—Let all mortal flesh keep silent
—Save us, O Lord
—The promise which was made
Maurice Besley—The night is come
A. H. Brewer—Evening Service in D
E. T. Chapman—All creatures of our God and King
Darke—*Benedictus*
—Communion Service in F
—O gladsome light
Walford Davies—God be in my head
—If any man hath not the spirit
—I vow to thee, my country
F. T. Durrant—The strife is o'er

[196]

Dyson—Morning Service in D
Elgar—Jesus, Lord of life and glory
   —Light of the world
Balfour Gardiner—Evening hymn
Basil Harwood—Communion Service in Ab
       —Evening Service in Ab
Holst—Eternal Father
   —Lullay, my liking
   —*Te Deum*
John Ireland—Greater love hath no man
C. S. Littlejohn—Communion Service
Marchant—*Te Deum*
Oldroyd—Mass of the quiet hour
Cyril Scott—*Benedicite*
Geoffrey Shaw—Hail to thee, Beth'lem
      —How far is it to Bethlehem
      —The day draws on
Martin Shaw—Arise in us
    —I sing of a maiden
C. V. Stanford—And I saw another angel
      —Communion Service in Bb
      —Evening Service in Bb
      —Jesus Christ is risen today
      —*Te Deum* in Bb
      —When God of old
Charles Stewart—Communion Service
John E. West—Hide me under the shadow
    —O everlasting light
    —O God of love
R. Vaughan Williams—At the Name of Jesus
       —Communion Service in D
       —Down in yon forest
       —Evening Service in C
       —Festival *Te Deum*
       —Five mystical songs
       —Let us now praise famous men
       —The pilgrim pavement
       —*Te Deum* in G
       —Valiant for truth
Charles Wood—*Expectans expectavi*
      —Father all holy
      —Glory and honor
      —Hail, gladdening light
      —O thou the central orb
      —St. Mark Passion

MID-TWENTIETH CENTURY

AMERICAN WORKS:

Ronald Arnatt—*Benedictus es, Domine**
    —*Christo paremus cantica**
    —Evening Service*
    —*Jesu, dulcis memoria**
Samuel Barber—Let down the bars, O death
Paul Callaway—An hymn of heavenly love†
    —Communion Service in D major†
    —Evening Service†
    —Hark the glad sound*†
    —O saving Victim†
Candlyn—Bread of the world
    —Communion Service in Db
Richard Clem—Before the ending of the day*†
    —O God, when darkness falls*†
Richard (Wayne) Dirksen—*Cantate Domino**†
    —Christ, our passover*†
    —Christians to the Paschal Victim*†
    —*Deus misereatur**†
    —An Easter Alleluia*†
    —Evening Service*†
    —*Jam sol recedit**†
Garth Edmundson—Evening Service in E*
Cecil Effinger—Sing we merrily
Harold Friedell—*Benedictus es, Domine*
    —King of glory
    —Lute-book lullaby
Henry H. Hungerford—*Benedictus es, Domine*
Philip James—By the waters of Babylon
    —The Lord is my shepherd
Hugh Mackinnon—I hear along our street
Robert Sanders—Recessional
Leo Sowerby—*Benedictus*
    —*Benedictus es, Domine* in Bb
    —*Benedictus es, Domine* in C
    —Come, Holy Ghost*
    —Communion Service
    —Evening Service in D
    —Forsaken of man
    —I was glad when they said unto me*
    —I will lift up mine eyes
    —*Jubilate Deo*
    —Like the beams
    —Now there lightens upon us
    —O dearest Jesus

—*Te Deum* in D minor
—*Tu es vas electionis*
C. Sumner Spalding—Ah, dearest Jesus*†
　　　　　　—Cleanse thou me from secret faults*†
William Strickland—*Benedictus es, Domine*
　　　　　　—*Jubilate Deo*
Randall Thompson—Alleluia
Clarence Watters—*Laudate pueri*
William Y. Webbe—*Benedictus es, Domine*
　　　　　　—Lord, let thy spirit

ENGLISH WORKS:

Benjamin Britten—Ceremony of Carols
　　　　　　—*Te Deum*
Bullock—Christ, the fair glory
　　—Evening Service
　　—O most merciful
　　—*Te Deum* in D
Howells—Morning Service in E♭
　　—Evening Service in E
　　—Evening Service in E♭
　　—A spotless rose
Henry Ley—*Te Deum*
Robin Milford—By the waters of Babylon
　　　　　—Up to those bright and gladsome hills
Ernest J. Moeran—Morning Service in E♭
Eric Thiman—Communion Service
　　　　　—Evening Service in D♭
　　　　　—O Christ the heaven's eternal king
　　　　　—The holly and the ivy
　　　　　—The strife is o'er
Peter Warlock (Philip Heseltine)—Balulalow
　　　　　　　　　—Bethlehem Down
　　　　　　　　　—*Corpus Christi*

CANADIAN WORKS:

Graham George—*Benedictus es, Domine*
Alfred E. Whitehead—*Benedicite*
　　　　　　—Jesus, the very thought of thee
Healey Willan—Behold the tabernacle of God
　　　　　—*Benedictus es, Domine* in E♭
　　　　　—*Benedictus es, Domine* (fauxbourdon)
　　　　　—Evening Service in B♭
　　　　　—Hail, true Body
　　　　　—In the name of our God
　　　　　—Lo, in the time appointed
　　　　　—Look down

[199]

—*Missa de Sancta Maria Magdalena*
—O how glorious
—O King of glory
—O sacred feast
—O saving Victim
—*Te Deum* in B♭
—The three kings
—While all things were in quiet silence

RUSSIAN WORKS:

Bortniansky—Cherubim song
—Divine praise
Gretchaninoff—The cherubic hymn
A. Kastalsky—O gladsome light
(Walter Parratt, ed.)—Give rest, O Christ
Rachmaninoff—Cherubim song
—Glory be to God
—Glory to the Trinity
Shvedov—With heart uplifted
Stravinsky—Mass
Tschaikowsky—How blest are they
—Hymn to the Trinity
—O praise the name
Chesnokov—Cherubic hymn
—Salvation belongeth

APPENDIX C

Biographies of American Church Musicians

SAMUEL ATKINSON BALDWIN (1862-1949) was born in Lake City, Minnesota, on January 25, 1862. After four years of study at the Dresden Conservatory, he served as organist-choirmaster at Plymouth Church, Chicago (1885-1889), People's Church, St. Paul (1889-1895), and Church of the Intercession, New York (1895-1902). He then succeeded Dudley Buck at Holy Trinity Church, Brooklyn, serving there until 1911. In 1907 he was appointed to the chair of music at the College of the City of New York, where he inaugurated a famous series of semi-weekly organ recitals which continued until his retirement in 1932. He composed for the orchestra, choir, and solo voice. His anthem *Tarry with me* has been very popular. He was a founder, fellow, and warden (1903-5) of the American Guild of Organists, whose history he compiled in 1946. He died in New York on September 15, 1949.

EDWARD SHIPPEN BARNES (1887-†) was born in Seabright, New Jersey, on September 14, 1887. He studied at Yale under Jepsen and Parker, then at the Schola Cantorum in Paris under d'Indy, Vierne, and Decaux (1910-11). Returning to this country, he became a fellow of the American Guild of Organists in 1917. He has served as organist-choirmaster in New York at the Church of the Incarnation (1911-12) and at Rutgers Presbyterian Church (1913-24), at St. Stephen's Church, Philadelphia (1924-38), and at First Presbyterian Church, Santa Monica, California, since 1938. He has composed several symphonies for orchestra, suites and smaller works for the organ, cantatas, services and anthems for choir. He has also published a number of articles on the

†1958.

organ, a *School of Organ Playing,* and has edited several collections of anthems.

CAROLINE (LATTIN) BEARDSLEY (1860-1944) was born on May 21, 1860, in Huntington, Connecticut. She began her career as an organist when twelve years of age at the local Congregational church. Two years later she moved to St. Paul's Episcopal Church. She married Elmer Beardsley in 1881, becoming a widow eight years later. On December 3, 1883, she became organist-choirmaster of the Second (United) Congregational Church of Bridgeport, Connecticut. From 1909 to 1938 she also served at the B'nai Israel Temple. An expert sight-reader, she was in great demand as an accompanist. Yearly from 1920 to 1929 she gave an outstanding Lenten recital series at the United Church, bringing many distinguished organists to Bridgeport. In 1936 she was awarded a civic medal by municipal authorities. She retired on Christmas Day, 1938, after fifty-five years of service. She died on February 21, 1944, and was buried in Stratford, Connecticut. There is a portrait and short account of her work in *The Diapason,* XXX, 1 (December, 1938), 10.

WILLIAM BILLINGS (1746-1800).

[See pages 49-50.]

SETH BINGHAM (1882-) was born in Bloomfield, New Jersey, on April 16, 1882. He studied at Yale University under Parker, earning his Bachelor of Arts degree in 1904 and the Bachelor of Music degree in 1908. During 1906-7 he studied in Paris under Guilmant, D'Indy, and Widor. He became a fellow of the American Guild of Organists in 1909, subsequently serving as their vice-president and national chairman of the convention and expansion committees. He served as organist-choirmaster at St. Paul's Church, New Haven (1902-6), at Rye Presbyterian Church (1909-12) and since 1912 at New York's Madison Avenue Presbyterian Church. He taught organ at Yale, 1908-19, and since 1920 has been an associate professor of music at Columbia University. He has composed extensively for all mediums. There is a list of his works in the article by Walter Blodgett in *The Diapason,* XLII, 3 and 4 (February and March, 1951).

JOHN W. BISCHOFF (1850-1909) was born in Chicago on November 27, 1850. He lost his sight as a result of measles when two years old. He attended the Wisconsin Institute for the blind and then went to London where he studied organ under Cresswold. In 1875 he became organist-choirmaster of the First Congregational Church in Washington, D. C., playing on the new Odell organ shown in Plate XVIII and taking the leadership in the concert life of the city. One of the founders of the American Guild of Organists, he composed many piano pieces, songs, and anthems for his quartet choir. He died in 1909 after thirty-four years of service to the church.

WILLIAM BATCHELDER BRADBURY (1816-1868) was born in York, Maine, on October 6, 1816. When seventeen, he went to Boston and studied at the Boston Academy under Mason and Sumner Hill. In 1841 he became organist of the First Baptist Church in New York City. There he organized free singing classes, similar to those of Mason in Boston, which resulted in the introduction of music in the New York public schools. From 1847 to 1849 he studied in Leipzig, sending interesting letters back to *The New York Observer* and other periodicals. Returning to this country, he spent his time in teaching and writing, compiling some fifty-nine tune-books during the remainder of his lifetime. With others, he founded the Bradbury Piano Company, which was later absorbed by Knabe. He died in Montclair, New Jersey, on January 7, 1868. His "Creed for a Church Musician" is quoted on page 109.

JAMES BRENNER (*d.* 1780).
[See Note 4 of Chapter VI, page 247.]

JOHN HYATT BREWER (1856-1931) was born in Brooklyn on January 18, 1856. He was a boy soprano in various Brooklyn and New York choirs during the years 1864-1871, and studied under Dudley Buck whom he later succeeded as conductor of Brooklyn's Apollo Club. He served as organist-choirmaster in the City Park Chapel (1871-3), Church of the Messiah (1873-7), Clinton Avenue Congregational Church (1877-81), and thereafter at the Lafayette Avenue Presbyterian Church where, for many years, his quartet and chorus choir presented six or eight oratorios annually. He was a founder, fellow, and warden (1905-8) of the American Guild of Organists. A charter member of the music section of the Brooklyn Institute, he was elected its fellow in 1906. New York University awarded him its Doctor of Music degree in 1914. He composed over two hundred songs, quartets, anthems, cantatas, and other pieces. He died in Brooklyn on November 30, 1931.

DUDLEY BUCK (1839-1909).
[See pages 114-15.]

PAUL (SMITH) CALLAWAY (1909-) was born in Atlanta, Illinois, on August 16, 1909. He started playing the organ when thirteen, at the First Congregational Church in Rock Falls, Illinois. After study at Westminster College and William Jewell College, he moved to New York in 1930 for organ work under T. Tertius Noble, later studying with Marcel Dupré, David McK. Williams, and Leo Sowerby. He became a fellow of the American Guild of Organists in 1932. He served as organist-choirmaster of St. Thomas' Chapel, New York, 1930-35, and at St. Mark's Cathedral, Grand Rapids, Michigan, 1935-39. Since 1939 he has served at Washington Cathedral where he has developed one of the outstanding choirs in the country, a Chamber Chorus, and the Cathedral Choral Society. He has been much in demand as an organ recitalist, and has taught summers at Wa-Li-Ro, the Wellesley Conference, and the Evergreen School of Church Music. During World War II, he served as an army bandmaster. He has been a member of the Hymnal Commission of the Episcopal Church.

T. FREDERICK H. CANDLYN (1892-†) was born in England, in December, 1892. He served as assistant organist of Doncaster Parish Church, and received the Bachelor of Music degree from the University of Durham before coming to this country. In 1914 he played in various New York churches, and then settled in Albany as organist-

†1964.
[204]

choirmaster of St. Paul's Church. He served in the United States Army from 1917 to 1919, then returned to St. Paul's. He served on the staff of New York University from 1919 to 1943. He became organist-choirmaster of St. Thomas' Church, New York, in 1943, succeeding T. Tertius Noble. He has composed about one hundred vocal and instrumental compositions, including many anthems and services.

WILLIAM CRANE CARL (1865-1936) was born in Bloomfield, New Jersey, on March 2, 1865. He was a pupil of Samuel P. Warren in New York, and of Guilmant in Paris. He was organist of the First Presbyterian Church in Newark, New Jersey, from 1882 to 1890, and of First Presbyterian Church in New York from 1892 until his death on December 8, 1936. A founder of the American Guild of Organists, he also founded the Guilmant Organ School of New York in 1899, which he directed for many years. He was largely responsible for the American tours of Guilmant and Bonnet. His *Masterpieces for the Organ* (1898), was a pioneer historical anthology. In 1911 he received the honorary Doctor of Music degree from New York University, and in 1924 was made a Chevalier of the French Légion d'Honneur.

BENJAMIN CARR (1768-1831).
[See pages 106-07.]

F. MELIUS CHRISTIANSEN (1871-†).
[See pages 161-62.]

CHARLES EDWIN CLEMENS (1858-1933) was born in Plymouth, England, on March 12, 1858. He studied at the Royal College of Music under Weekes, Martin, and Bridge. When eleven, he was the organist of Christ Church, Davenport, England. From 1889 to 1896, he was organist-choirmaster of the English Church in Berlin, and taught organ at the Klindworth Conservatory. In 1896 he came to Cleveland, Ohio, first serving at St. Paul's Church, and after 1911 at the Euclid Avenue Presbyterian Church. After 1898, he also taught at Western Reserve University, from which he received an honorary Doctor of Music degree in 1916. He published two popular works on the organ: *Modern*

†1955.

Progressive Pedal Technique (2 vols.) in 1894, and *The Modern School for the Organ* in 1903. He died in Cleveland on December 26, 1933. There is a portrait and discussion of his work by Carleton H. Bullis in *The Diapason,* XX, 8 (July, 1929), 29.

JOSEPH WADDELL CLOKEY (1890-†) was born in New Albany, Indiana, on August 28, 1890. He graduated from Miami University in 1912 and then earned diplomas in organ and theory at the Cincinnati Conservatory, graduating in 1915. He taught organ and theory at Miami University (1915-1926) and at Pomona College (1926-1939). Returning to Miami University, he served as dean of the School of Fine Arts until his retirement in 1946. He has composed extensively for chorus, solo voice, organ, chamber ensembles, and orchestra. He has also composed operas, sacred cantatas, and an interesting sacred drama with music, *A Rose from Syria.* He has served as organist-choirmaster in a number of smaller churches, a fact which is reflected in the performability of his works. His pamphlet, *In Every Corner Sing* (New York: Morehouse-Gorham Co., 1945) is an excellent outline of church music for the layman, and equally useful for the amateur church musician. It should be read by every member of a music committee.

HENRY STEPHEN CUTLER (1824-1902) was born in Boston on October 13, 1824. After some preparatory study in music, he went to Frankfurt in 1844 and then to England, where he became interested in cathedral choirs. Returning to Boston in 1846, he became organist, first of old Grace Church, and then of the Church of the Advent, where he organized a vested choir of men and boys. In November, 1858 he went to Trinity Church, New York, serving there until June 30, 1865. There he also established a choir of men and boys, and introduced vestments, as described in Chapter X. His career at Trinity ended rather unfortunately; he accepted an engagement for a month's concert tour, only to have the vestry dismiss him "for absence without leave." (*Cf.* Messiter, *History of the Choir and Music of Trinity Church,* p. 110.) Subsequently, Cutler held positions at Christ Church, New York; St. Ann's, Brooklyn; St. Stephen's, Providence; St. Mark's, Philadelphia; Zion Church, New York; and St. Paul's, Troy, New York. He retired

†1960. [206]

in 1885 and lived in Boston until his death on December 5, 1902. Columbia University conferred the Doctor of Music degree on him in 1864. He published the *Trinity Psalter* (1864) and *Trinity Anthems* (1865), the latter containing some of the twenty-two anthems he had composed for use at Trinity Church. His portrait is at Plate IX.

ERIC DELAMARTER (1880-1953) was born in Lansing, Michigan, on February 18, 1880. He studied with Middleschulte in Chicago, and with Guilmant and Widor in Paris (1901-02). He served as organist-choirmaster in the New England Congregational Church in Chicago (1900-12), the First Church of Christ, Scientist (1912-14), and then for twenty-two years at the Fourth Presbyterian Church in Chicago. During this same period, he was the assistant conductor of the Chicago Symphony Orchestra and other musical organizations. In 1936 he resigned from all church work, partly due to the lack of appreciation which his idealism received, and devoted himself to symphonic work and composition. He wrote extensively for all mediums. His short responses and choral prayers for the non-liturgical service are outstanding. He received the honorary Doctor of Music degree from Wooster College. He died in Orlando, Florida, on May 17, 1953.

VERNON DE TAR (1905-) was born on May 6, 1905, in Detroit, Michigan. He began organ study there under Charles Frederick Morse, and then went to Syracuse University where he graduated with the degree of Bachelor of Music in 1927, studying under Adolf Frey, George Parker, and William Berwald. Going to New York, he studied piano with Franklin Cannon, organ with David McK. Williams, and theory with Clement Gale. He became a fellow of the American Guild of Organists in 1931, and has subsequently served as an examiner and a member of its national council. He directed choral groups at St. Bartholomew's Community House and served as summer organist at that church from 1928 to 1930. He has been organist-choirmaster of St. Luke's Church (1929-32), Calvary Episcopal Church (1932-39), and, since 1939, the Church of the Ascension, where he was instrumental in establishing, in 1948, their annual prize competition for outstanding works in the field of church music. He has taught organ and church music at the Juilliard School of Music since 1946, and is also an organ instructor at Union Theological Seminary's School of Sacred Music. He has composed two communion services, several anthems, and other service music. He is a member of the Joint Commission on Church Music of the Episcopal Church.

CLARENCE DICKINSON (1873-†) was born in Lafayette, Indiana, on May 7, 1873. He began to play the organ at the age of ten in a Cincinnati Presbyterian church where his father was minister. He attended Miami University and Northwestern University (A.B. 1894; honorary M.A., 1909; Mus.D., 1917). He studied composition in Chicago with Weidig and organ with Harrison Wild, playing at the Sixth Presbyterian Church, Evanston, and the Hyde Park Church, Chicago. In 1898 he studied in Berlin under Heinrich Reimann and Otto Singer, then in Paris under Guilmant, Vierne, and Moszkowski (1899-1900). He returned to Chicago in 1901 as organist-choirmaster of St. James' Church and director of the Cosmopolitan School of Music. He also directed the Aurora and Dubuque Musical Clubs, the Chicago English Opera Company, the music for the Chicago Sunday Evening Club, and founded the Chicago Musical Art Society. He moved to New York in 1909, entering on his long career as organist-choirmaster of Brick Presbyterian Church and Temple Beth-El. For a time he also conducted the Mendelssohn Glee Club and the Bach Festival of Montclair, New Jersey. In 1912 he became a professor at the Union Theological Seminary where he founded the School of Sacred Music, only retiring from the directorship in 1945, at which time the Seminary established the Clarence and Helen A. Dickinson Chair of Sacred Music in his honor. Other honors have included a Doctor of Music degree from Ohio Wesleyan University, a Doctor of Letters from Miami University, and selection as "The Hoosier of 1950." He was one of the founders of the American Guild of Organists. He has played many recitals in Europe as well as in America. For many years he has given two famous series in New York, the Historical Lecture-Recitals at Union Seminary and the Friday Noon Hours of Music at Brick Church. One of the outstanding arrangers and editors of sacred music, he has published a series of 260 *Sacred*

†1969. [208]

Choruses Ancient and Modern, Forty Antiphons, and many original anthems, carols, and other pieces. For the organ he has edited the *Historical Recital Series,* composed the *Storm King Symphony* and many smaller works. He has also written *The Technique and Art of Organ Playing* and *The Choir Loft and the Pulpit.* In 1904 he married Helen A. Snyder, who has since been his collaborator in lectures and writing, being responsible for most of the texts or translations used in his choral works. A full list of his compositions has been published by the H. W. Gray Company of New York. His portrait is at Plate XVI.

ROLAND DIGGLE (1887-†) was born in London on January 1, 1887, and studied at the Royal Academy of Music. He came to America in 1904, and has served as organist-choirmaster of St. John's Church, Wichita, Kansas (1908-11), St. John's Cathedral, Quincy, Illinois (1911-14), and since 1914 at St. John's Church, Los Angeles. He received the Doctor of Music degree from the University of the State of New York in 1914. He has published many works for organ, choir, and orchestra, and was for a time a member of the Episcopal Hymnal Commission. *The American Organist,* XXI (1938), 239-40, contains a biographical sketch and partial list of his compositions.

(CHARLES) WINFRED DOUGLAS (1867-1944).

[See pages 160-61.]

JACOB ECKHARD (1757-1833) was born at Eschewege in Hesse Cassel, Germany, on November 24, 1757. He came to America in 1776 as an organist in Richmond. In 1786 he moved to a post at St. John's Lutheran Church, Charleston, South Carolina, and soon became active in the life of that community. He joined the Freemasons and the German Friendly Society, serving the latter as treasurer from 1802 until his death in November, 1833. He organized benefit concerts for the refugees from Santo Domingo, appeared as pianist in various recitals, and directed the annual concert for the Charleston Orphan House. In 1809, he was persuaded to accept a call to the superior organ

†1954.

at St. Michael's Church, at a yearly salary of $350. There he compiled the manuscript described in Chapter XI, and served faithfully throughout the remainder of his life.

GARTH EDMUNDSON (1895-) was born on April 11, 1895, in Prospect, Pennsylvania. He studied at Cincinnati Conservatory and with Joseph Bonnet, Lynwood Farnam, Harvey Gaul, and Isidor Philipp. From 1918 to 1940 he was organist-choirmaster at the First Baptist Church of Newcastle, Pennsylvania, and from 1930 to 1940 also served in the local Roman Catholic church. Since 1941 he has served at the First Presbyterian Church of Newcastle. He has composed some two hundred organ and choral works, his choral preludes on plainsong and German chorale themes being outstanding.

C. HAROLD EINECKE (1904-) was born in Quincy, Illinois, on March 13, 1904. He received his Bachelor of Music degree from Columbia University and has been a fellow of Westminster Choir College. He received the honorary Doctor of Music degree from Grand Rapids University. Among his teachers have been Charles Doersam, Lilian Carpenter, G. Darlington Richards, Edwin Stanley Seder, Edwin Arthur Kraft, John Finley Williamson, and Joseph Bonnet. He has also studied in England under William Drew, Adrian Boult, and Ralph Vaughan Williams. During his college days he served as organist-choirmaster at the Church of the Holy Communion, New York, and at Christ Church, Rye, New York. He then served at Salem Evangelical-Reformed Church of Quincy, Illinois (1925-29), First (Park) Congregational Church, Grand Rapids, Michigan (1930-45), Pilgrim Congregational Church, Saint Louis (1945-47), First Presbyterian Church, Santa Ana, California (1848-50), and since 1950 at the First Methodist Church of Santa Barbara, California. He has lectured widely on the subject of music and worship, and written articles for *The American Organist* and various church papers. He has served on the Illinois State Commission on Music Therapy, the Art Commission in Grand Rapids, and the Arts Guild of the Congregational-Christian Churches of America. Since 1950 he has also been resident organist of the Art Museum and director of the Choral Society in Santa Barbara.

Elwood Baker, The Washington Evening Star

PLATE XIX. The Choir of Washington Cathedral on the occasion of the presentation of a cross and candlesticks from the late George VI (1951)

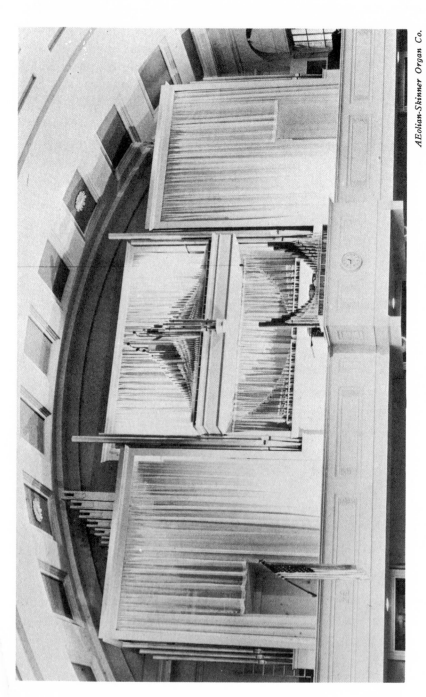

AEolian-Skinner Organ Co.

PLATE XX. The AEolian-Skinner Organ, St. Paul's Cathedral, Boston
A Recent Example of Modern Case-design

EDMUND SERENO ENDER (1886-) was born in New Haven, Connecticut, on July 22, 1886, where his father sang in the choir of Trinity Church. He studied at Yale under H. B. Jepson and Horatio Parker, and upon graduating he studied further in Berlin and Oxford. He taught music at South Dakota State College (1910-1912), was organist-choirmaster of Gethsemane Church, Minneapolis (1912-18), then professor of music at Carleton College, Northfield, Minnesota. Since 1921 he has been organist-choirmaster of St. Paul's Church, Baltimore, director of music at Goucher College, and an instructor at Peabody Conservatory.

W. LYNNWOOD FARNAM (1885-1930).
[See pages 159-60.]

(JAMES) MILES FARROW (1871-1953).
[See page 158.]

WILLIAM JOSEPH FINN, C.S.P. (1881-[†]) was born in Boston on September 7, 1881. He studied at St. Charles College, St. Thomas College, and Catholic University of America, with musical studies at the New England Conservatory and in London, Paris, and Rome. He was ordained in the Roman Catholic priesthood in 1906. His first choir work was at the Mission Church, Boston, where he was organist-choirmaster from 1902 to 1904. The following two years he served at St. Paul's Roman Catholic Church in Washington, and worked with various student groups. In 1906 he was assigned to Old St. Mary's— the Paulist Church in Chicago—where he developed his famous choir of men and boys, the Paulist Choristers. In his autobiography, *Sharps and Flats in Five Decades* (New York: Harper; 1947), Father Finn tells, by way of an anecdote of those early years, about the excitement of an Irish cable-car operator on Chicago's Indiana Avenue line while watching an impromptu raid of the St. Mary's boys on Harrison Wild's Episcopal boys at Grace Church. National fame came to the Paulist Choristers in 1918 as the result of a six-month tour to raise money for the restoration of war-damaged churches in France. Following the

[†]1961.

[211]

tour, Father Finn and many of his choristers transferred to the Paulist Church in New York City, where for five years he maintained the only Roman Catholic choir school in the country. With the advent of radio, his choir broadcast many concerts over the air. He was transferred back to Chicago in 1940. Recent years have seen a number of Paulist choirs conducted by his former pupils, with Father Finn devoting most of his own time to writing and lecturing. He is the author of a *Manual of Church Music* (1905), *An Epitome of Some Principles of Choral Technique* (1935), *The Art of the Choral Conductor* (1939), *Child Voice Training* (1944), and *The Conductor Raises His Baton* (1944). He was made Magister Cantorum by the Vatican in 1912. The August, 1934, issue of *Caecilia,* LX (1934), 287-331, is devoted to a discussion of his career.

ARTHUR WILLIAM FOOTE (1853-1937) is so well known today in the field of secular music that he is seldom remembered as a church musician. Born in Salem, Massachusetts, on March 5, 1853, he graduated from Harvard and studied with Stephen Emery, B. J. Lang, and J. K. Paine. From 1878 until 1910 he was organist at the First Unitarian Church, Boston. He was one of the founders of the American Guild of Organists and its president from 1909 to 1912. A fellow of the American Academy of Arts and Sciences, he received the honorary Doctor of Music degree from Trinity College, Hartford, in 1919. He composed well in all fields, with uniformly high quality. Besides various canticles, there are around twenty-five anthems of which "Still, still with thee," "God is our refuge," "And there were shepherds," and "Awake, thou that sleepest" have been especially popular. There are some twenty organ works of which the most significant is the *Suite in D,* Opus 54. He wrote and collaborated in several theory text-books. On Thanksgiving Day, 1914, organists throughout the country played his *Festival March in F* by common agreement in thanksgiving for his recovery from serious illness. He died in Boston on April 8, 1937. An autobiography was published in 1946.

HARVEY B. GAUL (1881-1945) was born in New York City on April 11, 1881. He should not be confused with the older English composer,

Alfred R. Gaul, whose cantata, *The Holy City,* was popular a genera-tion or so ago. Harvey Gaul first studied with Le Jeune and Dudley Buck, then in England with Armes and Alfred Gaul. From 1900 to 1908 he was organist-choirmaster of Emmanuel Church, Cleveland, director of the Hough Choral Club, and critic for the *News.* The next two years were spent in Paris, studying with Decaux, Guilmant, d'Indy, and Widor, and serving at St. Luke's Chapel. In 1910 he went to Pitts-burgh's Calvary Church, where he served the remainder of his life. He also taught at Carnegie Institute of Technology and other schools, and wrote extensively for various local newspapers. He composed over four hundred works, instrumental as well as choral, many being based on folk melodies. Outstanding is his *Prayer of Thanksgiving.* In 1941 the mayor of Pittsburgh proclaimed March 28th as "Harvey Gaul Day" in his honor. He received the honorary Doctor of Music degree from the University of Pittsburgh. Death came on December 1, 1945, as a result of injuries received in an automobile accident.

GRAHAM GEORGE (1912-) was born in Norwich, England, and came to Canada in 1928. He studied under Alfred Whitehead from 1932 to 1936. In 1934 he became an associate, and two years later a fellow, of the Canadian College of Organists. At the University of Toronto he earned the Bachelor of Music degree in 1936, the Doctor of Music degree in 1939, and won the Lallemand Prize for orchestral composition in 1938. During the Second World War he served overseas with the Canadian armed forces. Since 1946 he has taught at Queen's University and served as organist-choirmaster of St. James' Church, Kingston, Ontario. He has composed a number of anthems and other service music, as well as orchestral works, of which his *Variations for Strings,* won the C.A.P.A.C. Music Award for 1943.

(HAROLD) BECKET GIBBS (1868-†) was born in England on August 2, 1868. He began the study of plainsong under H. B. Briggs in 1890, two years later becoming a life member of the English Plainsong and Mediaeval Music Society. In 1893 he made the first of many visits to the Benedictine Abbey at Solesmes, forming a lifelong friendship with Dom Mocquereau. In 1905 he lectured at the first summer school that

†1956.

the Solesmes monks held at Quarr Abbey on the Isle of Wight. Under the sponsorship of the Plainsong and Mediaeval Music Society, he held many "plainsong missions" throughout England, working with both Anglican and Roman Catholic groups. In 1900 he founded the London Plainsong Choir. His last position in England was as organist-choir-master of St. Marie's Church, Sheffield. His coming to America was due to the direct appeal of Pope Pius X, who wished to have some of the English choirmasters come to this country to aid in creating conditions necessary for the success of his *Motu Proprio* of 1903. Gibbs first served at the Roman Catholic cathedral in Covington, Kentucky, where in 1905 he founded the Gregorian Congregation, a society which met monthly until he moved to New York in 1918. He had been in Covington but a short time when he was persuaded to move to the cathedral in Cincinnati and to give courses in church music at the Cincinnati Conservatory. Long active in the work of the Society of St. Gregory, he was Dom Mocquereau's accompanist at the International Congress of 1920 in New York. In 1915 he received the Doctorate in Gregorian Chant from the Pontifical Institute in Rome. He has served in a number of churches in the New York area and has taught in many summer institutes and other schools, including the Pius X School of Liturgical Music. For many years he has directed the Quilisma Club, sponsored by the Liturgical Arts Society. He is the author of a course in Gregorian aesthetics in the Catholic Choirmaster Correspondence Course and has published articles on "Congregational singing" in *Church Music,* I (1905/6), 21-33, "Music at Low Mass" in *The Catholic Choirmaster,* XXVI (September, 1940), 107-8, 111, and "The foibles of organists" in *Caecilia,* LXV (1938), 139-141.

WALTER BOND GILBERT (1829-1910) was born in Exeter, England, on April 21, 1829. He studied with Angel, Wesley, and Bishop, taking an Oxford degree in 1854. He was one of the founders of the Royal College of Organists, and played in a number of English churches before coming to New York to play at Trinity Chapel. He was highly respected during the remainder of the century as player, composer, and editor, although his anthem style was the homophonic simplicity of the early Victorians, scarcely distinguishable from his hymn-tunes, and with no independent organ part. He edited *The Parish Church Manual* (1854), *The Canticles* (1856), *The Church Chorister* (1872), *The Hymnal* (1872), and *The Psalter* (1882). His oratorio *St. John* appeared in 1857, *The Restoration of Israel* in 1859, and his *Organ Preludes and Fugues* in 1880. He received the Doctor of Music degrees from both the University of Toronto (1886) and Oxford University (1888). He was pensioned in 1899 and subsequently returned to England. He died in Oxford on March 2, 1910.

WILLIAM WALLACE GILCHRIST (1846-1916) was active in the last decades of the nineteenth century, but his compositions have a style which is well in advance of others of his own era. He was born in Jersey City on January 8, 1846, and studied with H. A. Clarke at the University of Pennsylvania. Thereafter his life was closely affiliated with the musical activities of Philadelphia. He was organist-choir-master at St. Clement's Church (1873-77), then at Christ Church, Germantown (1877-82). After 1882 he taught at the Philadelphia Academy of Music and served at the Swedenborgian Church. In 1874 he organized and for forty years directed the Philadelphia Mendelssohn Club. His choral compositions won early recognition, a setting of Psalm XLVI winning a thousand-dollar prize at the Cincinnati Festival in 1882. He wrote many fine anthems and also three oratorios: *The Easter Idyll, The Lamb of God* (1909), and *The Christmas Oratorio* (1911). With James A. Moore he edited *The Hymnal Companion to the Prayer Book* for the Reformed Episcopal Church in 1885, and a Presbyterian hymnal in 1895. He received an honorary Doctor of Music degree from the University of Pennsylvania in 1896, and was a founder of the American Guild of Organists. He died at Easton, Pennsylvania, on December 19, 1916. His career is discussed by W. H. Hall in the *New Music Review*, XVI (1917), 470-1.

(JOHN) WALLACE GOODRICH (1871-1952) was born in Newton, Massachusetts, on May 27, 1871. He studied first with Petersilea, Dunham, and Chadwick, while serving as organist at the Newton Baptist Church (1886-9) and the Eliot Church (Congregational) in Newton (1889-94). He then spent a year in Munich under Rheinberger and Abel, followed by a year in Paris with Widor. The years 1896 and 1897 were spent in Leipzig as a coach and ballet conductor at the Stadt-Theater. Returning to Boston, he became an organ instructor at the New England Conservatory and organist to the Boston Symphony Orchestra. In 1905 and 1906 he was acting director of the Conservatory, the following year becoming dean of the faculty. In 1930 he succeeded Chadwick as director of the Conservatory. He retired in 1942 and died on June 6, 1952. Organist-choirmaster at the Church of the Messiah (1901-2) and at Trinity Church, Boston (1902-9), he retained an active interest in the problems of church music throughout his academic career, giving many organ recitals, conducting, lecturing, and writing articles in this field. In 1902 he founded, and until 1907 conducted, the Choral Art Society of Boston, one of the first organizations in the country devoted to *a cappella* singing. He composed a number of anthems and a requiem mass. He published translations of Pirro's *J. S. Bach and His Works for the Organ* (1902), and of Niedermeyer and D'Ortigue's *Gregorian Accompaniment* (1905). He wrote *The Organ in France* (1917), and history, *The Parish of the Advent in the City of Boston* (1944), where he was a member of the corporation, music committee, and junior warden. He was a member of the Episcopal Church's Hymnal Commission from 1916 to 1918, and secretary of its Joint Commission on Church Music from its inception in 1919 until 1949. In the latter capacity he was active in the preparation of *The Choral Service* (1927), *The American Psalter* (1929), and several issues of *A List of Texts of Anthems Approved by the General Conventions . . . of the Protestant Episcopal Church*. He was a fellow of the American Academy of Arts and Sciences and a Chevalier of the French Légion d'Honneur. He received the honorary Doctor of Music degree from Northwestern University in 1931.

WALTER HENRY HALL (1862-1935).

[See page 156.]

WILLIAM CHURCHILL HAMMOND (1860-1949) was born in Rockville, Connecticut, on November 25, 1860. He studied organ with Nathan H.

Allen in Hartford and Samuel P. Warren in New York. From 1890 to 1900 he taught organ at Smith College, and from 1900 until his retirement in 1937 was head of the music department of Mount Holyoke College, where he received the honorary Doctor of Music degree in 1925. From 1924 to 1936 the annual carol concert of his Mount Holyoke Glee Club was a New York tradition. For sixty-four years— from 1885 until his death in 1949—he served as organist-choirmaster of the Second Congregational Church in Holyoke, Massachusetts. He was one of the founders of the American Guild of Organists. Death came to him on Easter Even, April 16, 1949, only a few hours after he had played for the Good Friday services.

CHARLES F. HANSEN (1867-1947) was born in Lafayette, Indiana. Blind from birth, he went to the State School of the Blind, at Indianapolis, when ten years old. Early interested in the organ, he studied under Robert A. Newland, and first played at the Fletcher Place Methodist Church, using a reed organ. He played for two years at the Mayflower Congregational Church of Indianapolis—this time on a pipe organ. He served at the Meridian Street Methodist Church from 1887 to 1897. Upon his teacher's retirement in January, 1898, he went to the Second Presbyterian Church where he was organist and director of the quartet choir until a few weeks before his death on May 24, 1947. He composed a number of choral responses and hymn tunes. Pupils flocked to him from all parts of the state. He did considerable recital work, being particularly adept at playing "bird song" descants to hymn tunes. He received an honorary Doctor of Music degree from Hanover College.

LOUIS H. HAST (? -1890) was born in the Upper Palatinate, Germany, and spent his boyhood in Spires (Speyer) where an uncle was the archbishop. Coming over to Kentucky, he first taught music in Bardstown, settling at Louisville in 1851. There he soon became an outstanding leader and pioneer in the introduction of finer music into that section of the South. He organized and directed many concerts of chamber, choral and orchestral music, a Beethoven Club, La Reunion Musicale, and a Philharmonic Society. From 1878 to 1889 he was the organist-choirmaster of Christ Church Cathedral, and trained the choir to sing plainsong and *a cappella* motets, as well as works like the Handel *Dettingen Te Deum*. His music library is preserved in the University of Louisville.

THOMAS HASTINGS (1784-1872) was born October 15, 1784, at Washington, Connecticut, the son of a country physician. When about twelve years of age he moved with his parents by ox-sledge to Clinton, New York, where he lived the rigorous life of what was then the frontier. An albino, and very near-sighted, he taught himself the rudiments of music. At eighteen, he was leading a country choir and had begun to compile tune-books. In 1816 he became connected with the Oneida County Musical Society, for which he compiled the *Utica Collection,* a work that went through a number of later editions under the title *Musica Sacra.* From 1823 to 1832 he was the editor of the Utica *Western Recorder,* a weekly paper which gave him many opportunities to spread the gospel of good singing. Moving to New York City in 1832, he joined forces with Lowell Mason and produced the *Spiritual Songs for Social Worship.* In 1836 he founded *The Musical Magazine,* in which he gave further expression to his high ideals for sacred music. Already, in his *Dissertation on Musical Taste* (1822), he had set forth tenets which, widely read over a period of thirty years, exerted considerable influence throughout the country. His *History of Forty Choirs* (1854) consists of sketches illustrative of his own experiences with choirs, clergy, directors, and congregations. In 1858, New York University conferred on him the Doctor of Music degree. He is said to have written 600 hymn texts and to have composed some 1,000 tunes, besides issuing 50 volumes of music. For 40 years he was an integral part of the life of New York, whence his influence radiated throughout the United States. Death came on May 15, 1872. His diary for the years 1832-46 is preserved with other relics at Union Theological Seminary in New York. There is a biography by Mary Browning Scanlon in the *Musical Quarterly,* XXXII (1946), 265-77.

EDWARD HODGES (1796-1867).
[See pages 110-11.]

JOHN SEBASTIAN BACH HODGES (1830-1915) the son of Edward Hodges, was born in the cloisters of Bristol Cathedral, England, and was brought to this country in 1845. He graduated from Columbia College (A.B., 1850; M.A., 1853), and from the General Theological Seminary in 1854. Racine College honored him with the Doctor of Sacred Theology degree in 1867. Ordained deacon in 1854 and priest in 1855, he was an assistant at Trinity Church, Pittsburgh, from 1854 to 1856. For the next three years he taught at Nashotah House Seminary, Wisconsin, also serving at the Church of the Holy Communion, Chicago. In 1860 he became rector of Grace Church, Newark, New Jersey. In 1870 he began a thirty-five year tenure at St. Paul's Church, Baltimore, where he was instrumental in building an outstanding choir of men and boys. He retired in 1906 and died in Baltimore on May 1, 1915. He was active in the work of the Episcopal Hymnal commissions of 1874 and 1892. He composed over one hundred hymn-tunes and anthems, compiled *The Book of Common Praise* (1868), and the collection, *Hymn Tunes,* revised edition 1903.

OLIVER HOLDEN (1765-1844).
[See page 51.]

JOHN HENRY HOPKINS, JR. (1820-1891) was born in Pittsburgh on October 28, 1820, the eldest son of pioneer parents—the father from Dublin and the mother from Hamburg. His father was successively an ironmaster, school teacher, lawyer, priest, the second Bishop of Vermont, and Presiding Bishop of the Episcoal Church. The son reflected the artistic talents of both parents in music, poetry, and art. After graduation from the University of Vermont in 1839 he worked as a reporter in New York while studying law. From 1842 to 1844 he tutored the children of Bishop Elliott in Savannah, returning to take his Master of Arts degree from the University of Vermont in 1845. He graduated from the General Theological Seminary in 1850 and was ordained deacon. From 1855 to 1857 he served as the first instructor in church music at that seminary. He founded the *Church Journal* and was its editor from 1853 to 1868. During these years he took an active interest in the Church Choral Society and the New York Ecclesiological Society, where his artistic talents revealed themselves through his designs for stained-glass windows, episcopal seals, and a wide variety of other church *ornamenta*. Simultaneously his musical talents led to the writing and composing of a number of fine hymn texts and tunes, anthems, and services. He was ordained priest in 1872, and thereafter served as rector of Trinity Church, Plattsburg, New York (1872-6) and Christ Church, Williamsport, Pennsylvania (1876-87). He died at a friend's home near Hudson, New York, on August 14, 1891. Well known for his carol "We three kings of Orient are," Hopkins was one of the leaders in the development of Episcopal Church hymnody during the mid-nineteenth century. His *Carols, Hymns, and Songs,* first published in 1863, went to a fourth edition (1883). His *Canticles Noted with Accompanying Harmonies* (1866) likewise went through several editions. His collected *Poems by the Wayside* was published in 1883. In 1887 he edited Bishop John Freeman Young's *Great Hymns of the Church.* His biography was written by Charles Filkins Sweet, *A Champion of the Cross* (New York: Pott, 1894).

FRANCIS HOPKINSON (1737-1791).

[See pages 47-9.]

GEORGE K. JACKSON (1745-1823) had been a boy chorister in the English Chapel Royal, and later a teacher and author of harmony texts. He sang tenor at the Handel Commemoration of 1784, and received the Doctor of Music degree from St. Andrew's College in 1791. Five years later, he came over to Norfolk, Virginia, where he taught and played the organ. After a short time, he moved up the coast, playing successively in churches at Alexandria, Virginia, Baltimore, Philadelphia, Elizabeth, New Jersey, and New York, where, in 1804, he was serving at St. George's Chapel. In 1812 he removed to Boston, where he played in turn at the Brattle Street Church, King's Chapel, Trinity Church, and St. John's Church. He compiled several tune-books and was instrumental in obtaining publication of Lowell Mason's first collection by the Boston Handel and Haydn Society. A collection of his music is preserved in the library of the Harvard Musical Association.

PHILIP (FREDERICK WRIGHT) JAMES (1890-) was born in Jersey City on May 17, 1890. He graduated from the College of the City of New York, and served overseas during the First World War. He has served as organist-choirmaster of St. Luke's Church, Montclair, New Jersey (1919-21), and St. Mark's-in-the-Bouwerie, New York (1922-23). He conducted the Victor Herbert Opera Company (1919-22), the New Jersey Symphony Orchestra (1922-29), the Brooklyn Orchestral Society (1927-30), and the Bamberger Little Symphony of Radio Station WOR, Newark (1929-36). Since 1933 he has been chairman of the music department at Washington Square College of New York University. He has won numerous prizes for his orchestral composition, and has composed a number of cantatas and anthems. He became a fellow of the American Guild of Organists in 1910, and received an honorary Doctor of Music degree from the New York College of Music in 1946.

JOHN HARRIS KNOWLES (1832-1908) was born in Cork, Ireland, on April 24, 1832. When eighteen, he came to Chicago and three years later began to study for the ministry. For a while, during his student days at General Theological Seminary, he sang in Cutler's choir at Trinity Church. After his ordination, he served for a time in Aurora and Naperville, Illinois. In 1867, he went to the cathedral in Chicago as canon precentor, where he initiated the work discussed on page 78. In 1884 he became rector of St. Clement's Church, Chicago, leaving in the nineties to join the staff of Trinity Parish in New York. His last years were spent as curate of St. Chrysostom's Chapel. He died in New York on July 6, 1908. There is a portrait of Knowles in Granville L. Howe, *A Hundred Years of Music in America* (Chicago: 1889), p. 266.

FELIX LAMOND (1864-1940).
[See pages 156-57.]

BENJAMIN JOHNSON LANG (1837-1909), teacher of Arthur Foote and Ethelbert Nevin, was the outstanding Boston musician for an entire generation. He was born in Salem, Massachusetts, on December 28, 1837, and studied in Europe with Satter, Jaell, and Liszt. He composed many works, including an oratorio, *David,* but permitted almost none of them to be published—rightly judging them to have no lasting merit. In Boston he was organist at Dr. Neale's church, Old South Church, and at the South Congregational Church before going to King's Chapel in 1885. He was also organist for the Handel and Haydn Society (1859-95) and its director (1895-7). He founded and directed the Boston Apollo Club (1871-1901), the Cecilia Club (1874-1907), and was one of the founders of the American Guild of Organists. He died in Boston on April 3, 1909.

CHANNING LEFEBVRE (1895-†) was born in Richmond, Virginia, on September 30, 1895. He studied organ under Harold D. Phillips at Peabody Conservatory, Baltimore, and under Gaston Dethier at the Institute of Musical Art in New York. In 1912 he became assistant organist under Miles Farrow at the Cathedral of St. John the Divine, leaving in 1917 to serve at sea with the United States Navy. After the war he served for two years as organist-choirmaster at St. Luke's Church, Montclair, New Jersey, moving to Trinity Church, New York, on May 1, 1922. During his years at Trinity he introduced the use of plainsong and built up an extensive repertory of sixteenth-century polyphonic works by Palestrina, Byrd, Gibbons, and others. He founded the Down Town Glee Club in 1927 and directed it until 1941; he has directed the University Glee Club of New York since 1927. He resigned from Trinity on September 15, 1941, to become the director of music at St. Paul's School, Concord, New Hampshire. A fellow of the American Guild of Organists since 1915, he has been its secretary, chairman of the examination committee, and warden (1939-41). He has served for many years on the Joint Commission on Church Music of the Episcopal Church. He has composed a Communion Service in A flat, numerous anthems, secular works for mixed, male, and women's chorus, and many arrangements of folk-songs.

GEORGE FITZ CURWOOD LE JEUNE (1841-1904) was born in London on June 18, 1841, the son of an eminent composer and organist. He studied with Barnby and Macfarren in London, and with the cathedral organist in Montreal. Coming to the United States, he served at the

†1967.

Pearl Street Church, Hartford, at St. Luke's Church, Philadelphia, and, from 1871 to 1876, at the Anthon Memorial Church, New York. While at St. Luke's, he lived in the same house with J. Kendrick Pyne who was building a boy choir at St. Mark's Church at the time. He put Pyne's methods to good use when he moved to St. John's Chapel, New York, in 1786, developing one of the outstanding boy choirs in the country. A great exponent of elaborate services, complete Schubert, Mozart, and Haydn masses were the regular bill for his Sunday programs. Among his pupils were Harvey B. Gaul, Felix Lamond, and George E. Stubbs. He composed a Communion Service in C, a number of anthems, and a collection, *Twenty-four Hymns*. He died on Staten Island, New York, on April 11, 1904.

PETER CHRISTIAN LUTKIN (1858-1931) was born on March 27, 1858, in Thompsonville, Wisconsin, of Danish parents. In 1869 the family moved to Chicago, where he served as a choir boy under Canon Knowles. At fourteen he became the organist at St. James' Church. His talent attracted the attention of friends who made it possible for him to study abroad from 1881 to 1884. Returning to Chicago, he was organist-choirmaster for Father Knowles at St. Clement's Church (1884-1891) and again at St. James' (1891-1896). From 1885 to 1895 he was director of the theory department at the American Conservatory. In 1896 the trustees of Northwestern University set up a School of Music under his direction. There his pioneering work exerted a profound influence upon the development of music education at the collegiate level in this country. His *a cappella* choir, founded in 1906, was long pre-eminent in its field. In 1908 he established the annual North Shore Festivals, which he continued to direct until 1930. His interest in church music was always intense, as witnessed by the strength of the department established by him at Northwestern. He served on the hymnal commissions of both the Episcopal and Methodist churches. As a composer, he left a number of canticles, anthems, hymn tunes, and instrumental compositions. Lutkin received an honorary Doctor of Music degree from Syracuse University in 1900. He was a founder of the American Guild of Organists, and was active in the work of the Music Teachers' National Association, being its president in 1911 and 1920. He died in Evanston, Illinois, on December 27, 1931, while engaged with Charles Macaulay Stuart in the preparation of a new hymnal. A memorial pamphlet with portrait, biography, and list of compositions was issued in 1932 as Bulletin No. VII of the Department of Church and Choral Music, Northwestern University.

JAMES LYON (1735-1794) first came to attention as a student at Princeton, where he composed a graduation ode in 1759. He settled in Philadelphia where, in 1762, he brought out the first tune-book in America to contain fuging tunes, as well as the first to be published outside New England and under purely commercial auspices. Shortly after his *Urania: Or a choice collection of Psalm Tunes, Anthems, or Hymns* appeared, Lyon became a Presbyterian minister and settled in Nova Scotia.

HUGH A. MACKINNON (1891-) was born in St. Johnsbury, Vermont, on May 20, 1891. He attended Dartmouth College (1910-14) and the Trinity School of Church Music, New York City (1914-16). There he studied organ under Felix Lamond, analysis with Alfred Madeley Richardson, counterpoint with Frank E. Ward, composition with Mark Andrews, ear-training with Ernest Ashe, and the boy voice with Beecher Aldrich. As a student he had played the organ and directed the choir at St. Andrew's Church, St. Johnsbury (1906-9), and played the organ at St. Thomas' Church, Hanover, New Hampshire (1911-12). He subsequently served as organist-choirmaster at St. Andrew's Church, Newark, New Jersey (1914-15), Church of the Transfiguration, New York (1915-16), St. Luke's Church, East Hampton, Long Island (1917-18), Grace Church, Utica, New York (1918-22), St. Matthew's Cathedral, Laramie, Wyoming (1929-42), and Grace Cathedral, San Francisco (1942-46). Since 1946 he has been in Laramie, teaching organ and theory at the University of Wyoming and playing the organ at St. Matthew's Cathedral. He became a fellow of the American Guild of Organists in 1916. He has composed some twenty-five anthems and carols, and ten songs.

LOWELL MASON (1792-1872) was born in Medfield, Massachusetts, on January 8, 1792. His music training was from two local tune-book compilers, Amos Albee, the local schoolmaster, and Oliver Shaw of nearby Dedham. He was also intimate with the village bandmaster, George Whitefield Adams, and a violinist, James Clark. At sixteen, he was leading the village choir and directing singing schools. In 1812 he moved to Savannah, where he worked in a bank and served as organist-choirmaster of the First Presbyterian Church. He studied harmony with F. L. Abel and compiled his first tune-book, based on William Gardiner's *Sacred Melodies.* This appeared, thanks to George K. Jackson's interest, in 1821 as *The Boston Handel & Haydn Society Collection of Church Music.* His *Address on Church Music,* given in 1826, is an interesting exhortation toward choir betterment. Mason moved to Boston in 1827, became president of the Handel and Haydn Society and for fourteen years served as choirmaster of Lyman Beecher's Bowdoin Street Church. His first children's book, *The Juvenile Psalmist,* appeared in 1829. Concerned over the need for juvenile instruction, he established in 1832 the Boston Academy of Music, which featured large singing classes for children. In 1838 he secured the introduction of music to the public school curriculum of Boston and in 1834 introduced an annual teacher-training class at the Academy, a work he later extended throughout the country by means of musical conventions, teacher's institutes, and musical normal institutes. Mason visited Europe twice—in 1837 to study at first hand the Pestalozzian methods of teaching, and during 1851-3 when he lectured in many cities. Returning, he made his home in Orange, New Jersey, where he died on August 11, 1872. New York University awarded him the Doctor of Music degree in 1855. His large library, acquired in the process of editing his many collections, is now in the School of Music at Yale University. His biography has been written by Arthur Lowndes Rich: *Lowell Mason, "the father of singing among the children"* (Chapel Hill: University of North Carolina Press, 1946). There is a complete index to his many hymn-tunes, compiled by his nephew, Henry Lowell Mason: *Hymn-tunes of Lowell Mason, a Bibliography* (Cambridge, Mass.: The University Press, 1944).

H. ALEXANDER MATTHEWS (1879-) was born in Cheltenham, England, on March 26, 1879. His early musical training, like that of his brother John Sebastian, was from his father, John Alexander Matthews, for over forty-five years conductor of the Cheltenham Festivals. He came over to Philadelphia in 1900, continuing music studies with Gilchrist and George A. A. West. He was organist-choirmaster of several churches, and for a time taught and directed music at the University of Pennsylvania. From 1916 to 1937 he served at the Church of St. Luke and The Epiphany. Since then he has served at St. Stephen's Church, conducted the Philadelphia Music Club Chorus, and directed the theory department of Clarke Conservatory of Music. He received honorary Doctor of Music degrees from Muhlenberg College (1920) and from the University of Pennsylvania. He is an associate of the American Guild of Organists and a member of the Philadelphia Art Alliance. He has composed over three hundred works—cantatas, anthems, solos, organ and piano pieces. Notable among these are his cantata *The City of God*, commissioned for the quadricentennial of the Reformation, his *Introits and Graduals of the Church Year*, and several groups of organ preludes on hymn tunes.

ABRAHAM MAXIM (1773-1829).

[See pages 50-1.]

ROBERT GUY McCUTCHAN (1877-†) was born in Mountayr, Iowa, on September 13, 1877. He graduated from Park College in 1898, and took a Bachelor of Music degree from Simpson College in 1904. He organized the music department at Baker University during the years 1904-10. Following a year of study in France and Germany, he became dean of the School of Music at DePauw University, where he remained until his retirement in 1937. During the First World War he was active in promoting community singing. He has been president of the Indiana Music Teachers' Association and the National Association of Church Choir Directors, and secretary of the Music Teachers' National Association. He organized and directed (1919-27) the Bay View (Michigan) Summer School of Music. He has served on a number of special commissions of the Methodist Church devoted to hymnody, liturgy, and music. He was music editor of *The Methodist Hymnal* of 1935,

†1958.

and of several smaller collections for church schools. He has written *Our Hymnody* (1937; second edition 1942) and many monographs and articles on church music.

GEORGE MEAD (1902-) was born in New York City on May 21, 1902. As a boy he sang in the Chapel of St. Cornelius the Centurion, Governor's Island. He attended Trinity School and Columbia College, receiving from the latter his Bachelor of Arts degree in 1923. Awarded the Baier Fellowship in Music at Columbia University, he proceeded to the Master of Arts degree in 1925. He became an associate of the American Guild of Organists in 1930. His principal teachers were Seth Bingham in theory, Daniel Gregory Mason in analysis, Channing Lefebvre and Charles Doersam in organ, George Bowden in voice, and Chalmers Clifton in conducting. He has served as assistant organist-choirmaster of Trinity Church (1925-35), organist-choirmaster of the Central Congregational Church, Brooklyn (1936-40), the First Unitarian Church, Brooklyn (1940-41), and since 1941 at Trinity Church, New York. He was also director of music at St. Agatha School (1930-41) and at Hofstra College (1936-40). He has been conductor of the Lyric Club of Newark, the Scarsdale Choral Society, the Brooklyn Heights Madrigal Club, the Down Town Glee Club since 1941, the Glee Club of the Friendly Sons of St. Patrick since 1934, and the Golden Hill Chorus since 1941. His *Fantasy,* for organ, was an American Guild of Organists-*Diapason* prize winner. He has composed a *Short Mass* in three parts, and several anthems, including *I have surely built thee an house,* for chorus and orchestra, on the occasion of the hundredth anniversary of the present Trinity Church building. Other works include his one-act *Brokers' Opera,* introits, carol arrangements, and various secular works for men's, women's, and mixed chorus. He has served on the national council of the American Guild of Organists and as chairman of their Committee on a Code of Ethics, and the Committee for Guild Sunday. He received an honorary Doctor of Music degree from Columbia University in 1945.

ARTHUR HENRY MESSITER (1834-1916) was born in Frome, Somerset, on April 12, 1834. He was articled to McKorkell of Northampton and

[227]

then studied under the Austrian Derfell. Coming to New York in 1863, he sang for a time under Cutler, then moved to Philadelphia where he played successively at St. Mark's, St. Paul's, Calvary Chapel, and St. James the Less. He was called to Trinity Church, New York, in 1866 at the age of thirty-two. There he built on the foundation laid by Cutler, at times attempting too much, as in the use of Macfarren's "Procession of the Ark" from *David* as a processional anthem, but soon recognizing the faulty usage. In his chanting, he must have come close to the modern concept of speech rhythm. A purist and excellent accompanist, he maintained remarkably high standards at Trinity Church. He also composed a few worthy anthems. After 1897, he lived in retirement in New York, publishing in 1906 the *History of the Choir and Music of Trinity Church*. He died on July 2, 1916.

NICOLA ALOYSIUS MONTANI (1880-1948) in many respects was the inheritor of Singenberger's mantle, especially in the East. He was born in Utica, New York, on November 6, 1880. His musical training was under Perosi and Capocci in Rome (1900-04) and under the plainsong specialists Dom Mocquereau and Dom Eudine during the years 1905-06, when the Solesmes monks were living on the Isle of Wight. Returning to America, he settled in Philadelphia where he served as organist-choirmaster of the Church of Saint John the Evangelist from 1906 to 1923. He served at the Paulist Church in New York City during 1923-24, then spent the remainder of his life teaching music in various seminaries and colleges, conducting festivals, and in editorial work. In 1913 he was active in founding the Society of St. Gregory; for over twenty-five years he was the editor of its journal, *The Catholic Choirmaster*. He also edited the *St. Gregory Hymnal*, the *Catholic Choirbook*, liturgical music catalogs for G. Schirmer & Co., and the Boston Music Company, wrote *The Art of A Cappella Singing* and *Essentials in Sight Singing* (1931), and composed eight masses, a *Stabat Mater*, various motets and other pieces. He was associated with the Pontifical Institute of Sacred Music, and in 1926 was made Knight Commander of the Order of St. Sylvester. He died on January 11, 1948. There are articles on his career in *Caecilia*, LXI (1935), 335-381, and *The Catholic Choirmaster*, XXXIV (1948), 5-8, 36.

THOMAS TERTIUS NOBLE (1867-1953).
[See pages 157-58.]

HENRY KEMBLE OLIVER (1800-1885) was born at Beverly, Massachusetts, on November 24, 1800. He studied at Boston Latin School and at Phillips Andover Academy, spent two years at Harvard, and graduated from Dartmouth in 1818. Harvard conferred the Master of Arts degree on him in 1862 and Dartmouth the Doctor of Music degree in 1883. When but ten years old he was singing regularly in the Park Street Church. In 1823 he became organist of St. Peter's Church, Salem, Massachusetts. Two years later he went to the North Church, Boston, where he served for twenty years. After that, he served for fifteen years in the Unitarian Church of Lawrence, Massachusetts. A leader in civic affairs as well as musician and teacher, he was mayor of both Lawrence and Salem, and was state treasurer from 1861 to 1865. In Salem, he conducted a boy's school which he later converted into a school for girls. He organized the Mozart Association and the Salem Glee Club. He died in Salem on August 12, 1885. With Tuckerman and Bancroft he published the *National Lyre* (1848). His *Hymn and Psalm Tunes* first appeared in 1860, his *Original Hymn Tunes* in 1875. A biography by Jesse Henry Jones was published in 1886.

HORATIO WILLIAM PARKER (1863-1919).
[See pages 154-55.]

JAMES CUTLER DUNN PARKER (1828-1916) was organist-choirmaster at Trinity Church, Boston, from 1864 to 1891, and taught at the New England Conservatory and Boston University until his retirement in 1912. He was born in Boston on June 2, 1828, graduated from Harvard in 1848 and then studied law for three years. He spent the years 1851 to 1854 in Leipzig, studying under Hauptmann, Richter, and Moscheles. His music was too sweet, but was good for its day; among his best works are the cantata *Redemption Hymn* (1877), and the oratorio *Life of Man* (1895), both long popular with choral societies. He translated Richter's *Manual of Harmony* and then published two of his own (in 1855 and 1870). He died in Brookline, Massachusetts, on November 27, 1916.

WALDO SELDON PRATT (1857-1939) was born in Philadelphia on November 10, 1857. He graduated from Williams College in 1878, and then spent two years in further study at Johns Hopkins University, majoring in art and the classics. After two more years as assistant director of the Metropolitan Museum of Art, he settled in 1882 in Hartford, where he lectured at the Theological Seminary for the remainder of his life. From 1905 to 1920 he also lectured at the Institute of Musical Art in New York. Long a member and officer of the Music Teacher's National Association, he lectured and directed choral groups in many cities. From 1912 to 1919 he was president of the American section of the International Music Society. He received the Doctor of Music degree from Syracuse University in 1898 and the Doctorate of Humane Letters from Williams College in 1929. He published many articles on church music. His *History of Music* (1907) was long a standard text, as were his *American Supplement to Grove's Dictionary of Music and Musicians* and his own *Encyclopedia of Music.* His final work was a detailed study entitled *The Music of the French Psalter* (1939). He died in Hartford on July 29, 1939.

RICHARD IRVEN PURVIS (1915-) was born in San Francisco on August 25, 1915. He studied at the Peabody Conservatory, Baltimore, then at the Curtis Institute of Music, Philadelphia. Going to England for further work, he studied at the Royal School of Church Music and at Quarr Abbey on the Isle of Wight. His principal teachers have been Wallace Sabin, Benjamin S. Moore, Alexander McCurdy, David McK. Williams, Charles Courboin, Sidney Nicholson, and Edward Bairstow. He played his first service when nine years old, in the Trinity Presbyterian Church of San Francisco. Two years later he became regular organist at St. James' Church, Oakland, and the following year appeared in recital in the San Francisco Civic Auditorium. He was organist-choirmaster of St. James' Church, Philadelphia, and head of the organ and music department at Episcopal Academy, Overbrook (1937-1941). Enlisting in the United States Army, he saw service in Europe as bandmaster of the 28th Infantry Division, spending the last six months of the war in a German prison camp. After the war he returned to his native San Francisco, where he has served as organist-choirmaster in St. Mark's Lutheran Church (1947-48) and since then at Grace Cathedral. He has composed two communion services, carols, and other services.

JAMES HOTCHKISS ROGERS (1857-1940) was a Cleveland organist, but his compositions made him nationally famous. He was born in Fair Haven, Connecticut, on February 7, 1857. He studied with Clarence Eddy in Chicago, Haupt and Loeschorn in Berlin, and Guilmant and Widor in Paris. In 1883 he settled in Cleveland, where he served as organist in the Euclid Avenue Temple and the First Unitarian Church. For many years he was also music critic for the Cleveland *Plain-Dealer*. An able teacher, he was a successful composer for choir and organ. He wrote in the quartet style so prevalent at the turn of the century, but with sufficient originality that many of his anthems are still popular. He also composed lighter works, such as "The Ninety and Nine," under the pseudonym of Edward Campion. He died in Pasadena, California, on November 28, 1940.

CARLO ROSSINI (1890-) was born in Osimo, Italy, on March 3, 1890, and was priested in 1913. During the First World War he served as a chaplain with the Italian Army. He studied plainsong, organ, and composition under Perosi, Casimiri, Dobici, and Dagnino at the Pontifical Institute of Sacred Music in Rome, receiving the degree of Master of Gregorian Chant in 1920. Coming to the United States in 1921, he was first associated with the Scalabrinian Fathers of St. Charles Borromeo, then went to the Church of the Epiphany, Pittsburgh, in 1923 as organist-choirmaster. The following year he organized the Pittsburgh Polyphonic Choir. From 1926 to 1949 he served at St. Paul's Cathedral in Pittsburgh, becoming chairman of the Diocesan Music Commission in 1930. Since 1949 he has been the Acting Secretary-General of the St. Caecilia Association in Rome. He received the Benemerenti Medal from Pius XII in 1951. He has composed over fifteen masses, many motets and anthems, and arranged ten volumes of liturgical music for the organ. He has also edited several choir-books and school text-books of plainsong, a volume of organ accompaniments to the *Kyriale* (1942), and *The Parochial Hymnal* (1936).

IRA DAVID SANKEY (1840-1908) was born on August 28, 1840, in Edenburg, Pennsylvania, going to New Castle, Pennsylvania, when seventeen. He had been "converted" at a revival meeting in King's Chapel Church a year earlier, and in New Castle soon became active as Sunday school superintendent and choir leader in the First Methodist Church. At that time (*ca.* 1858), members of his church still objected to the use of any musical instrument other than the tuning fork, and a few actually left the church when a reed organ was introduced several years later. When near twenty, he attended a musical convention conducted by William B. Bradbury at Farmington, Ohio. During the Civil War, he served with the 22nd Regiment of Pennsylvania Volunteers, then worked in the Internal Revenue Office at New Castle until he met Dwight L. Moody at a Young Men's Christian Association convention at Indianapolis in 1870. Moody was greatly impressed with Sankey's ability as a song leader, and after much urging was able to persuade Sankey to join his work in Chicago. In 1873 they made their first trip to England and thereafter toured both the United States and Great Britain, holding revival meetings wherever they went, until Moody's death in 1899. Sankey died on August 13, 1908, in Brooklyn. He was totally blind during his last five years. Sankey compiled a number of gospel song-books, including a series of six *Gospel Hymns* with James McGranahan and George C. Stebbins. Profits from the sale of these collections built Carrubber's Close Mission in Edinburgh, Scotland, two buildings for The Northfield Schools in Massachusetts, and assisted with those of the Y.M.C.A. and First Methodist Church in New Castle. There is a memorial window in the latter which portrays Sankey's famous gospel song "The ninety and nine." In 1941 the Lawrence County, Pennsylvania, Historical Society published the *Ira D. Sankey Centenary Proceedings.*

MARY CHERUBIM SCHAEFER, O.S.F. (1886-) was born in Slinger, Wisconsin, on January 11, 1886. She studied privately with Singenberger, Semmann, Zeitz, and at Marquette University, earning the Bachelor of Music degree in 1922. She joined the Sisters of St. Francis in 1903 and was professed in 1906. She served as organist-choirmaster in St. Lawrence's Church, Milwaukee (1904-09), and as director of music at St. Joseph's Convent (1909-24). She founded and directed the St. Joseph's Conservatory of Music (1924-33) and its College of Music, now known as the Alverno College of Music (1933-38). In 1938 she received the Caecilian Society Award. Since that year she has devoted all of her time to composing. She is the author of *Music Appreciation for Schools* (1933-36), *The Liturgical Choir Book* (1939), and *The Organist's Companion* (1945), and has composed many masses, hymns, and motets. The August, 1938, issue of *Caecilia*, LXV (1938), 245-280, is devoted to discussions of her work.

J. ALFRED SCHEHL (1882-[†]) was born in Cincinnati on July 12, 1882, the son of John A. Schehl, long a prominent organist in German-American Catholic circles. He studied at St. Francis Xavier College and at Cincinnati Conservatory. His music career began as a violinist in the Cincinnati Symphony Orchestra (1898-1908), and as chorus director and accompanist for the May Music Festival (1906-12). He was organist-choirmaster first at Holy Trinity Church (1899-1904), then at St. John's Church (1904-12). Since 1912 he has served at St. Lawrence's Church. He has also been professor of organ at the Archdiocese Teacher's College, and director of music at Elder High School. He became an associate of the American Guild of Organists in 1916. In 1937 he was the general chairman of its convention in Cincinnati. He has composed a number of masses and other works, and was the editor of the *St. Caecilia Hymnal* (1929), a work containing many of the old German Catholic chorales and *Singmessen* for use at Low Mass.

HARRY ROWE SHELLEY (1858-1947).
    [See page 154.]

ERNEST ARTHUR SIMON (1862-1950) was born in London, England, on July 15, 1862. He first settled in Chicago, then went to Louisville, Kentucky, where he was organist-choirmaster at Christ Church Cathedral for forty-five years (1901-46), profoundly influencing church music throughout that area. He died in Louisville on May 2, 1950.

JOHN BAPTIST SINGENBERGER (1848-1924).
    [See pages 107-8.]

[†]1959.

LEO SOWERBY (1895-†).
[See pages 164-65.]

BARRETT SPACH (1898-‡) was born in Chicago on November 13, 1898. He studied at the University of Chicago, transferring to the David Mannes School in New York where he was a member of the first graduating class in 1924. During the next two years he taught at the Cincinnati Conservatory and served as organist in Calvary Church, Cincinnati. There followed three years of study in Paris under Nadia Boulanger. Returning to Chicago in 1929, he became associate organist-choirmaster of the Fourth Presbyterian Church under Eric Delamarter, succeeding him upon his retirement in 1935. He was associate professor of church music at the Chicago Theological Seminary (1942-45), director of concerts of Renaissance and Baroque music at the Newberry Library (1945-47), and since 1946 has been professor and chairman of the organ department at Northwestern University.

GEORGE EDWARD STUBBS (1857-1937).
[See pages 155-56.]

VAN DENMAN THOMPSON (1890-) studied at Colby College, Maine, and the New England Conservatory. He began teaching at Woodland College, Jonesboro, Arkansas, in 1910, moving to DePauw University at Greencastle, Indiana, the following year. He received an honorary Doctor of Music degree from DePauw in 1935 and since 1937 has been director of their School of Music. He became a fellow of the American Guild of Organists in 1919. He has composed extensively for organ, piano, and voice—songs, motets, anthems, and cantatas, as well as an oratorio, *The Evangel of the New World,* based on the history of Methodism.

ANDREW TIETJEN (1911-1953) was born in New York City. He sang as a boy in St. Thomas' Church, studying in its choir school, and then at Trinity School and Columbia University. As his voice changed he continued music study with T. Tertius Noble in New York, becoming his assistant at sixteen. He served as organist-choirmaster at St. Thomas'

†1968.
‡1963. [234]

Chapel, then at All Angel's Church (1937-1941), Chapel of the Intercession (1941-43), and as associate organist of Trinity Church until his premature death on April 13, 1953. He was a fellow of Trinity College, London. He served with the United States Army during the Second World War. After his return from military service, he founded and directed the mixed choir known as the Trinity Choir of St. Paul's Chapel, which broadcast each Sunday morning over the Columbia Broadcasting System.

H. EVERETT TITCOMB (1884-) was born in Amesbury, Massachusetts, on June 30, 1884. He studied first with his sister, Ruth Titcomb, then with T. P. Currier, J. T. Whelan, and S. B. Whitney. He sang as a boy in St. James' Church, Amesbury, becoming its organist in 1900. After three years, he went to the Church of the Messiah, Auburndale, and then, in 1909, to Christ Church, Andover. In 1910 he entered upon his long career as organist-choirmaster at the Mission Church of St. John the Evangelist in Boston, where, working with the loyal cooperation of the Cowley Fathers (the Society of St. John the Evangelist), he has for more than forty years demonstrated the potential beauties of the music of the liturgy. In 1938 his choir was organized as a Schola Cantorum, giving concerts of liturgical music and holding an annual festival on St. Gregory's Day, March twelfth. Titcomb has taught for some years at the Wellesley Conference School of Church Music, serving for two years as its dean. He lectured at the Redlands University Conference in 1947, and at the Cranbrook (Michigan) Conference in 1949. He is an instructor in liturgical music and choir training at the New England Conservatory and is assistant professor of church music at Boston University's School of Music. He composed an important *Victory Te Deum* for the conclusion of the Second World War, many anthems and organ works, as well as *A Choirmaster's Notebook on Anglican Services and Liturgical Music.* For a number of years he was a member of the Episcopal Joint Commission on Church Music and of the Massachusetts Diocesan Commission. There is a list of his earlier works in *The American Organist,* XXII (1939), 374-5. For a further appreciation of his work, *cf.* the memorial issue of *Cowley,* XXIII (Autumn, 1950), which includes several portraits.

[235]

JOHN IRELAND TUCKER (1819-1895).
[See pages 111-12.]

WILLIAM TUCKEY (1708-1781).
[See page 51.]

WILLIAM HENRY WALTER (1825-1893) was born at Newark, New Jersey, on July 1, 1825. As a boy organist, he played at a Presbyterian church and at Grace Episcopal Church in Newark. He became a pupil of Hodges, and in 1842 went to the Church of the Epiphany, New York City, thence to St. John's Chapel, St. Paul's Chapel, and Trinity Chapel until 1869. Beginning in 1865, he was also organist at Columbia University, having received the Doctor of Music degree from that institution the previous year. In later years he did much editing and compiling: *A Manual of Church Music* (1860), *Chorals and Hymns, Hymnal with tunes old and new, Selections of Psalms . . . with chants* (1857), *The Common Prayer, with Ritual Song* (1868), and others. He composed masses, services, and anthems, and arranged for the publishing of several of Hodges' works during his illness. In 1862 he founded the short-lived Church Choir Union for combined choir programs.

JUSTINE BAYARD (CUTTING) WARD (1879-) was born in Morristown, New Jersey, on August 7, 1879. She was educated privately, and entered the Roman Catholic Church in 1904. Becoming interested in church music, she studied with Herman Hans Wetzler (1918-1921), Dom Mocquereau (1921-1929), and at the Pontifical Institute of Sacred Music in Rome, where she received the Doctorate of Gregorian Chant in 1925. In 1918 she was instrumental, with Mother Stevens, in founding the Pius X School of Liturgical Music, where she developed her famous Ward Method of teaching plainsong. Since then she has been active as an author and teacher, preparing materials and introducing them into parochial school systems in this country and abroad. She has received two papal crosses—Pro Ecclesia et Pontifice, and Knight of Malta.

[236]

GEORGE WILLIAM WARREN (1828-1902) was born in Albany on August 17, 1828, and was largely self-taught in music. He began his career as organist of St. Peter's Church, Albany, serving there from 1846 to 1858, and at St. Paul's from 1858 to 1860. During the next decade he was organist-choirmaster at Holy Trinity, Brooklyn, leaving in 1870 for three decades at St. Thomas' Church, New York City. There his music was colorful and popular, but devoid of taste (*Cf.* page 94). His *Warren's Hymns and Tunes, as sung at St. Thomas's Church* appeared in 1888. He received an honorary Doctor of Music degree from Racine College. He retired in 1900, and died in New York on March 17, 1902.

RICHARD HENRY WARREN (1859-1933) was born in Albany on September 17, 1859, the son and pupil of George William Warren. He was organist-choirmaster at All Soul's Church, New York (1880-6), at St. Bartholomew's (1886-1905), and, after 1907, at the Church of the Ascension. He founded the Church Choral Society in 1886, conducting it until 1895 and again from 1903 to 1907. With this group he brought out many important works, some for their first American performance. Parker's *Hora Novissima* (1893), was composed for it. His own compositions include several operettas, orchestral works, songs, and considerable church music. He died in South Chatham, Massachusetts, on December 3, 1933.

SAMUEL PROWSE WARREN (1841-1915), unrelated to the Warrens discussed above, was the son of Samuel Russel Warren (*d.* 1882), a Canadian organ builder. He was born in Montreal on February 18, 1841. During 1861-1864 he studied in Berlin under Haupt, Gustav Schumann, and Wieprecht. As a boy he played in St. Stephen's Chapel, Montreal, and the American Church. In 1865 he came to New York and served for two years as organist-choirmaster in All Soul's Church. In 1867 he moved to Grace Church, where his weekly recitals drew universal esteem. He transcribed many orchestral works for organ, and composed many songs and anthems for his quartet choir. He left Grace Church in 1894 when the vestry voted to replace the quartet with a boy choir, and went to the Munn Avenue Presbyterian Church in East Orange, New Jersey. He died in New York on October 7, 1915. He was one of the founders of the American Guild of Organists and the collector of a remarkable music library, a catalog of which has been published. There is an extended obituary and portrait in the *New Music Review*, XV (1915-6), 21-2.

ALFRED ERNEST WHITEHEAD (1887-) was born in Peterborough, England, on July 10, 1887. He was a boy chorister at the cathedral there, and subsequently studied with Haydn Keeton and Arthur Eaglefield Hull. He was organist-choirmaster at Trinity Congregational Church in Peterborough before coming to Truro, Nova Scotia. In 1913 he was appointed professor of organ at Mt. Allison University, Sackville, New Brunswick, also serving at the local Methodist Church. He has since served at St. Peter's Church, Sherbrooke (1916-1921), and Christ Church Cathedral, Montreal (1922-1947). In 1947 he returned to Mt. Allison University as dean of music. He was awarded the Doctor of Music degree in 1922 by the University of Toronto. He is a fellow of the Royal College of Organists, and is a past president of the Canadian College of Organists. He has published many works for the orchestra, choir, and organ.

GEORGE ELBRIDGE WHITING (1840-1923) was born in Holliston, Massachusetts, on September 14, 1840. He studied with George W. Morgan in New York, Best in Liverpool, and Haupt and Radecke in Berlin. He taught at the New England Conservatory from 1875 until 1897 except for three years (1879-82) at Cincinnati's College of Music. He composed a few works for orchestra and more extensively for organ and choir. From 1876, save for the years in Cincinnati, he served as organist-choirmaster at the Church of the Immaculate Conception, Boston, where his elaborate "concert vespers" attracted large audiences. He resigned in 1910 because of Pius X's encyclical on church music, and died in Cambridge, Massachusetts, on October 14, 1923.

SAMUEL BRENTON WHITNEY (1842-1914) was born at Woodstock, Vermont, on June 4, 1842. He studied under John Knowles Paine and then taught organ and church music at the New England Conservatory. In 1871 he became organist and choirmaster at the Church of the Advent, Boston, serving in the latter capacity for twenty-six years, and as organist twelve years longer. Although neither a great composer nor a brilliant organist, he excelled in the musical quality of his improvisation and in his Bach playing. He accompanied the services with great sympathy, making the Advent's music nationally famous. With J. C. D. Parker and others he founded the Massachusetts Choir Festival Association, and maintained its work for many years. He was also a founder of the American Guild of Organists. He died in Brattleboro, Vermont, on August 3, 1914.

HARRISON MAJOR WILD (1861-1929) was born in Hoboken, New Jersey, on March 6, 1861. He studied in Chicago under Liebling, Creswold, and Eddy, then spent the year 1878-9 in Leipzig under Richter and Rust. Returning to Chicago, he was organist-choirmaster at Ascension Church for five years, at Unity Church for thirteen years, and after 1895 at Grace Church, where he made the musical services especially notable. He was one of the founders of the American Guild of Organists, dean of its western chapter, and after 1898 conductor of Chicago's outstanding Apollo Club and several other choral groups. He began to be bothered with deafness *ca.* 1926, and gradually gave up his extensive teaching and choral conducting. Increasingly discouraged as his deafness became more acute, he took his own life on March 1, 1929. There is a portrait and biographical sketch in *The Diapason,* XX, 5 (April, 1929), 1-2.

HEALEY WILLAN (1880-[†]).
[See page 163.]

DAVID McK. WILLIAMS (1887-).
[See pages 158-59.]

(FRANK) WALTER WILLIAMS (1901-[‡]) was born in Newark, New Jersey, on August 30, 1901. He graduated from Harvard in 1923, then spent several years of study in Paris. Becoming organist-choirmaster of

[†]1968.
[‡]1960.

St. Stephen's Church, Providence, he established St. Dunstan's Choir School there in 1928. He was ordained deacon in 1929, and priest in 1930. He was also a music instructor at Brown University (1930-33), and an instructor in the history of sacred music at New England Conservatory (1929-39). Leaving St. Dunstan's in 1935, he became an assistant at Christ Church, Cambridge, Massachusetts, and music instructor at the Episcopal Theological School (1937-39). From 1939 to 1943 he was assistant rector of St. Paul's Church, Oakland, California, and lecturer on religious music at the Church Divinity School of the Pacific. He was rector of St. Mark's Church, Denver, from 1943 to 1950. Since October 1950 he has been executive secretary of the Leadership Training Division, Department of Christian Education of the National Council of the Episcopal Church. He has taught in the summer conferences at Wellesley, Blue Mountain, Chatham Hall, and Evergreen, being dean of the latter's School of Church Music since 1940. He was a member of the Joint Commission on Church Music from 1931 to 1949. He edited the St. Dunstan series of sacred music, in which he introduced a number of works from the sixteenth-century Spanish polyphonists.

JOHN FREDERICK WOLLE (1863-1933), pioneer American director of Bach's choral music, was born on April 4, 1863, in Bethlehem, Pennsylvania, where he studied in the local Moravian parochial school. He served as organist-choirmaster of Trinity Episcopal Church, Bethlehem, from 1881 to 1884, and then spent a year in organ study under Rheinberger in Munich. Returning to Bethlehem, he was organist of the Moravian Church and (from 1887) of Lehigh University until 1905. In 1882 he had been instrumental in organizing a choral union which dissolved in 1892. Six years later he became the founder and conductor of the Bethlehem Bach Choir, which gave, on March 27, 1900, the first complete performance in America of Bach's *B Minor Mass*. From 1905 to 1911 he occupied the chair of music at the University of California. Returning to Bethlehem, he reorganized the Bach Choir and from 1912 until his death on January 12, 1933, conducted the famous Bach Festivals at Lehigh University. He received honorary Doctor of Music degrees from the Moravian College in 1904, from the University

APPENDIX D

Notes and Bibliography

CHAPTER I

1. Jacob M. Coopersmith, "Music and musicians of the Dominican Republic," *The Musical Quarterly*, XXXI (1945), 71-88, 212-26.

2. Gilbert Chase, *The Music of Spain* (New York: W. W. Norton, 1941) Chapter XVII, "Hispanic music in the Americas."

3. Alejo Carpentier, "Music in Cuba," *The Musical Quarterly*, XXXIII (1947), 365-80.

4. Lota M. Spell, "Music in the Cathedral of Mexico in the Sixteenth Century," *Hispanic American Historical Review*, XXVI (1946), 293-319.

5. End-papers, from the copy preserved in the New York Public Library, show the title page and the first music page of Pablos' *Ordinarium*.

6. A copy is in the John Carter Brown Memorial Library, Providence, R. I.

7. Dorothy L. Pillsbury, "Christmas at San Felipe," *The Cathedral Age,* XXVI, 4 (Christmas, 1951), 22-3.

8. José de J. Núñez y Dominguez, "The Alabado and Alabanzes," *Mexican Folkways,* II, 5 (December, 1926), 12-22, reproduces a broadside with the original Spanish text and an Aztec version by Fr. Margil. The latter's biography has been compiled by Eduardo Enrique Ríos (México: Antigua librería Robredo de J. Porrúa e hijos, 1941).

9. Anna McGill, "Old Mission Music," *The Musical Quarterly,* XXIV (1938), 192; Gabriel Saldíva, *Historia de la Música en México* (México: Publicaciones del Departamento de Bellas Artes, 1934) p. 125-6.

10. Juan B. Rael, *The New Mexican Alabado* (Stanford University Press, 1951).

11. Several versions have been published in recent years. Excerpts from a presentation at the Church of Our Lady of Guadalupe, San Antonio, Texas, were recorded by John Lomax in 1935. Other songs from the play were recorded by Lomax at Cotulla, Texas, in 1934. The latter are available in the recordings issued by the Archive of American Folk Song, Library of Congress (Record no 24).

12. Dorothy L. Pillsbury, "Ancient Christmas Customs in New World," *The Cathedral Age,* XXIV, 4 (Christmas, 1949), 12-3.

13. Owen Francis Da Silva, *Mission Music of California* (Los Angeles: W. F. Lewis, 1941). Some of this music has recently been made available on recordings.

14. Zephyrin Engelhardt, *Mission San Juan Bautista* (Mission Santa Barbara, Cal., 1931) Appendix F: "Church Music at the Missions," p. 133.

15. Da Silva, p. 30.

16. From "Monterey" in R. L. Stevenson's *Across the Plains,* first published as "The Old Pacific Capital," *Fraser's Magazine,* CII [N.S. 22] (November, 1880), 647.

CHAPTER II

1. This evolution is traced in detail by Waldo Selden Pratt, *The Music of the French Psalter of 1562* (Columbia University Press, 1939).

2. Charles W. Baird, *History of the Huguenot Emigration to America* (New York: Dodd, Mead & Co., 1885) I, 68.

3. Cited by Pratt, p. 21 note.

4. *Cf.* p. 49.

5. Francis Fletcher, "The World Encompassed by Sir Francis Drake," in H. S. Burrage, ed., *Early English and French Voyages,* (New York: Scribner's, 1906), p. 163.

6. *Cf.* Pratt, p. 70-1, and the references he cites.

7. Millar Patrick, *Four Centuries of Scottish Psalmody* (London: Geoffrey Cumberlege—Oxford University Press, 1949) Chapter X.

8. This does not apply to their attitude towards secular music; *cf.* Percy Scholes, *The Puritans and Music* (London: H. Milford—Oxford University Press, 1934).

9. Patrick, Chapter X.

10. Symmes, *Reasonableness of Regular Singing* (1720); *cf.* the next chapter.

11. Henry Wilder Foote, *Three Centuries of American Hymnody* (Harvard University Press, 1940) Appendix A. *Cf.* Chapter IX below.

12. Quoted from a *History of Worcester* in George Hood's *A History of Music in New England* (Boston: Wilkins, Carter & Co., 1846), p. 183-4.

13. Edward N. West, "History and development of music in the American Church," *Historical Magazine of the Protestant Episcopal Church,* XIV (1945), p. 22.

CHAPTER III

1. Foote, *op. cit.,* p. 91 ff.

2. *Cf.* Chapter VII. Similar opposition as late as 1858 is cited on p. 232.

3. Quoted in detail by Foote, *op. cit.,* Appendix B.

4. For an analysis of the materials of 18th century music instruction, *cf.* Allen Perdue Britton, *Theoretical Introductions in American Tune-books to 1800* (University of Michigan microfilm, 1949); see also Sirvart Poladian, "Rev. John Tufts and Three-part Psalmody in America," *Journal of the American Musicological Society,* IV (1951), 276-7.

5. Nathaniel Duren Gould, *Church Music in America* (Boston: A. N. Johnson, 1853).

6. Horace C. Hovey, ed., *Origins and Annals of "The Old South" First Presbyterian Church and Parish, in Newburyport, Mass.* (Boston: Damrell & Upham, 1896), p. 54.

7. Silas Leroy Blake, *The Later History of the First Church of Christ* (New London: Day Publ. Co., 1900), p. 229f.

8. *Cf.* p. 103.

9. Irving Lowens, "Daniel Read's World: The letters of an early American Composer," *Music Library Association Notes,* 2nd series, IX (March, 1952), 233-248.

10. *Cf.* p. 57.

11. Oscar Sonneck, *Early Concert Life in America* (Leipzig: Breitkopf & Härtel, 1907).

12. Kenneth H. MacDermott, *Old Church Gallery Minstrels* (London: S. P. C. K., 1948).

13. *Ibid.*

14. Foote, *op. cit.,* p. 113.

15. *Ibid.,* p. 176.

16. *Cf.* p. 35.

17. Quoted by Hood, *op. cit.,* p. 138.

18. *Cf.* p. 224.

19. Hopkinson is discussed further in Chapter VI.

20. *Cf.* Frank Metcalf, *American Psalmody* (New York: C. F. Heartman, 1917) and the article "Tune-books" in W. S. Pratt's *American Supplement* to *Grove's Dictionary of Music and Musicians* (New York: Macmillan, 1935).

CHAPTER IV

1. *Cf.* p. 50.

2. Irving Lowens, *The Fuging-Tune, America's Lost Music* (consulted in manuscript). Some of these have been separately published in his series of *Early American Choral Music* (New York: E. B. Marks Music Corp.).

3. *Cf.* p. 51.

4. *Cf.* Plate XI.

5. *The Golden Sheaf, No. 2* (Boston: Advent Christian Publication Society, 1916).

6. *Cf.* Chapter XII.

7. Allen P. Britton, "The Musical Idiom in Early American Tunebooks," abstracted in *The Journal of the American Musicological Society,* III (1950), 286.

8. *Cf.* pp. 108-9 and Chapter XIX.

CHAPTER V

1. Reproduced in *Church Music and Musical Life in Pennsylvania,* I. prepared by the Committee on Historical Research, Pennsylvania Society of the Colonial Dames of America. See also Albert G. Hess, "Observations on the ms. 'The Lamenting Voice of the Hidden Love,'" *Journal of the American Musicological Society,* V (1952), 211-23.

2. *Cf.* pp. 53-4.

3. *Church Music and Musical Life in Pennsylvania,* II, 83.

4. "An Historical Sketch of Ephrata," *Hazard's Register of Pennsylvania,* XV, 11 (March, 1835), 161-7.

5. English translations will be found in *Church Music and Musical Life in Penn.*, II, 46-59.

6. *Cf.* Plate III.

7. For a full discussion, *cf.* Allen Anders Seipt, *Schwenkfelder Hymnology* (Philadelphia: Americana Germanica Press, 1909).

8. *Cf.* p. 25.

9. The Rev. Bernhard A. Grube compiled and published a *Harmony of the Gospels and a Collection of Hymns* (1763) in the Delaware language. In 1803, the Rev. David Zeisberger published another *Collection of Hymns for the Use of the Christian Indians* in Delaware and English.

10. Two of his works are available in modern editions from the Music Division of the New York Public Library.

11. Rufus A. Grider, *Historical Notes on Music in Bethlehem, Pennsylvania, from 1741 to 1871* (Philadelphia: Pile, 1873).

12. James Constantine Pilling's *Bibliography of the Algonquian Languages* (1891) lists two manuscript collections of chants prepared by 18th century French-Canadian missionaries.

13. *Jesuit Relations*, LVI, 133 (Rueben G. Thwaites, ed.; Cleveland: Burrows Bros., 1899).

14. George Thornton Edwards, *Music and Musicians of Maine* (Portland: Southworth Press, 1928), p. 6-8.

15. J. Vincent Higginson, *Hymnody in the American Indian Missions.* New York: The Hymn Society of America, 1954. (*Papers of the Hymn Society*, 18.)

16. Hugh T. Henry, "Music of the Roman Catholic Church in Pennsylvania in the 18th Century," *Church Music and Musical Life in Penn.*, III, 2, 301-30.

17. Jean Lefevre de Cheverus, later to become the first Bishop of Boston and then Cardinal Archbishop of Bordeaux. His works cited here are only known bibliographically. We have not been able to locate copies of them for examination.

18. William W. Manross, *A History of the American Episcopal Church* (New York: Morehouse-Gorham Co., 1950), p. 172.

19. Bird Wilson, *Memoir of the Life of William White* (Philadelphia: James Kay, 1839), p. 349.

20. Henry Mason Brooks, *Olden-Time Music* (Boston: Ticknor, 1888), p. 78.

21. Laurence Thomas Cole, "Trinity School and Trinity Parish," *Historical Magazine of the P. E. Church*, XVI (1947), 96-9.

22. Arthur H. Messiter, *A History of the Choir and Music of Trinity Church* (New York: Gorham, 1906).

23. George W. Williams, *St. Michael's, Charleston, 1751-1951* (Columbia: University of South Carolina Press, 1951), p. 208.

CHAPTER VI

1. *Cf.* Oscar Sonneck, *Francis Hopkinson and James Lyon* (Washington: McQueen, 1905); reprinted in *Church Music and Musical Life in Penn.*, III, 2, 439:

However small the reputation I shall derive from this work, I cannot, I believe, be refused the credit of being the first native of the United States who has produced a musical composition.

Note that Hopkinson's use of the term "native" excludes the music of Kelpius and Beissel (*cf.* Chapter V). He may even have meant the first in the new Republic, since he writes "of the United States."

2. For further biographical information, *cf. ibid.;* also Otto Albrecht, "Francis Hopkinson, Musician, Poet, and Patriot, 1737-1937," *University of Pennsylvania Library Chronicle,* VI, 1 (March, 1938), 3-15; Everett Hastings, *Life and Works of Francis Hopkinson* (University of Chicago Press, 1926). His portrait is reproduced in Plate IV.

3. *Cf.* p. 25.

4. James Brenner was Hopkinson's music teacher. According to Sonneck, he arrived in Philadelphia from England in 1763. The following year he gave a benefit concert for the organ fund of St. Peter's Church, probably becoming its first organist. After *ca.* 1774, he shifted to Christ Church's organ. He died in September, 1780.

5. Sonneck, *op. cit.,* p. 59-62.

6. *Cf.* pp. 10-11.

7. Discussed by Carleton Sprague Smith in connection with "The 1774 Psalm Book of the Reformed Protestant Dutch Church in New York City," *The Musical Quarterly,* XXXIV (1948), 84-96.

8. Such are the three works by Billings which Clarence Dickinson edited for the Music Press, Inc. (MP-62) under the misleading title, *Three Fuguing Tunes.*

9. Arthur H. Messiter, *A History of the Choir and Music of Trinity Church* (New York: Gorham, 1906), p. 19-31.

10. Oscar Sonneck, *A Bibliography of Early Secular American Music* (revised by William Treat Upton; The Library of Congress, 1945), p. 309, 394.

11. *Ibid.,* p. 27.

CHAPTER VII

1. *Cf.* Plate V, showing the interior of Christ Church, Philadelphia, looking west from the Communion Rail. This is the organ used by Francis Hopkinson. Note the fine baroque case in contrast with the more austere English cases shown in Plates II and VI.

2. *Church Music and Musical Life in Pennsylvania,* II, 271.

3. *Papers Read Before the Lancaster County Historical Society* XXX (1926), 3-11.

4. Herbert Boyce Satcher, "Music in the Episcopal Church . . . ," *Church Music and Musical Life in Pennsylvania,* III, 2, 229 ff. The case, as shown in Plate V, was not altered.

5. Sonneck, *Early Concert Life,* p. 9.

6. Christine Merrick Ayars, *Contributions to the Art of Music in America by the Music Industries of Boston* (New York: H. W. Wilson Co., 1937), p. 140-1.

7. Mary Kent Davey Babcock, "The organs and organ builders of Christ Church, Boston: 1736-1945," *Historical Magazine of the Protestant Episcopal*

Church, XIV (1945), 241-63; "Early organists of Christ Church, Boston: 1736-1824," *ibid.*, XIV (1945), 337-51.

8. *E.g.* Hood, *History of Music in New England*, p. 152.

9. Babcock, *op. cit.*

10. Virginia Larkin Redway, "Charles Theodore Pachelbell, musical emigrant," *Journal of the American Musicological Society*, V (1952), 32-6.

11. William King Covell, "The Organs of Trinity Church, Newport, R. I., U.S.A.," *The Organ* [London] XIV (1935), 245-55.

12. Andrew Freeman, "John Snetzler and his Organs," *The Organ* [London] XIV (1934-5), 34-42, 92-101, 163-71. The present *History* adds three instruments to those listed by Freeman.

13. Gardiner M. Day, *The Biography of a Church* (Cambridge, Mass.: Riverside Press, 1951), p. 30.

14. Further details on Trinity Church's music will be found in Andrew Tietjen, "The Pipe Organs of Trinity Church," *Trinity Parish Herald*, I, 6 (December, 1946), 3-4; Edward N. West, "The Music of Old Trinity," *Historical Magazine of the P. E. Church*, XVI (1947), 100-24; Messiter, *op. cit.*

15. George W. Williams, *St. Michael's, Charleston, 1751-1951* (University of South Carolina Press, 1951).

16. Boyce's anthems and arrangements were advertised in the *South Carolina Gazette* during 1767.

17. Redway, *op. cit.*

18. Brooks, *Olden-time Music*, p. 107.

19. Engelhardt, *Mission San Juan Bautista*, p. 42.

20. Elbridge Henry Goss, *Early Bells of Massachusetts* (Boston: D. Clapp & Sons, 1874); Eva A. Speare, *Historic Bells in New Hampshire* (Plymouth, N. H.: 1944).

21. Arthur H. Nichols, "Christ Church Bells," *New England Historical and Genealogical Register* (January, 1904).

22. Arthur H. Nichols, *Bells of Paul and Joseph W. Revere* (Boston: 1911).

23. *Cf.* Francis S. Rodgers, *The Bells of St. Michael's* (Charleston, S. C.: The Quinn Press, 1935), also George W. Williams, *op. cit.*

24. Satcher, *op. cit.*

25. Marie T. Walsh, *The Mission Bells of California* (San Francisco: Harr Wagner, 1934).

CHAPTER VIII

1. Plate XII shows Lowell Mason's *Carmina Sacra* (1841) opened at *Naomi*, one of the most popular of 19th century tunes in this country.

2. Such a rack may be seen across the rear gallery in front of the organ in Plate II.

3. Joseph Bennett, *A Short History of Cheap Music, as exemplified in the records of the house of Novello, Ewer, & Co.* (London: Novello, Ewer & Co., 1887).

4. For the history of music publishing in the United States, see William

Arms Fisher, *150 Years of Music Publishing in the U. S.* (Boston: Oliver Ditson, 1933).

5. This has always been a marked desideratum, since the choirmaster otherwise is likely to be led astray by the deluge of sample copies of current works which are sent to him by the music publishers.

6. From the preface of May, 1902.

CHAPTER IX

1. Williams, *St. Michael's*, p. 214.

2. Morgan Dix, *A History of the Parish of Trinity Church* (New York: Putnam, 1898-1950), IV, 331.

3. Lowell Mason, *An Address on Church Music* (New York: Mason & Law, 1851).

4. Some of this may have been caused by the inversion of the parts as printed in the tune-books, *cf.* p. 68.

5. Helen Martha Wright, *Two Hundredth Anniversary; Reminiscences of the First Presbyterian Church, Mendham, New Jersey* (Jersey City: 1938).

6. Belle Thomas, *The First Hundred Years, a History of the First Presbyterian Church, Muncie, Indiana* (Muncie: Scott Printing Co., 1938).

7. Wilson Waters, *History of St. Luke's Church, Marietta, Ohio* (Marietta: J. Mueller, 1884).

CHAPTER X

1. Anne Ayres, *The Life and Work of William Augustus Muhlenberg* (New York: Harper, 1880), p. 148, 193-5.

2. Edward N. West, "History and Development of Music in the American Church," *Historical Magazine*, XIV (1945), 15-37. *Cf.* Plate VII.

3. Ayres, *op. cit.*

4. Christopher W. Knauff, *Doctor Tucker, Priest-Musician* (New York: Randolph, 1897), p. 144 ff.

5. West, *op. cit.*

6. Wallace Goodrich, *The Parish of the Advent in the City of Boston* (Boston: 1944), p. 123-42. *Cf.* Plate VII.

7. West, *op. cit.*

8. Messiter, *op. cit.*, p. 84-90.

9. Peter Christian Lutkin, *Music in the Church* (Milwaukee: Young Churchman, 1910), p. 184-219.

10. G. E. Stubbs in the *New Music Review*, XIII (1914), 413-5.

11. John Punnett Peters, *Annals of St. Michael's* (New York: Putnam, 1907).

12. Arthur B. Kinsolving, *A Short History of the Boys School of St. Paul's Parish, Baltimore, Maryland, 1899-1945* (n.p.).

13. Not to be confused with the Church Music Association founded in 1869 by George Templeton Strong for the concert production of oratorios and other

large sacred choral works. Conducted by James Pech [Peck] and Charles E. Horsley, it merged with the New York Oratorio Society in 1874.

14. Knauff, *op. cit.*

15. Goodrich, *op. cit.*

16. Messiter, *op. cit.*

17. *Journal of the . . . Protestant Episcopal Church in the U. S. A. General Convention*, 1868, p. 40.

18. *Ibid.*, 1871, p. 598-601.

19. Lutkin, *op. cit.*

20. Charles W. Evans, *History of St. Paul's Church, Buffalo, New York* (Buffalo: Matthews-Northup, 1903).

CHAPTER XI

1. Messiter, *op. cit.*, p. 26.

2. Albert G. Mackey, *The History of Freemasonry in South Carolina* (Charleston: Walker, Evans & Cogswell, 1936).

3. *Hymns of praise sung by the youth of the Evangelical Lutheran Zion's Congregational of Loonenburg, in the county of Albany, State of New-York, on the occasion when their church organ was refitted* . . . (Hudson: A. Stoddard, 1792).

4. *Cf.* pp. 209-10.

5. *Cf.* p. 51.

6. Messiter, *op. cit.*, p. 38. It continued to be sung elsewhere, and was re-published at least once during the 20th century.

7. The *Sanctus* from this Mass was sung by request at a service of the Episcopal General Convention of 1880, meeting at St. George's Church, New York. The Presiding Bishop (Benjamin B. Smith of Kentucky) was so shocked that, after the choir had finished, he said the *Sanctus* all over again.

8. In an interview during the intermission period of the Columbia Broadcasting System's Sunday afternoon symphony program on July 29, 1950, Richard Wagner's granddaughter stated that in Europe they thought the use of these pieces for weddings was a Hollywood joke—quoted in *Music for Church Weddings* (Greenwich, Conn.: Seabury Press, 1952) issued by the Joint Commission on Church Music of the Episcopal Church.

9. West, *Historical Magazine*, XVI (1947), 119.

10. Lutkin, *op. cit.*, p. 198-9.

11. A work falsely attributed to J. S. Bach; it was actually composed by Georg Gottfried Wagner.

12. Robert H. Lord, *History of the Archdiocese of Boston* (New York: Sheed & Ward, 1944), II, 376.

13. Quoted, with names deleted, by W. F. P. Stockley in an article on "The Pope and Reform in Church Music," *American Ecclesiastical Review*, XXX (1904), 386. Other similar atrocities are cited by Montani in his "Early Church Music in America," *Catholic Choirmaster*, XIV (1928), 7-11.

14. "Catholic Choirs and Choir Music in Philadelphia," *Records of the American Catholic Historical Society of Philadelphia*, II (1886-8), 115-126.

15. *Cf.* p. 40.

16. *Cf.* p. 70.

17. *Cf.* pp. 107-8.

18. This papal decree of 1903, like the earlier ones of John XXII in 1324-5 and the 22nd session of the Council of Trent in 1562, laid down basic principles to be observed in the composition and performance of sacred music. Copies of the decree may be found printed with the *White Lists, cf.* p. 140. Its principles were reaffirmed in 1947 by Pius XII in his encyclical letter "Mediator Dei."

19. J. Vincent Higginson, "The American Caecilia Society," *Catholic Choirmaster*, XXVIII (1942), 107-9, 114.

CHAPTER XII

1. George Pullen Jackson, *White and Negro Spirituals, their Life Span and Kinship; tracing 200 years of untrammeled song making and singing among our country folk* (New York: J. J. Augustin, 1943).

2. Jackson, *Spiritual Folk-Songs of Early America* (New York: J. J. Augustin, 1937).

3. Jackson, *Down-East Spirituals and Others* (New York: J. J. Augustin, 1939).

4. Jackson, *White Spirituals in the Southern Uplands* (Chapel Hill: University of North Carolina Press, 1933). Also Irving Lowens, "John Wyeth's *Repository of Sacred Music, Part Second:* A Northern Precursor of Southern Folk Hymnody," *Journal of the American Musicological Society*, V (1952), 114-31.

5. Jackson, *The Story of The Sacred Harp, 1844-1944* (Nashville: Vanderbilt University Press, 1944).

6. Jackson, *White and Negro Spirituals.*

7. *Grove's Dictionary of Music and Musicians* (1928 ed.), III, 611a.

8. *Cf.* p. 23.

9. Jackson, *White Spirituals,* Chapter II.

10. *Cf.* p. 30.

11. Jackson, *White Spirituals.*

12. Arthur L. Stevenson, *The Story of Southern Hymnology* (Roanoke, Va.: Stone Printing Co., 1931), p. 67-90.

CHAPTER XIII

1. No comprehensive figures are available on church musician's salaries save for a sketchy tabulation of comparative salaries paid the ministers, sextons, clerks, etc., in various churches in Anton Paul Allwardt's manuscript dissertation on *Sacred Music in New York City, 1800-1850* (Union Theological Seminary, 1950).

2. *Cf.* p. 40.

3. Virginia Redway, "The Carrs, American Music Publishers," *The Musical Quarterly*, XVIII (1932), 150-77, includes a full list of his compositions.

4. *Cf.* p. 100.

5. Albert Lohmann in *Caecilia*, LI (July-August, 1924), 31-3; see also J. Vincent Higginson in *The Catholic Choirmaster*, XXVII (1941), 101-4, and *ibid.*, XXVIII (1942), 6-9, 54.

6. Later developments of this industry, in the gospel song trade, have already been discussed in Chapter XII.

7. *Cf.* Plate XII.

8. Quoted in Knauff, *Doctor Tucker*, p. 249.

9. Stephen P. Dorsey, *Early English Churches in America, 1607-1807* (New York: Oxford, 1952).

10. Messiter, *op. cit.*, p. 300. *Cf.* pp. 123-24.

11. Faustina Hodges, *Edward Hodges* (New York: Putnam, 1896).

12. Stubbs, writing in the *New Music Review*, XV (1916), 294-6.

13. Knauff, *op. cit.*

14. See also p. 79.

15. Granville L. Howe, *A Hundred Years of Music in America* (Chicago: 1889), p. 266-9.

CHAPTER XIV

1. Andrew Tietjen, "The Pipe Organs of Trinity Church," *Trinity Parish Herald*, I, 6 (December, 1946), 3-4; Edward N. West, "The Music of Old Trinity," *Historical Magazine*, XVI (1947), 108-10.

2. Henry Lowell Mason, *The History and Development of the American Cabinet Organ* (n.p.: 190?).

3. George Laing Miller, *The Recent Revolution in Organ Building* (New York: Charles Francis Press, 1913); Leslie Leet, *An Introduction to the Organ* (Cranford, N. J.: Allen, 1940); William Harrison Barnes, *The Contemporary American Organ*, 4th edition (New York: J. Fischer, 1948); William Leslie Sumner, *The Organ* (London: MacDonald, 1952).

4. Gustav F. Dohring, "The Roosevelt Organ Works," *The American Organist*, XXXV (September, October, 1952), 293-6, 331-4. The reader may be interested to know that Hilbourne and Frank were first cousins to President Theodore Roosevelt.

5. *The American Organist*, XXV (March, 1942), 75-80; XXVI (January, February, March, 1943), 9-11, 33-5, 57-9; XXVII (August, 1944), 177-9; XXIX (December, 1946), 379-80; XXX (March, April, May, June, 1947), 87-8, 123-5, 155-6, 191-2; XXXII (May, June, 1949), 155-6, 189-91.

CHAPTER XV

1. *Cf.* Plate XVII.

2. J. C. Beckel, *Amateur's Organ School* (Boston: Oliver Ditson Co., 1850), p. 30 ff. Spellings and punctuation have been corrected in this quotation since Beckel's work was badly edited.

3. Henry C. Lahee, *The Organ and its Masters* (Boston: Page, 1927).

4. Henry E. Krehbiel, *Review of the New York Musical Season, 1885-1886* (New York and London: Novello, Ewer & Co., 1886).

5. *Cf.* pp. 150-52.

6. Biographies of these men will be found in Appendix C.

CHAPTER XVI

1. Archibald T. Davison, *Protestant Church Music in America* (Boston: E. C. Schirmer, 1933).

2. Florence Smith, *Protestant Church Music* (Butler, Ind.: Higley Press, 1949).

3. *Music Teachers' National Association Proceedings,* XXIII (1928), 67-80.

4. Reported in detail in *The Diapason,* XIV, 10 (September, 1923), 9; XIV, 11 (October, 1923), 9; XV, 1 (December, 1923), 4.

5. Howard Hanson, "The American Orchestral Repertory," *M.T.N.A. Proceedings,* XXXI (1936), 336-42.

6. E. S. Barnes, "American Composers of Church and Choral Music since 1876," *M.T.N.A. Proceedings,* XXIII (1928), 101-20.

7. Paul Henry Lang in *The Musical Quarterly,* XXXI (1945), 517-35.

8. John Henry Mueller, *The American Symphony Orchestra* (Bloomington: Indiana University Press, 1951).

9. *Cf.* p. 134.

10. These votes are due to a single work, as listed in the next table.

11. J. Vincent Higginson, "History of the Society of St. Gregory," *Catholic Choirmaster,* XXVI (1940), 57-9, 160-3.

12. *Sharps and Flats in Five Decades* (New York: Harper, 1947), p. 323.

13. *Cf.* pp. 211-12, also John C. Selner, "Paulist Choristers," *Catholic Choirmaster,* XXXVII (1951), 99-101, 140.

14. *Cf.* the discussion by Fr. Selner, "Sacred Music in Seminaries," *ibid.,* XXXVII (1951), 53-4.

15. The choir and its routine are described in Chapter XXI.

16. *Cf.* pp. 150-52.

CHAPTER XVII

1. *Cf.* Ellouise W. Skinner, *Sacred Music at Union Theological Seminary, 1836-1953* (New York: Union Theological Seminary, 1953).

2. *Catholic Choirmaster,* XXXIV (1948), 9.

3. Philip T. Weller, "Early Church Music in the United States," *Caecilia,* LXVI (1939), 297-304.

4. These are detailed in the history of *The Hymnal* by Herbert Boyce Satcher in *The Hymnal 1940 Companion,* p. xix-xxvii.

5. Samuel A. Baldwin, *The Story of the American Guild of Organists* (New York: H. W. Gray Co., 1946).

CHAPTER XVIII

1. An attempt was made in 1910 by Frederic E. J. Lloyd to compile a *Church Musician's Directory* on a national scale. Only one volume appeared and that was but a sketchy listing.

2. *Cf. Horatio Parker, a Memoir for his Grandchildren* (New York: Putnam, 1942) compiled from his letters and papers by Isabel Parker Semler. This includes a full list of his works.

3. *Cf.* pp. 164-65.

4. *The Monastic Diurnal Noted* (Kenosha: St. Mary's Convent, 1952).

5. There is an obituary in *The Catholic Choirmaster*, XXXII (1946), 60-1, 92.

6. *Musical Canada*, IX, 12 (December, 1928), 3-4, has an interesting description of Willan's work at St. Mary Magdalene.

7. There is a biography by Burnett Tuthill and a list of earlier works in *The Musical Quarterly*, XXIV (1938), 249-64.

CHAPTER XIX

1. For convenience of reference, all texts and tunes mentioned in this chapter may be found in the Episcopal *Hymnal 1940*, although in nearly every case they may also be found in several other modern hymnals. Their history is traced in *The Hymnal 1940 Companion* (New York: The Church Pension Fund, 1949).

2. *Cf.* the chronological table of texts and tunes in *The Hymnal 1940 Companion*, p. xii-xix.

3. *Cf.* pp. 89-90.

4. Books especially constructed to facilitate this were described on page 68.

5. *Cf.* Chapter XII.

6. *Hymnal 1940 Companion*, p. xxvii.

7. Howard Chandler Robbins, *The Way of Light* (New York: Morehouse-Gorham Co., 1933).

CHAPTER XX

1. *Cf.* p. 137. The plainsong setting of the Communion Service composed by John Merbecke in 1550 for the first Book of Common Prayer has become increasingly popular for such services.

2. Martin Luther, *Deudsche Messe und ordnung Gottes diensts* (Wittenberg: 1526). *Cf.* Paul Nettl, *Luther and Music* (Philadelphia: Muhlenberg Press, 1948), p. 78-82.

CHAPTER XXI

1. *Diamond Jubilee of Trinity Evangelical Lutheran Church, Indianapolis, December 5, 1950* (n.p.: 1950).

2. Examples of literature used for publicity purposes are available from Dr. Einecke.

3. Details about the Cathedral's music through the years will be found in the files of *The Cathedral Age*.

CHAPTER XXII

1. Quoted from *Music in Church; a report of a committee appointed in 1948 by the Archbishops of Canterbury and York* (Westminster: The Church Information Board, 1951).

[254]

Index

All churches and other institutions, with the exception of schools, are entered under the name of the city or town where they are located. Schools are entered under their own name directly.

Composers and music titles listed in Appendix B are not separately listed here, nor are those found in the references under "Music lists" below.

Modern authors and their works cited in the Bibliography (Appendix D) are not included here.

INDEX

35646